Beyond the Security Dilemma

Ending America's Cold War

JASON G. RALPH
Institute of Politics and International Studies
University of Leeds, UK

Ashgate

Aldershot • Burlington USA • Singapore • Sydney

Published by
Ashgate Publishing Limited
Gower House
Croft Road
Aldershot
Hampshire GU11 3HR
England

Ashgate Publishing Company
131 Main Street
Burlington, VT 05401-5600 USA

Ashgate website: http://www.ashgate.com

British Library Cataloguing in Publication Data
Ralph, Jason G.
   Beyond the security dilemma : ending America's cold war. -
   (Critical security series)
   1.National security - United States 2.United States -
   Foreign relations - 1945-1989
   I.Title
   327.7'3'09045

Library of Congress Control Number: 00-111395

ISBN 0 7546 1249 X

Printed and bound in Great Britain by
Antony Rowe Ltd., Chippenham, Wiltshire

Books are to be returned on or before
the last date below.

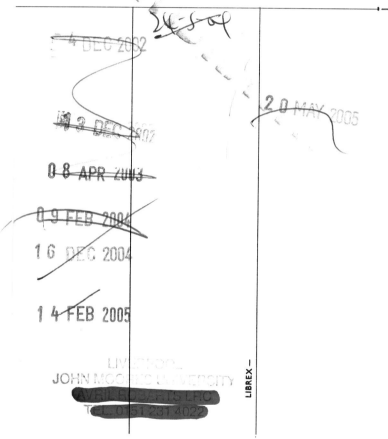

BEYOND THE SECURITY DILEMMA

For Mom, Dad and Heidi

Critical Security Series

Contents

Preface

The concept of the security dilemma has been used by the discipline of Strategic Studies to explain why security competition is an inherent feature of the international system. This book challenges that assumption theoretically and empirically. It redefines the security dilemma to account for the social and political contingency of reality and thereby reveal the immanent possibility of mitigating uncertainty between states and even constructing security communities. The book engages recent literature on transnational coalitions to demonstrate how the security dilemma can be mitigated and how the domestic structure of states is central to that process. Ultimately, military considerations are only one dimension of the security dilemma. Political and socioeconomic reform is central to constructing long term peace between states. Security communities rest on internationalist and democratic systems of governance that are responsive to the needs and aspirations of individuals. The book expands the definition of the security dilemma in a way that incorporates the difficulties of defending and promoting democracy and thus recognises its normative character. Against this background an assessment is made of American policy in ending the Cold War and laying the foundations for post-Cold War security communities.

This book is a product of many influences. I have been very fortunate in receiving inspiration, encouragement and support from institutions and individuals. The book is based on research I engaged while doing an M.Sc. in Strategic Studies at the Department of International Politics, University of Wales, Aberystwyth, and a Ph.D. at the Department of War Studies, King's College London. Both degrees were funded by the Economic and Social Research Council. I had additional financial support from the MacArthur Foundation. My original idea was inspired by Nick Wheeler's 'The Study of War' class and his work on the security dilemma with Ken Booth. My time at Aberystwyth gave me the skills and self-confidence to exceed many of the expectations that I had for my future. I would like to thank the Department of International Politics as a whole and Len Scott in particular for encouraging me to think beyond those expectations. Dr.Beatrice Heuser was my supervisor at King's. I also benefited from discussions with Christopher Dandeker, Michael MccGwire, Patrick Morgan and William Lee while studying in London.

Much of the empirical research for this book was done in the United States. I would like to thank the staff of the Ronald Reagan Library, the National Security Archives, the Library of Congress, the Hoover Institute and the Seeley G. Mudd Manuscript Library, Princeton University. A number of practitioners took time out of their busy schedules to talk to me. I would like to thank, Vice-President, Richard Cheney, National Security Adviser, Condoleezza Rice, Ambassador William Crowe, Ambassador Edward Rowney, General Brent Scowcroft, Secretary Frank Carlucci and Judge William Webster. I also benefited from discussions with Bruce Blair, Paula Dobriansky, Arnold Kanter, John Lenczowski and Sven Kraemer. My time in Washington was made much more enjoyable by the friends I made on Capitol Hill. I would like to thank the staff of Senator Murkowski's office, in particular Maggie Smolen, for their help.

Finally, I would like to thank my close friends and family. Through my own failings my friends are probably unaware of how much they have informed the writing of this book. Yet their friendship has been constant throughout this process, as has the love and support of Aunty Marg. When I left home to start my studies, when I pursued them by travelling to Russia and the U.S., and when I prepared to talk to 'important' people, I didn't know what to expect. The more I study and travel the more I realise who is important and how much home means to me. One particularly inspirational tutor has inspired me to demonstrate the 'courage of my confusions'. It's a task made a lot easier by knowing that many important things are simple, that personal anchorages do exist and some feelings never change. This book is dedicated to my Mom, Dad, Heidi and our love. "You just know."

List of Abbreviations

ABM	Anti-ballistic missile
ACDA	Arms Control and Disarmament Agency
ASEAN	Association of South East Asian Nations
ASW	Anti-submarine warfare
BMD	Ballistic missile defence
CFE	Conventional forces in Europe
CIA	Central Intelligence Agency
CPD	Committee on the Present Danger
CPSU	Communist Party of the Soviet Union
CSCE	Conference on Security and Cooperation in Europe
DCI	Director of Central Intelligence
DIA	Defense Intelligence Agency
FOTL	Follow-on-to-Lance
GDR	German Democratic Republic
GRIT	Graduated reduction in tension
ICBM	Intercontinental ballistic missile
IMF	International Monetary Fund
INF	Intermediate range nuclear forces
JCS	Joint Chiefs of Staff
KGB	*Komitet Gosudarstvennoy Bezopastnosti* (Committee of State Security)
LRTNW	Long-range theatre nuclear weapons
MAD	Mutually assured destruction
MFN	Most favoured nation
MIRV	Multiple independently targeted reentry vehicle
MLF	Multilateral Force
MND	Minimum nuclear deterrence
NAFTA	North American Free Trade Association
NATO	North Atlantic Treaty Organization
NIE	National intelligence estimate
NOD	Non offensive defence
NPD	Non provocative defence

NPT	Non-Proliferation Treaty
NSC	National Security Council
NSD	National Security Directive (Bush)
NSDD	National Security Decision Directive (Reagan)
NSDM	National Security Decision Memorandum (Nixon)
OSCE	Organisation for Security and Cooperation in Europe
PD	Presidential directive (Carter)
PFIAB	Presidential Foreign Intelligence Advisory Board
RYAN	Raketno-Yadernoye Napadenie (nuclear missile attack)
SADS	Soviet-American Disarmament Study Group
SALT	Strategic Arms Limitation Treaty
SDI	Strategic Defense Initiative
SEED	Support for East European Democracy
SLBM	Sea-launched ballistic missile
SNF	Short range nuclear forces
SNIE	Special national intelligence estimate
SOVA	Office of Soviet Analysis
START	Strategic Arms Reduction Treaty
TNW	Theatre nuclear weapon
UN	United Nations

Cannot both
Co-exist?

The world
in which
Secrecy has to be
carried out in
change should come
natural to politi

1 Critical Security Studies and the Security Dilemma

> Philosophers have only interpreted the world, in various ways; the
> point is to change it.
>
> Karl Marx[1]

Critical Security Studies seeks to broaden the academic agenda in a manner
that explores immanent possibilities for peaceful change (Krause and
Williams, 1996; 1997; Wyn Jones, 1995). This book redefines the concept
of the security dilemma to reveal the possibility of transcending those
social structures that, according to the Realist dominated discipline of
traditional Security Studies, condemns social groupings to live in
permanent conflict. Theoretically, then, the book is normatively inspired
by the critical agenda of changing as well as interpreting the world. It
proposes a new definition of the security dilemma that embraces this
idealism without denying reality. In fact, by highlighting the openness of
the future it claims greater realism than the traditional concept.

The future can be characterised by peace or conflict. As both
scenarios are contingent on social practices neither can be considered
permanent. It is the character of those social practices, however, that
determines whether conflict or peace prevails. The book's foundation,
then, is that change is the only constant feature of politics (Booth, 1999).
The way the world was, is and will be, has nothing to do with preordained
immutable structures, but was, is and will be the result of contested social
practices. Anarchy, the social context of state behaviour, is what states
make of it (Wendt, 1992). States are not, as Neorealists claim, condemned
to an existence characterised by a constant zero-sum competition for
security. States need not necessarily define their security in opposition to
others. In security communities, particular conceptions of security do not
exist, peace is only defined in terms of universal security and the
expectation of peaceful change is guaranteed. As a concept that can
highlight relations between states *at certain times*, therefore, the security
dilemma must, if it is to be of any use to students of Security Studies, be

1

able to accommodate the prospect of change. Additionally, in a security community where political units 'know' that they are not threatened by each other, the uncertainty that characterises a security dilemma does not exist. If it is to tell us anything at all about reality, therefore, the security dilemma must be redefined in a way that contains within itself the possibility of its own irrelevance.

The Traditional Security Dilemma

This book does not deny the existence of security dilemmas, yet it contests the Realist view that security dilemmas are a structural feature of anarchy. The traditional concept serves to highlight the structural reasons why states are forced to become power-maximising rational egoists who define security in zero sum terms. It tells us that states can never be certain of the intentions of other states. This unresolvable uncertainty forces states to rely on their own devices to guarantee their security. Herbert Butterfield (1951, p.21) considered the inability to 'enter into the other man's counter fear' as the central feature of the security dilemma. Describing the situation he called 'Hobbesian fear', he wrote:

> you know that you yourself mean him no harm, and that you want nothing from him save guarantees for your own safety; and it is never possible for you to realize or remember properly that since he cannot see inside your mind, he can never have the same assurance of your intentions that you have. As this operates on both sides the Chinese puzzle is complete in all its interlockings - and neither party sees the nature of the predicament he is in, for each only imagines that the other party is being hostile and unreasonable.

Uncertainty as to the intentions of the other side leads to a reliance on one's own power to guarantee security. In this self-help environment the only language that is respected is that of material power as it is the ultimate arbiter of any dispute. 'Striving to attain security' John Herz (1950, p.157) wrote:

> ... [states] are driven to acquire more and more power in order to escape the impact of the power of others. This, in turn, renders the others more insecure and compels them to prepare for the worst. Since none can ever feel entirely secure in such a world of competing units, power competition ensues, and the vicious circle of security and power accumulation is on.

The inability to be certain as to the intentions of other states, in other words, leads all states to rely on military power in an effort to guarantee security. Yet this solution is, according to the security dilemma thesis, invariably unsatisfactory. 'When states seek the ability to defend themselves, they get too much and too little' writes Robert Jervis. 'Too much because they gain the ability to carry out aggression; too little because others, being menaced, will increase their own arms and so reduce the first state's security' (Jervis, 1976 pp.63-64). This illusory incompatibility between two benign states characterises the tragedy of the traditional concept (Collins, 1997).

controversial

Critical Security Studies: knowledge and power

Critical Security Studies also highlights the fact that 'all theory is for someone and for some purpose' (Cox, 1986, p.207). It is argued here that the traditional concept of the security dilemma is *for* those who have a particular interest in conflict. By convincing society that conflict is a constant feature of international politics *because* of the security dilemma, those particular interests have been able to legitimate their practices even though they provide unsatisfactory solutions and make others insecure.

By exposing this instrumental purpose of the traditional security dilemma and its related concepts like the deterrence and spiral models, this book exposes motives behind these concepts that are not wholly related to the uncertainty of the anarchic system. Uncertainty is often a secondary motive that is used to legitimise approaches to security that suit the interests of a particular intellectual community[2]. In this sense an appropriate 'security dilemma' is often sort for a particular security 'solution'[3]. For instance, those that stand to profit from increased defence spending are those that are, at the very least, predisposed to the argument that an uncertain international environment demands a self-help policy of rearmament. At most they will cynically manufacture uncertainty or more likely manufacture what they claim is a clear threat to the national interest in order to encourage support for their preferred solution.

Exposing the instrumental way in which the security dilemma is used by certain agents to advance their particular interests, not only opens up possibilities for state agency but specifically identifies those political constituencies that are obstacles to alternative approaches. In other words, the reliance on a military approach to security and the resignation to the unsatisfactory solutions that such an approach offers, is not determined by the international system. Rather it is a consequence of particular groups that have the political power to define 'the national interest' in a way that is satisfactory to them if not to the nation as a whole. Finding a solution that satisfies all is the key to transcending the security dilemma. It is argued here that this depends on the political marginalisation of those who have exclusivist concepts of security and have a particular interest in enduring conflict.

Yet it would be incorrect to argue that the particular interests that thrive on conflict are the only obstacles to security cooperation. Prudence, that is caution in the face of uncertainty, can be justified even when it is an unavoidable political ally of special interests. While the particular interests of certain groups may cause them to blindly advocate power politics, others may define their state's interests in universal terms and advocate a policy of security cooperation. The strength of their advocacy may be limited, however, by the fear that their idealism will be exploited by states that are less inclined to cooperate. This genuine dilemma takes the following form:

> should the other's military preparations be matched and so risk an arms race and the further build-up of mistrust, danger, and cost, or should a wait-and-see policy be adopted thereby risking exposure to coercion or attack as a result of relative weakness? (Booth and Wheeler, 1992, p.31)

The main point of this book is not to deny the existence of such a dilemma, but to identify the ways in which it finds practical (rather than abstract theoretical) expression and from that to identify possibilities for resolving uncertainty and finding satisfactory security solutions.

The Security Studies discipline has let the concept of the security dilemma be hijacked by particular interests. By making the theoretical assumption that all states are rational actors in a system that dictates self-help, and that self-help demands the accumulation of material power, traditional Security Studies has provided political support for those constituencies that control and profit by that power. Propagating the traditional security dilemma concept has allowed these constituencies to argue that they are working within the best of all possible worlds. Because of the security dilemma power competition has been seen as inevitable.

A critical definition of the security dilemma, however, recognises that states (or any other political unit for that matter) are not actors that pursue one particular view of rationality. Groups within states will disagree on the desirability and possibility of cooperation. This disagreement in effect reflects the state's uncertainty. Particular groups will, for reasons that may be different, argue that cooperation is impossible, conciliatory gestures naïve and a strong defence posture necessary. Other groups may, again for different reasons, see greater possibilities of cooperation and advocate policies designed to facilitate that.

Seeing the dilemma in these terms, as a political dispute over what constitutes the state's interests and how best to pursue those interests, reveals the immanent possibility that uncertainty can be transcended and the security dilemma resolved. Reaching that conclusion is assisted by the realisation that what goes for the subject of the security dilemma is likely to apply to the object of the dilemma. In other words, the same kind of debate that characterises one state's security dilemma also characterises the dilemma of the state that is being observed. There may be political constituencies within that state that also wish to define its interests in universal terms. These constituencies, had they political control of the state, would be more than willing to reciprocate cooperative policies if they could convince others that such policies were lasting and genuine.

Chapter two looks at this process in detail. By way of introduction it is important to realise that political constituencies which hold non-exclusive conceptions of the national interest do exist across states and can transform interests and identities so that war and security competition becomes unthinkable. Their political opposition to statist, elitist, exclusivist definitions of security demonstrates that the self-help, militarist rationality identified by Neorealists is not universal. Redefining the security dilemma in a manner that reflects the contested nature of a politically contingent reality, is necessary both to interpret the world and to demonstrate the possibility of changing it.

Ending America's Cold War

The focus on American security policy has both an interpretive and normative motive. Chapter three's assessment of American defence policy, for instance, illustrates how America's security dilemma is best seen in terms of a political battle between advocates of different strategies. This debate was not influenced by Soviet behaviour alone. The domestic context of the American political system, the institutional structures that framed the debate and the political culture that influenced the significance of particular ideas all influenced the character of America's security dilemma. Chapter three also demonstrates how that debate was further influenced by ideas that originated independently of the American discourse. The influence of transnational coalitions that sought to penetrate the policymaking communities of both superpowers is discussed in detail. As 'policy entrepreneurs' (Checkel, 1997), these intellectual communities sought to mitigate the uncertainty of the security dilemma by embedding the practices of security cooperation in the policymaking communities of both superpowers. As chapter three demonstrates, their political significance within the superpower bureaucracies was central to the way the Cold War ended.

The second reason for focusing on American security policy is normative. The main aim of this book is to investigate the possibilities of transcending the security dilemma and creating the conditions for an enduring peace. A focus on the U.S.-Soviet relationship is used as a case study in this respect. Yet the main reason lies in the potential for American agency that has increased since the collapse of Soviet power. International security is increasingly influenced by decisions taken in Washington. The end of the Cold War was instigated by Gorbachev's reforms and the subsequent change in Soviet identity. Yet the timing of the end and the nature of the post-Cold War order was largely determined by American policy and its dominant position in the international system. Whether these policies created the conditions for lasting peace is considered in detail.

Critical Security Studies, to repeat, is about broadening the academic agenda in a manner that explores immanent possibilities for peaceful change. To fully assess the role American policy played in ending the Cold War and laying the foundations for a larger security community, this book looks at three dimensions of that policy: the military, the political and the economic dimension. Again the motive for this is both interpretive and normative. The Cold War was fundamentally an ideological conflict. The power politics that characterised the security policies of both superpowers was secondary to social processes that decided what was worth defending and what was considered a threat to those interests. Focusing solely on the military dimension of America's security dilemma, that is how best to deter a Soviet military attack without appearing to be threatening, cannot explain why the Soviet Union was considered a threat to the U.S. and its allies. Certainly it had the nuclear capability to physically destroy the U.S., but then so did the U.K. and France. The 'meaning' of their military capabilities was completely different to that of the Soviet nuclear arsenal (Wendt, 1992). The Cold War was a consequence, not as Neorealists would have it, of the distribution of material capabilities in the system, but of the social meaning those capabilities acquired in the context of the ideological conflict.

Part of the American dilemma of course was not merely interpreting Soviet capabilities and intentions, nor indeed was it merely a matter of deciding how best to respond to the perceived challenge. America's dilemma was also constituted by the debate on what exactly the U.S. government was trying to defend. Again focusing on the military dimension and its role in defending territory can only tell half a Cold War story. America's purpose was seen by most, though by no means all, in terms of defending and promoting a political and socioeconomic system that it believed would lay the foundations for a worthwhile and therefore enduring peace. The fundamental dilemma for the United States therefore, was not only how to deter a military attack on the territory of those states that contributed to this ideological agenda, but how to do so without compromising its own commitment to that same agenda.

To some the power relationship with the Soviet Union, expressed in crude material terms, was all important. Even though the need to balance Soviet power would sometimes compromise liberal principles, for instance it would centralise political power at home and support authoritarian regimes abroad, these trade-offs were considered necessary to avoid the greater evil that was Soviet hegemony. To others the threat to American values came less from the Soviet military than from the overreactions of American Realists who were willing to compromise those principles in the name of power politics.

The fundamental point here is that the security dilemma is a normative dilemma. The U.S. need not have been threatened by the Soviet Union if it was willing to compromise the ideological principles that caused the conflict. Yet those principles were, of course, at the core of America's political identity. They were what defined America and helped determine its national interest. If peace was to be enduring it had to be worthwhile and to the liberal consensus that dominated the American political discourse, 'worthwhile' was defined in terms of liberal democracy and free markets. Faced by the power of the Soviet state, however, prudence dictated an element of compromise.

While the intensity of the dilemma varied, its character remained the same. For instance, the liberal philosophy that was said to guarantee justice and order in the United States was sometimes compromised in the name of national security. Likewise, the liberal principles of national self-determination, non-discrimination and democratic governance that were said to guarantee international order were also sometimes compromised in order to manage relations with the Soviet Union. As chapter five demonstrates, however, U.S. foreign policy was, particularly in its relations with Western Europe, unwilling to fully compromise these principles in the name of power politics.

In this regard the U.S.-Soviet relationship was not characterised by illusory incompatibility. While 'misperception' certainly played a role at the level of military doctrine (those who stood to profit by arms races were of course often willingly deceived), there was always a limit to the concessions either side could make in the name of peaceful coexistence. As both sides believed the ideology of the other was morally wrong and believed that such injustices were a threat to peace, compromising ideological principles in the name of security was simply irrational. The dilemma, to repeat, was how to defend and promote values that provided the foundation for a worthwhile and therefore enduring peace, without provoking the material power of an ideological opponent in a manner that caused greater disorder and a greater injustice.

Ultimately the Cold War could only end when a common identity was adopted across both superpowers. This was the revolutionary role played by Gorbachev in the Soviet Union and the New Political Thinkers across Europe. Their advocacy of non-provocative defence was central to mitigating the uncertainty of the military dimension and decreasing the tension that had for so long characterised the East-West relationship. Yet it was their advocacy of political pluralism and their opposition to Communist Party dogma that was decisive in ending the Cold War.

As chapters three and five demonstrate, the success of democratisation was inherently linked to disarmament. A fact that had long been realised by European peace movements and only belatedly, and even then only partially, recognised by the U.S. government. By demonstrating a willingness to end the monopoly of the Communist Party and by doing nothing to stop the rise of the liberal activists across Eastern Europe, New Thinkers in the Soviet government made it easier for liberals in the U.S. to make a case for disarmament. Reducing the tension of the military relationship in turn facilitated the process of reform across Eastern Europe. Trying to end the military stand-off assisted the process of political reform, but it was also very much dependent on the direction of political and socio-economic processes that were autonomous of arms control.

Beyond the Security Dilemma

How to consolidate the democratic revolutions of 1989 and preserve the principles that had created peace across Western Europe without provoking an undemocratic backlash characterised America's late Cold War security dilemma. Chapter five in particular details how U.S. diplomacy approached the dilemmas caused by the collapse of the Eastern bloc, the prospect of the reunification of Germany and the distintegration of the Soviet Union. In assessing the role of the U.S. during this period, this book is largely complimentary of the immediate role played by the Bush administration. Its prudent commitment to extending the liberal order that had provided the foundations for peace in Western Europe should not be underestimated. Yet prudence is a virtue associated with inaction. The diplomacy surrounding German unification represents the high point of Bush's success, but for the most part the democratic, pro-Western direction of the 1989 revolutions was not a consequence of direct American action.

The actions of the Superpowers are remarkable for what they didn't do as much as for what they did. Indirectly, the relative political and socioeconomic success of the West provided popular support for the reformers across Eastern Europe. The political direction of the 1989 revolutions, however, came from a political commitment across European civil society to ideas that were independent of the American experience.

Certainly activists across European civil society were inspired by elements of the American model. But their interpretation of democracy meant pursuing an ideal and not the particular ideology of another state. Bush's claim, during his 1989 visit to Poland, that the idea of 'America' was alive and kicking in Poland was not, in this regard, wholly accurate. As Mary Kaldor notes, the idea that inspired transnational activists across Eastern Europe was 'democracy' which did not always coincide with interpretations of 'America'. Central to the political ambitions of democratic activists across Eastern Europe and the Soviet Union was 'responsiveness'. In the 1980s this translated into protests against unresponsive totalitarian states, something the U.S. could relate to and support. These aspirations were not inconsistent with the anti-statist, laissez-faire ideology of Americanism. With the collapse of the totalitarian state, however, the liberalisation and privatisation that American's usually equate with democracy risked isolating many European democrats. As Kaldor puts it:

> Instead of forging a new more responsive relationship between state and society as the civil society theorists of the 1980s had anticipated, the state simply withdrew from large parts of society. ... What emerged were new political currents based on the appeal to prejudice and fear, new criminal and mafia groups, new anti-cultures of guilt and insecurity, which have included deep and perhaps paradoxical resentment of the confident victors of 1989.

By withdrawing militarily in 1989, U.S. foreign policy created a relatively secure political space for further Soviet withdrawals. In that space democracy was expected to flourish and indeed the governments and state structures that replaced communist rule were, for the most part, more responsive to the needs and aspirations of their citizens. By promoting an international economy that demands minimal state intervention, moreover, U.S. foreign policy demonstrated a faith in capitalism's ability to liberate the individual while avoiding the social injustice that makes certain states unresponsive to certain sections of society. As the above quote suggests, however, this faith may have been misplaced. The withdrawal of the state has left democratic society vulnerable to 'new political currents' that thrive on the social and economic dislocation caused by neoliberal reforms.

By equating democracy with neoliberal conceptions of the state's role in the international economy, American foreign policy has been blinded by unwarranted assumptions that stem from a particular reading of its own political and social development. Chapter six argues that these assumptions are informing American agency in a way that is helping to create social structures that are unresponsive to the needs and aspirations of many individuals. In this sense, American agency is failing to promote the conditions necessary for the creation of a security community. While American hegemony has in the past helped construct the norms on which a security community is based, those that dominate contemporary policy have 'forgotten' the lessons of those successes. This again is a consequence of particular groups defining the national and international interest in a manner that suits their narrow interests at the expense of others.

Critical Security Studies: the human dimension

What justifies this criticism of U.S. hegemony? The main purpose of this book is to highlight practical ways of moving beyond the security dilemma and towards a security community where uncertainty is removed because war is unthinkable and there are dependable expectations of peaceful change. Towards that end this book is further inspired by the emphasis Critical Security Studies places on human as opposed to state security (Booth, 1991a; Wyn Jones, 1995, pp.310-311). Social structures like states, cultures and societies are in a constant process of being constituted, reconstituted or deconstructed. Individual human beings, on the other hand, are 'permanent and indestructible in a sense in which groupings of them of this or that sort are not' (Bull, 1995, p.21). In other words, social groupings cannot exist independent of human beings, but human agency can exist independent of social structures and individuals will use that power to change society in a way that suits their interests. If social structures are unresponsive to the needs and aspirations of individuals then those individuals will feel threatened, insecure and likely to take actions that undermine those social structures.

This book, whether the author likes it or not, is part of that social process. As 'knowledge' it, like any other book, holds a significant position when it comes to passing judgment on social structures and reconstituting society. Rather than deny the social responsibility that comes with 'knowledge', this book fully accepts that the ideas advanced here will, to paraphrase Cox, be used by someone for some purpose. The intended purpose of this book is to help identify social practices that create peace. The second part of Cox's point, however, demands the question, peace for whom? The perspective of an intellectual in a university should be no narrower than that which the institute he or she works in implies – the universal (Booth, 1991b, p.539). The security of a social group, whether it is the state, nation, society or culture, can only be the referent object of Security Studies to the extent that those groups contribute to the security of all. Advocating practices that protect a particular group at the expense of another is not the object of Security Studies. How can it be when someone's *insecurity* is an inevitable consequence?

Ultimately the referent object of Security Studies should be the individual, not, as it has been, the state. A commentator has no right to declare a security community between states if individuals within those states feel threatened by their government. A security community cannot exist solely on the mutual understanding of elites, particularly if those elites deny individuals their basic needs and dismiss their aspirations without consideration. Chapter four argues that 'responsiveness' is fundamental to the creation of a security community. If individual needs and aspirations are heard in a dialogue of all individuals in a society, and if society is seen to respond to those requirements in a manner that doesn't deny anyone else access to that dialogue, then it is likely that individuals will be reassured[4]. Perhaps more importantly, individuals or groups that are unwilling to compromise particular interests that have the effect of excluding others from this dialogue, can be justifiably identified as an obstacle to achieving the ideal of a security community.

It is on this basis that this book passes judgement on American hegemony. A security community rests on its ability to respond to the voices of individuals whose lives are affected by it. Actions that involve more individuals in such a dialogue are to be welcomed. In this respect America's liberal hegemony, its emphasis on multilateral decision making between democratic states and its promotion of a capitalist system that helps undermine authoritarian conceptions of truth, has the potential for extending and consolidating security communities. The major criticism of U.S. policy, however is that it is unaware of the dangers involved in replacing statist modes of exclusion with those that are a consequence of the free market. This, in part, is a consequence of the role capitalism has played in America's own political evolution and the importance it plays in America's own identity.

This point contributes to a more general conclusion. Progress towards a security community was initiated by the fundamental rethink of Soviet identity that was enacted by Gorbachev. Yet while Communism was often instrumental in legitimising the rule of Soviet elites, the idea itself had the power, independent of Soviet agency, to mobilise individuals against unresponsive capitalist structures. The collapse of the Soviet Union not only removed the material power of Soviet agency, but also discredited the idea that had informed the use of that power. To conclude from this that the reason for communism's initial appeal was simply the manipulation by political elites would be mistaken. It would be a further mistake to argue that the decline of communism's appeal meant victory for the kind of free market capitalism that occupies the other end of the political spectrum. It was the nature of *communism's* particular response to the failure of capitalism that was discredited, not the fact that *a response* was required to address the unresponsive nature of capitalism. Capitalism was and is largely unresponsive to the needs and aspirations of many individuals. The collapse of the Soviet Union has done nothing to change that fact.

This is not to conclude that communism is about to make a come back, that it will embed itself in the ideology of a materially powerful state and contest American hegemony. We need not expect Cold War history to repeat itself. The liberal order as Deudney and Ikenberry (1999) note, is for the forseeable future secure from any such challenge. Yet the liberal hegemony is far from meeting the criteria this book sets for the construction of a security community. Central to that criticism is the role American hegemony plays in managing the international economy and the influence that has on transnational civil society. Its multilateral and internationalist approach to global order is to be welcomed, but so long as the voices that dominate that dialogue are statist elites and transnational capitalists, then that order is likely to offer security for some at the expense of others.

Recognising this relationship between capitalism and democratisation contradicts much of what Americans understand about their own political experience. To recognise the exceptional nature of that experience, however, is also to recognise America's partial responsibility for the Cold War. The capitalist system that was consistent with an American definition of democracy was not easily exported abroad, and when American policy sought impose that particular conception through intervention and material coercion it was considered imperialist. It was this that contributed to the appeal of Communism. As noted above, for the Cold War to end a fundamental change in the identity of a Superpower was required. That happened in 1991 with the collapse of the Soviet Union. For the end of the Cold War to be succeeded by a security community, however, the identity of both Superpowers had to change. That has not happened. There are structures at the very core of America's identity that stop it from being the responsive and responsible hegemon that contributes to the construction of a global security community.

Chapter Outline

This book, then, seeks to move Security Studies beyond the traditional security dilemma in several ways. Chapter two redefines the actual concept that allows a better interpretation of a politically contested reality. Furthermore, by identifying a state's dilemma in terms of the political debate between different conceptions of reality and different approaches towards managing and changing that reality, the new definition of the security dilemma contains within itself the possibility of its own irrelevance. In other words, political debate is a way of identifying a state's uncertainty. Recognising the contingency of that debate, however, is to recognise the possibility that uncertainty can be resolved and the security dilemma transcended. Chapter three, shows how such a conception of the security dilemma can shed interpretive light on America's approach to the military dimension of its conflict with the Soviet Union. Furthermore, it demonstrates how transnational coalitions could influence the character of either side's dilemma in a manner that contributed to a mutual understanding and the mitigation of uncertainty.

A focus on the military dimension only gives a partial understanding of both the Cold War and the necessary foundations of a security community. Chapter three argues that the Bush administration could only reciprocate Gorbachev's disarmament programme when the Realist-Liberal coalition that informed U.S. policy became convinced that the reduced Soviet military threat was irreversible. Disarmament alone could not achieve this. American policymakers had to see changes in the domestic structure and political identity of the Soviet Union. Beyond that the American policymaking community would only be reassured once the Soviet Union adopted a liberal democratic identity. Again the political agency for these reforms came from across transnational civil society.

Chapter four expands on these conclusions by contesting the idea that dependable expectations of peaceful change can be guaranteed by mutual understandings between elites. The Cold War could only end once the U.S. was reassured that the Soviet Union was irreversibly on the path to liberal democracy. Yet the role of democracy in constructing a security community goes beyond identifying common characteristics between states. As noted above the decisive role played by democracy is its ability to include all individuals in a dialogue on their future and thereby respond in a way that gives them a vested interest in peace. Promoting a system of governance that is guided by this Habermasian ideal is considered the foundation of a security community.

Chapters five and six judge American hegemony on this basis. Focusing on the political dimension of America's Cold War security dilemma, serves two purposes. Firstly it demonstrates clearly the normative aspect of the dilemma. With the collapse of Soviet influence the Bush administration sought to consolidate and extend the transatlantic security community by committing itself to the Wilsonian principles of democracy, self-determination and non-discrimination, even though that risked the reversal of Soviet reform and the possibility of a renewed Cold War. The prudent promotion of a liberal democratic community based on multilateral international institutions is considered consistent with the duties of a responsible hegemon. This benign view of America's role is supported by liberals who argue that the penetrated nature of American hegemony encourages responsiveness and consequently creates confidence in American leadership.

Chapter six takes a more critical perspective. It takes a closer look at the kinds of groups that have actually penetrated American hegemony. It argues that the institutional and cultural structures at the heart of America's political identity have given the voices of a transnational capitalist elite disproportionate attention in the dialogue that has constructed contemporary world order. As a consequence the contemporary system of global governance lacks responsiveness and as such question marks hang over the future desirability of American hegemony. Finally, chapter seven concludes by offering a summary of America's role and poses some specific questions for further research.

Notes

[1] Cited in Wyn Jones, 1995, p.299.

[2] This point is informed by the recent literature on ideas and policy change, in particular the literature on epistemic and intellectual communities (Adler, 1992; Haas, 1992). Epistemic communities are networks of professionals with recognised expertise in a particular domain. An epistemic approach to International Relations explores the interaction between domestic and international sources of state behaviour and argues that ideas play a central role in shaping policy. Here, ideas are defined as 'consensual knowledge', which is a shared set of beliefs about a particular cause-effect relationship held by all members of an epistemic community (Checkel, 1997, p.4). Following Risse-Kappen, however, I use the phrase intellectual community because 'epistemic community' implies value-free knowledge about cause and effect. As Risse-Kappen notes, the internal consensus of many communities that have sought to influence policy derive not from uncritical reflections of cause and effect, but from shared principled beliefs and values (Risse-Kappen 1994, p.194). Jack Matlock captures this understanding of the intellectual when writing about Andrei Sakharov and the response of the Russian people to his death. 'How could I translate terms so redolent of emotion as those Russian words … intelligentsia and intelligent? 'Intellectual' just doesn't do. In English, there is something cold and clinical about 'intellectual' when applied to a person. In Russia, intelligent – pronounced with a hard 'g' – is different, because it carries obligatory moral overtones. An intelligent is not just an 'intellectual' but a person of

learning and culture who is devoted to the good of society. Not a 'do-gooder', but a person with a moral compass' (Matlock, 1995, pp.280-281).
[3] This point is inspired by Freedman's general point on U.S. intelligence. That is an appropriate problem was often created by the intelligence services to fit an available solution (Freedman, 1977).
[4] On the Habermasian concept of a dialogic community that informs this standard see Linklater, 1996. It is discussed in detail in chapter four.

References

Adler, E. (1992), 'The Emergence of Cooperation: National Epistemic Communities and the International Evolution of the Idea of Arms Control', *International Organization*, Vol.46, pp.101-146.

Booth, K. (1991a), 'Security and emancipation', *Review of International Studies*, Vol.17, pp.313-326.

Booth, K. (1991b), 'Security in anarchy: utopian realism in theory and practice', *International Affairs*, Vol.67, pp.527-546.

Booth, K. (1999), 'Three Tyrannies', in Tim Dunne and Nicholas Wheeler (eds.), *Human Rights in Global Politics*, Cambridge University Press, Cambridge, pp.31-70.

Booth, K. and Wheeler, N. (1992), 'The Security Dilemma', in John Baylis and N.J.Rengger (eds.), *Dilemmas in World Politics. International Issues in a Changing World*, Oxford, pp. 29-60.

Bull, H. (1995), *The Anarchical Society. A Study of Order in World Politics*, Macmillan, London.

Butterfield, H. (1951), *History and Human Relations*, Collins, London.

Checkel, J.T. (1997), *Ideas and International Political Change. Soviet/Russian Behaviour and the End of the Cold War*, Yale University Press, New Haven and London.

Collins, A. (1997), *The Security Dilemma and the End of the Cold War*, Keele University Press, Edinburgh.

Cox, R.W. (1986), 'Social Forces, States and World Orders: Beyond International Relations Theory', in Robert O. Keohane, (ed.), *Neorealism and its Critics*, Columbia University Press, New York, pp.204-254.

Deudney, D. and Ikenberry, G.J. (1999), 'The nature and sources of liberal international order', *Review of International Studies*, Vol.25, pp.179-196.

Freedman, L. (1977), *US Intelligence and the Soviet Strategic Threat*, Macmillan, London.

Haas, P. (1992), 'Introduction: Epistemic Communities and International Policy Coordination', *International Organization*, Vol.46, pp.1-35.

Herz, J. (1950), 'Idealist Internationalism and the Security Dilemma', *World Politics*, Vol.2, pp.157-180.

Jervis, R. (1976), *Perception and Misperception in International Politics*, Princeton University Press, Princeton.

Krause, K. and Williams, M.C. (1996), 'Broadening the Agenda of Security Studies: Politics and Methods', *Mershon International Studies Review*, Vol.40, pp.229-254.

Krause, K. and Williams, M.C. (1997), 'From Strategy to Security: Foundations of Critical Security Studies', in Keith Krause and Michael C. Williams, *Critical Security Studies. Concepts and Cases*, University of Minnesota Press, 1997.

Linklater, A. (1996), 'The achievements of critical theory', in M.Zalewski, K.Booth and S.Smith (eds.), *After Positivism*, Cambridge University Press, Cambridge, pp.279-298.

Matlock, Jack F. (1995), *Autopsy of an Empire. The American Ambassador's Account of the Collapse of the Soviet Union*, Random House, New York.

Risse-Kappen, T. (1994), 'Ideas Do Not Float Freely: Transnational Coalitions, Domestic Structures and the End of the Cold War', *International Organization*, Vol.48 Spring 1994, pp.185-214.

Wendt, A. (1992), 'Anarchy is What States Make of It: The Social Construction of Power Politics', *International Organization*, Vol.46, pp.391-426.

Wyn Jones, R. (1995), ' "Message in a Bottle"? Theory and Praxis in Critical Security Studies', *Contemporary Security Policy*, Vol.16, pp.299-319.

2 The Security Dilemma: the military dimension

Introduction

This chapter moves beyond the security dilemma by offering a redefinition of the concept as it has been defined in the Security Studies literature. When identifying a dilemma, the traditional literature has tended to focus on the consequences of policy, illusory incompatibility, rather than on the policymaking process. It is argued here, however, that this stance is epistemelogically untenable. The dilemma is best seen in terms of uncertainty. This is identified as a political debate between government bureaucracies, intellectual communities and policy entrepreneurs who advocate what they see as the most appropriate course of action.

Beyond the Traditional Definition

Alan Collins (1995 pp.11-15) identifies four characteristics of a security dilemma: uncertainty of intentions, no appropriate policies, decrease in the security of others, and decrease in the security of all. To Collins the unintentional effect of decreasing the security of another so that it sees malign rather than benign intent, is central to the concept of the security dilemma. Thus, 'benign intent lies at the core of the security dilemma; the incompatibility that states perceive is illusory' (Collins, 1995, pp.10-11). This is consistent with earlier definitions. In addition to Herz, cited in the introduction, Jervis also writes that the 'unintended and undesired consequences of actions meant to be defensive constitutes the "security dilemma"'(Jervis, 1979 p.66). It is this point that is contentious. Booth and Wheeler, label such unintended consequences a 'security paradox'(Collins, 1995 p.12). They reserve the label 'security dilemma' for those situations characterised by uncertainty and unsatisfactory solutions. This would seem appropriate given the epistemological difficulties of identifying another state as benign and consequently claiming that a situation is characterised by illusory incompatibility.

According to Collins it is possible to interpret events with a degree of objectivity that enables the observer to pass judgement on the accuracy of other accounts[1]. In other words, a third party that has objective knowledge of the state sees other perceptions of that state as correct or illusory. This then allows that third party to identify a situation where two states misinterpret the benign intentions of each other as a security dilemma. The first question concerns the place of 'uncertainty' alongside 'illusory incompatibility' as conditions for a security dilemma. If a state has 'decided' that its intentions and interests are incompatible with another, then surely it has resolved its uncertainty. The condition of incompatibility suggests certainty. State's interests are either compatible or they are not. If a state is uncertain then it cannot decide whether or not incompatibility is real or illusory. The point is that uncertainty or illusory incompatibility is the key condition of a security dilemma. It is simply illogical to say uncertainty and illusory incompatibility are necessary before a situation can be identified as a security dilemma.

The second criticism attacks the positivist claim that an observer can detach him or herself from the uncertainty that characterises other observations. By identifying an objective truth to the intentions of another state, an observer can describe the incompatibility of states as illusory. The post-positivist view that has informed recent work in Security Studies (see Wyn Jones, 1995), however, maintains that knowledge is inevitably part of a social setting. In this context claims to objectivity become political. Consider the claim that American perceptions of the Soviet Union in the late 1980s were characterised by 'illusory incompatibility'. Had such an analysis been given to Margaret Thatcher for instance, or to others of the same preconception, it would have been dismissed as appeasement (Ralph, 1999).

Collins (1996 p.14) cites Theodore Roosevelt's view that the German Kaiser had misperceived British intentions as evidence that the British and German relationship in 1904 was characterised by illusory incompatibility. By what standard does Collins privilege Roosevelt's view over the Kaiser's? Had Roosevelt 'informed' the Kaiser of the 'true' situation the Kaiser would undoubtedly have treated the information in a political context if not necessarily with distrust. The point is that knowledge is political, and as such the resolution of uncertainty is a political issue. For this reason the 'dilemma' is defined by the uncertainty that confronts a state's 'decision' and that is reflected in the political interaction of those with different views on security.

Where Collins considers uncertainty as one of four defining characteristics, Booth and Wheeler consider uncertainty to be the central characteristic of the security dilemma. They write:

> If the threat posed by one state to another, be it inadvertent or deliberate, is accurately perceived by the potential or actual target state, then the situation cannot be classified as a security 'dilemma'. It is simply a security 'problem', albeit perhaps a difficult one. *Whatever the actual intentions* of the state engaging in the military preparations, it is the unresolvable uncertainty in the mind of the potential or actual target state about the meaning of the other's intentions and capabilities which creates the 'dilemma' (1992 p.31, emphasis added).

To illustrate the importance of uncertainty, Collins (1996 p.13) uses the Butterfield quote cited in the introduction (1951 p.21). In other words, because it is impossible for the other to see inside one's mind it can never be certain as to one's intentions.

The security dilemma is indeed characterised by uncertainty. By using the word 'mind', however, these authors are in danger of confusing levels of analysis[2]. The security dilemma as discussed here exists at the level of the state. This book more specifically deals with *America's* security dilemma, not that of any particular President, Congressman or woman. In this sense it is inappropriate to discuss 'uncertainty in *the mind* of another'. A state like America is a political not a psychological entity. It is made up of individuals who may or may not be uncertain. The point is, however, if politically significant individuals resolve their uncertainty in different ways the state is still uncertain and its policy is likely to be confused, incoherent or completely non-existent.

The nature of an individual's uncertainty, moreover, is not necessarily that of the 'other-minds' problem. An influential decision-maker in one state does not fear the leader of another state. He or she fears the power of a state that may or may not be a result of that particular leadership. In that sense the uncertainty that attends the dilemma of interpretation (Booth and Wheeler, 1992) is only partially an 'other-minds' problem. It is clearly illustrated in chapter's three and five, for example, that little doubt surrounded the intentions of Mikhail Gorbachev and his close advisers. The doubt within the American foreign policy community was prompted by the question of whether Gorbachev would be in a political position to implement his preferred policy. America's uncertainty was reflected in a debate between optimists and pessimists in Washington who argued over the political position of reformers and traditionalists in Moscow.

When one talks about a security dilemma between states, therefore, one cannot necessarily identify it in terms of the 'other-minds' problem. A state's uncertainty may be reflected in the psychological uncertainty of influential decision-makers. In identifying that psychological uncertainty, however, academic observers then face an 'other-minds' problem of their own. Of more significance is the problem of identifying those individuals who speak for the state. Does it mean, for instance, that America faces a security dilemma because the President is uncertain about the intentions of another state? As chief executive and as commander-in-chief of the armed forces his uncertainty is likely to be reflected in state policy. It is different, however, if the situation is reversed. It cannot be claimed that America resolves its security dilemma when the President is certain as to the intentions of another state and certain in his response. The President alone does not determine U.S. foreign policy. The Constitution, it is often noted, invites the Presidency and Congress 'to struggle for the privilege of directing American foreign policy' (Corwin, 1940 p.200). Moreover, the influence of the bureaucracies, the media and the electorate on foreign policy has long been recognised. Should these politically significant institutions or politically significant individuals within those institutions adopt a different interpretation of another state or recommend a different policy, then America can be said to face a security dilemma. A state's security dilemma is reflected in the political dispute on how to interpret the threat and how best to respond.

If a state's security dilemma can only be epistemologically and ontologically identified in terms of a political battle for control of policy how does one distinguish it from a political problem? This leads to Collins' fourth characteristic: 'no appropriate policies'. A dilemma is characterised in terms of unsatisfactory solutions. That is, regardless of the course of action taken, the state will potentially lose something of value. Booth and Wheeler (1992 p.31) describe the dilemma of response as such:

> should the other's military preparations be matched and so risk an arms race and the further build-up of mistrust, danger, and cost, or should a wait-and-see policy be adopted thereby risking exposure to coercion or attack as a result of relative weakness?

To explore the nature of this dilemma it is appropriate to introduce a debate at the heart of the literature on the security dilemma.

Deterrence and Spiral Models

According to Robert Jervis, a spiral of mistrust between two benign and compatible states is a consequence of the anarchic system. As such a system cannot provide security guarantees, states can only be confident if they provide for their own security. As 'most means of self-protection simultaneously menace others', however, a status quo state risks provoking another state which would otherwise be benign. In other words, '[w]hen states seek the ability to defend themselves, they get too much and too little - too much because they gain the ability to carry out aggression; too little because others, being menaced, will increase their own arms and so reduce the first state's security' (Jervis, 1976 pp.63-64). This process continues when the first state, knowing its own intentions are benign, cannot understand why the other state feels it necessary to respond. It thus attributes that response to aggressive intentions and not only feels vindicated in its initial arms build-up but also feels under pressure to invest in more arms (Jervis, 1976 pp.69-74).

Thus, states come to see themselves in a deterrence rather than a spiral situation. That is each state believes the other is aggressive and must be deterred either through the threat of punishment or the denial of its presumed objective. The tragedy is, however, that the very measures taken to make deterrence effective - the clear communication of a credible threat to use force - is exactly what drives the spiral of mistrust (Jervis, 1978, pp.181-182). The only way of interrupting that process is to recognise the dynamics of the spiral and act in a manner that reassures the other side by unequivocally demonstrating benign intent (Jervis, 1976, pp.81-82). This is explored in greater detail below. That recognition, however, is clouded by a number of psychological factors that encourage faith in the prevailing paradigm and a reliance on doctrinal Realism.

Supported by the "Munich analogy" that emphasises the appropriateness of a deterrence policy, doctrinal Realism has a tendency to exaggerate the conflictual character of interstate relations (Booth and Wheeler, 1992; see also Jervis, 1982, p.360). Booth and Wheeler (1992) identify other such factors:

> *ethnocentrism*, which magnifies misperception, stereotyping, and nationalistic rivalries;...*strategic reductionism*, which takes the political out of interstate relations and reduces it to questions of military balance or imbalance; *worst-case forecasting*, which can magnify mutual fears; *secrecy*, which increases suspicion and the difficulty of accurate threat assessment; *zero-sum thinking*, which

promotes alarmism and rules out significant co-operation; and *implicit enemy imaging*, which leads to particular states being suspected by others whatever the character of their actions or non-actions.

The task of recognising a spiral situation is further complicated, not by misperception, but by the possibility that a deterrence posture is justified. There may be those in a policymaking community who argue that the other state is not benign. Its military build-up is not simply a reaction to that deployed against it, as advocates of the spiral model would argue. Rather its military build-up is a reflection of actual aggressive intent and any policy that mistakenly seeks to reassure the other side will be interpreted as weakness. That interpretation may in turn encourage the other state to believe it can gain its objective through the use of force[3].

In other words, the spiral model should be considered not as an objective observation but one particular interpretation that, if disputed, contributes to the political debate that represents a state's uncertainty. Given the political context that mediates knowledge, the spiral model can not be considered as *the only* description of the consequences of actions. While Collins' third party may be confident in identifying a situation as an unintended spiral of mistrust and the incompatibility of two states as illusory, the states involved face a dilemma of interpretation (is the other benign or malign?) and consequently a dilemma of response (deterrence or reassurance?). Those who argue for a benign interpretation and a reassuring response will cite the spiral model as an illustration of the 'unwanted effects' of a malign interpretation and deterrence posture[4]. Conversely those who argue for a malign interpretation and deterrence posture simply see the spiral model as naïve and may even dismiss it as a propaganda tactic of the adversary.

Unless there is a consensus view within a policymaking community that sees a situation in terms of the spiral model, claims to have identified 'illusory incompatibility' will be politically contested. The security dilemma is represented by this political debate. That debate is influenced by both the internal and external structural context. The former is considered in detail below. The next section, however, focuses on the distribution and, more specifically, the nature of power in the external environment.

Offence and Defence

In the anarchic international system there are no security guarantees. Neorealists argue that this forces states to pursue their own security through the maximisation of power. In other words, the spiral process outlined above forces states to adopt deterrence policies and socialises states so that they all become power-maximising egoists[5]. Benign appearances are dismissed merely as reflections of short-term expediency and advocates of reassurance policies become politically insignificant. The security dilemma is not the same as the spiral model, however, and should not be considered a Neorealist concept. Whereas Neorealists are certain as to the identity and intention of states, the key feature of the security dilemma is uncertainty.

The interpretation of another's intentions and the choice of appropriate response are, according to offence-defence theorists, influenced by the nature of military technology[6]. Robert Jervis (1978) argued that the spiral process that exacerbates mistrust could be mitigated when defensive military technology is dominant. He assesses the offence-defence balance in terms of money spent. He argues that 'if each dollar spent on offence can overcome each dollar spent on defence' then the offence will have the advantage (1978, p.188)[7]. Offensive dominance, he argues, increases mistrust and tightens the spiral as the cost of misinterpretation increases. In other words, if the offence has the advantage, conquest is easier. In this environment the costs of letting one's guard down increase. According to Jervis, this is likely to discourage states from risking a policy of reassurance.   If the level of mistrust is at such a level, and the offence is so dominant, a state may even decide to pre-empt what is interpreted as an inevitable attack by the other. This 'reciprocal fear of surprise attack' is the most potent and most dangerous driver of the spiral (1978, p.189).

The dynamics are reversed when the defence is dominant. In this situation the state that fears attack does not pre-empt since it would be less likely to succeed or success would involve military expenditure that is beyond its means (1978, p.190). Furthermore, because the defender has more faith in the ability of its forces to repel an attack it may be more likely to risk a policy designed to reassure the other side. In other words, the costs of the other state misperceiving that policy as a show of weakness would be less if defence held the advantage. Defensive dominance, therefore, not only mitigates mistrust by denying either side the ability to exploit weakness or to pre-empt their worst fears, but also encourages the adoption of what would otherwise have been considered a risky policy of reassuring the other side.

At this point it is important to note the influence of nuclear weapons on the offence-defence balance. Jervis makes the point (1978, pp.198-9) that with the development of ballistic nuclear missiles traditional defence was in effect redundant. Yet this, he argued, was 'a triumph not of the offence, but of deterrence. Attack makes no sense,' he continues, 'not because it can be beaten off [i.e. traditional defence], but because the attacker will be destroyed in return. In terms of the question under consideration here, the result is the equivalent of the primacy of the defence'. As Bradley Klein (1994, p.61) notes, 'in the deracinated logic of nuclear strategists, vulnerability was thus a virtue as it assured all countries that no one of them might achieve impunity should it choose to seize the initiative and attack'. In this sense technology that sought to address vulnerability, either by providing a defence against missiles or seeking to knock-out the other's missiles before they were launched, was now considered offensive. As Glaser (1990 p.74) put it, 'when countries depend on deterrence to maintain their security, forces that threaten the adversary's deterrent forces are offensive, while forces that enhance one's deterrent forces are defensive'.

Being acutely aware of the influence of nuclear weapons Jervis (1978 pp.198-210) adapted his offence-defence analysis. He argued that those nuclear weapons that were not accurate enough for counterforce targetting and therefore only suitable for a retaliatory/countervalue strike, should be considered defensive. By this logic he argued land-based Intercontinental Ballistic Missiles (ICBMs) were offensive and therefore destabilising, while Sea-Launched Ballistic Missiles (SLBMs) were defensive and therefore stabilising. He advocated that the United States interrupt a potential spiral of mistrust by forgoing the capability to attack Soviet defensive capability. For example, it should not invest in Anti-Submarine Warfare (ASW).

Jervis was of course writing in 1978, before the American D-5 Trident SLBM was deployed. Its increased accuracy would bring into question Jervis' logic (Cote, 1991). Yet regardless of the technical details, Jervis' faith in the 'nuclear revolution' was already questionable. Jervis for example, argued (1989) that mutually assured destruction (MAD) was, as he put it, 'a fact and not a policy'. In other words, the destructive potential of a nuclear conflict was enough to deter offensive intentions even with the increasing accuracy and counterforce capability of new generation missiles. Others, however, questioned the influence that the offence-defence balance had on the intentions of political actors. Colin Gray (1993 p.28) for example, clearly located malign or benign intentions at the domestic not systemic/technological level. He writes 'there has never been an aggressive weapon, only aggressive owners and operators of weapons'. According to this opinion, there is no universal interpretation of the reason a state invests in a particular weapon. SLBMs may be interpreted as defensive, but if one regards nuclear superiority and escalation dominance as providing political advantage, overinvestment of this particular 'defensive' weapon may be interpreted as offensive.

Chapter three clearly demonstrates that the interpretation of the nuclear revolution went to the heart of America's Cold War security dilemma. There were many voices in the American policymaking community who argued that the Soviet Union viewed nuclear weapons as offensive instruments to be used in a way that could coerce if not necessarily disarm the United States. Soviet policy was not the reaction of an insecure state that was preparing to defend its territory by denying the attacker an offensive capacity. Rather Soviet strategy was an attempt to use military power to advance a political agenda that was territorially expansionist. In effect these arguments questioned the existence of a nuclear revolution and pointed to Soviet strategy as evidence. Their lack of faith in minimal deterrence was usually met with a position that advocated preparations to fight a war once deterrence had failed. The 'maximalists' (Klein, 1994, pp.39-80) argued that only by militarily denying the other side its objective and actually prevailing in a conflict so that the aggressor was politically disadvantaged would the U.S. be able to deter the Soviets from pursuing its expansionist aims. To those who saw the Soviet Union as benign and insecure, or simply deterred by the reality of MAD, an American warfighting strategy was provocative. They feared the Cold War had followed the pattern of a spiral model and advocated more defensive postures. The political debate between advocates of these two positions characterised the military dimension of America's Cold War security dilemma.

Mitigating the Unwanted Effects of Uncertainty: common security

State behaviour is not determined by the systemic influences Neorealists identify (Wendt, 1992). Technology and its military application are not the only factors mediating the external influences on a state's behaviour. As Gray noted (1993 p.39), the influence of technology is dependent on the identity of the particular state. The utility of offence-defence theory in its strictest form, therefore, rests on the assumption of an egoistic and competitive state identity. Once that assumption is questioned its utility as a general theory is undermined. Lynn-Jones (1995, p.686), for example, admits that it cannot offer a monocausal explanation of all events.

Given the identity of a state, however, offence-defence theory does offer a coherent cause and effect logic that has informed many Realist approaches to security. Lynn-Jones (1995, pp.686-687), for example, writes that a 'state led by a leader with the aggressive designs of a Hitler, for example, is likely to be threatening in any international system, but it will be much more threatening when offence is relatively easy and inexpensive'. Likewise, a status quo state that is seeking to reassure another that its intentions are defensive will be able to make more concessions when the defence dominates as the risk and cost of being exploited will be less. In other words, when the defence dominates, defensive states will have greater incentive to pursue policies that interrupt the dynamics of the spiral model by resolving the uncertainty of the other side. It must be repeated, however, that these insights and the assumptions on which they are based (i.e. the identity of the other state) will be politically contested. In this sense offence-defence theory only has utility in as much as it articulates a particular approach of a particular intellectual community.

One particular community that used the insights of offence-defence theory to encourage cooperation between states and to mitigate the unwanted effects of uncertainty, tended to unite around the label 'common security'(Collins 1996, pp.59-63; Palme, 1982; Smoke and Kortunov, 1991; SIPRI, 1985; Buzan 1987). Its strategy included specific policies such as minimum deterrence, disarmament, arms control, non-offensive defence (NOD) (Wiseman, 1989; Boserup and Nield, 1990) and graduated reduction in tension (GRIT) (Osgood, 1962; Etzioni 1962). As Buzan (1987) points out, common security was a concept that united many of those concerned that the Cold War stand off in the 1980s was becoming increasingly unstable. As a response it offered an alternative that was potentially radical but not utopian like the world government proposals of earlier idealists.

The central debate among these thinkers was the place nuclear weapons should play in common security strategies. While some argued nuclear weapons were essential to maintain stability, others argued that nuclear weapons were the problem and not the solution. For example, Barry Buzan agreed with the idea that had united common security thinkers since it was espoused by the Palme Commission in 1982: state security was interdependent. Yet unlike Palme, Buzan argued that nuclear weapons were central to the recognition of that interdependence. He wrote in 1987: 'No clearer practical statement of security interdependence can be made than the commitment to national vulnerability that lies at the logical heart of MAD doctrine' (Buzan, 1987, p.268). Where Palme advocated nuclear disarmament, Buzan advocated a policy of Minimum Nuclear Deterrence (MND) that stabilised the shared understanding of mutual vulnerability.

The case for nuclear disarmament was made by, amongst others, Vayrynen, Bahr and Krass (SIPRI, 1985). They argued that MND had failed to tame the superpower spiral after the enthusiasm for that policy in the 1960s. They argued minimum deterrence would always give way to maximalist deterrence and the perceived need for a warfighting posture would always lead to a spiral of mistrust. The only way to stabilise a security relationship was to recognise its interdependent character and abolish threatening and provocative weapons. To Buzan, calls for nuclear disarmament in the 1980s were utopian given the problems and approaches of either Superpower. He claimed in 1987 that 'common security defined in terms of disarmament demands a shift so far into the unknown that the uncertainty associated with it automatically overwhelms any chance of its adoption' (Buzan, 1987, p.270). On the other hand MND offered a credible alternative.

Yet Buzan is forced to admit the logic of SIPRI's criticism of MND when examining the influence that political commitments such as alliances may have had on the choice of deterrence postures (Buzan, 1987, p.273). Chapter five demonstrates clearly the influence that America's commitment to the security of Western Europe had on its security policy. The implication of such political commitments is that they require power projection capabilities and doctrines of limited war that can be easily be interpreted in terms of a warfighting postures. While motivated by politically defensive reasons, a benign posture could none the less be easily misinterpreted as malign intent[8]. Buzan responds to such criticism by invoking non-provocative defence (NPD) to compensate for MNDs ambiguity. In response to those critics who argue MND leads to a warfighting posture as it seeks to address credibility gaps across the threat spectrum, Buzan argued that a robust conventional, non-provocative defence would eliminate the need for a nuclear response to most threats.

As technology evolved in the 1980s, many pointed to the possibility that precision guided weapons gave an advantage to the defence. NATO it was argued could afford to adopt a less threatening posture and abolish its nuclear deterrent (Windass, 1985). Buzan offered several points that suggested MND was still required even if NPD was adopted. First, NPD required fortified borders and defensive depth, yet NATO's key problem, the East/West German border, was conducive to neither. Second, a defensive posture that lacked a retaliatory or forward capability would fail to provide a credible deterrent. A potential aggressor would not be deterred if it knew that it had little to lose by fighting a battle on the opponent's territory. Moreover, such a posture would make it virtually impossible to regain lost territory (Buzan, 1987 pp.272-273; Collins, 1996, p.48). For these reasons Buzan advocated that NPD must be implemented in tandem with MND.

Yet the third weakness of NPD is left unaddressed by this approach. It again involves the problem of extended deterrence. If all members of an alliance adopted NPD then none would have the military reach to assist the other. Again, America's need to project military power on to the continent of Europe seemingly precluded its adoption of NPD. America's political commitments, in other words, posed an obstacle towards adopting a policy of common security along these lines. For this reason, Buzan (1987, pp.276-278) was forced to advocate the type of radical suggestion that he had earlier criticised as utopian. As the requirements of extended deterrence precluded NPD and if MND without NPD was seen as being provocative he effectively advocated cutting the link between America and Europe. Europe alone should adopt MND and NPD. This would remove the provocation that America's offensive capability seemed to create.

These issues are examined in more depth in the following chapter. The important point here is that in the 1980s certain strategies were developed with the intention of mitigating the spiral of mistrust that many thought characterised the Cold War. In this context, Buzan made the final point that should a common security policy be unambiguously adopted it would 'constitute a profound *political* challenge to one's opponent' (emphasis added). In other words, if the opponent did not reciprocate the policy of common security it would have increasing difficulty explaining its provocative posture and face 'internal pressures in favour of moves towards a common security norm'. Furthermore, the lack of reciprocation runs the risk of encouraging a more determined reaction from an opponent (Buzan, 1987, p.274). The idea that the impact of policies based on deterrence and spiral models is mediated in this way by internal political pressures, is picked up by Charles Glaser (1992) and examined in detail below. Before looking at Glaser's work, however, it is, in the light Buzan's point on the political impact of common security, important to introduce the concept of GRIT.

GRIT, Prisoners Dilemma and Security Regimes

Before common security became fashionable in the 1980s two authors explored the possibility of what became known as Graduated Reciprocation in Tension-Reduction (GRIT). Osgood (1962) argued that conciliatory policies would be able to reduce suspicion and tension between two benign states that were victims of misperception. The unilateral act of conciliation, however, would have to satisfy requirements of national security (this role was adopted by MND and NPD) but would decisively depend on reciprocation for success. The initiating state would therefore have to take sufficient risks to induce reciprocation from opponents and thereby reduce tension. Where Osgood called for a dramatic first conciliatory step and persistent efforts to induce reciprocation, Etzioni (1962) advocated a gradualist and more cautious approach that would assist communication and build understanding.

Reciprocation of cooperative moves is central to the neoliberal argument that states can cooperate under anarchy or, as some conceptualise it, prisoners dilemma. In prisoners dilemma the optimum *universal* outcome is for two states to cooperate. However, the optimum *particular* outcome is to defect while the other cooperates or to not reciprocate the other's concessions. Conversely, the worst possible particular outcome is to offer concessions that are not reciprocated. In an effort to avoid being exploited while seeking the benefits of exploitation, therefore, it is most likely that neither side offers cooperative concessions. Both sides end up in the worst possible situation. This 'payoff structure' can be altered, it was argued, if it can be guaranteed that future rewards outweigh immediate losses. If the game is repeated, in other words, future retaliation for defection or reward for reciprocity can alter a state's incentives (Axelrod, 1984).

Regimes, defined by Krasner (1983, p.2) as 'principles, norms, rules and decision-making procedures', can change

> the extent to which governments expect their present actions to affect the behaviour of others on future issues. The principles and rules of international regimes make governments concerned about precedents, increasing the likelihood that they will attempt to punish defectors. In this way, international regimes help link the future with the present (Axelrod and Keohane, 1993, p.94).

States will be more inclined to reciprocate cooperative moves, in other words, because they are aware that their long-term welfare depends on the expectations that their short term actions help to create. As time goes by, states privilege the long term gains from mutual cooperation over the short term and ultimately pyrrich gains of unilateral defection.

At this point, many neoliberals agree with Jervis who argues that security regimes are much more difficult to create than economic regimes. The 'high stakes' and 'unforgiving nature' of the military arena shortens the shadow of the future. That is, the costs of being exploited may be absolute thus removing the chance to retaliate against defection in the future. Moreover, the large and immediate gains of defection not only discourage moves to initiate cooperation, but make those states in a cooperative relationship extra sensitive to the relative gains of the other. As Grieco notes (1993 p.118), 'states are *positional* ... in character, and therefore Realists argue that, in addition to concerns about cheating, states in cooperative arrangements also worry that their partners might gain more from cooperation than they do'. With this in mind, Realists argue that states are guided by the maxim that 'today's friend might be tomorrow's enemy'. Unless the gains of cooperation are evenly distributed states will defect from cooperation even if their partner is in full compliance.

The persistent fear that states may be duped increases the tendency towards unilateral and secret military preparations that set additional obstacles to the initiation and monitoring of cooperative patterns. In the military arena, therefore, it is easier to create mutual suspicion than mutual trust. Spiral models, it would seem, are more common place than security regimes. If cooperation occurs it is more likely to be tacit and based on a prudent respect for the balance of power rather than expectations of cooperation[9].

Yet Jervis' and Grieco's analyses make unwarranted assumptions. They take the state's identity as given. The starting point for their analysis is to take the state as a rational, power-maximising egoist. This assumption underestimates the extent to which rationality is politically contested and underplays the potential influence that ideas (as opposed to interests defined in terms of material power) can have in changing the identity and interests of states in a way that fosters cooperation. To demonstrate the potential for such a process it is necessary first to refine the concepts at the heart of Jervis' analysis, the deterrence and spiral models, and to draw policy implications that are not based on a rationalist methodology.

The Politics of Political Consequences

Buzan's argument that domestic political pressure may force states to reciprocate GRIT-type strategies suggests Jervis and Grieco's dismissal of GRIT is too state-centric and too rationalist, in the sense that it neglects the influence of internal factors. The prospects for the reciprocation of a GRIT-type strategy and with it the applicability of the deterrence or spiral model are mediated by the internal politics of a state.

It is appropriate, therefore, to focus on sub-state actors for two reasons. Firstly, as was established at the outset, a state's security dilemma is identified by the political debate between different intellectual communities; and secondly, the subject of that debate is the political standing of similar communities in the other state. In other words, an intellectual community may see relations between two states in terms of a spiral model and advocate a reassurance policy. The chances of that policy being reciprocated, however, depend not on the rational calculations described by game theorists, but on the political consequences of that policy on the domestic power balance in the other state. In writing about the influence of the offence-defence balance, Glaser's recognition that the interests and intentions of that state are not set in stone and are themselves subject to political debate is crucial. The effectiveness of a reassurance policy is dependent on the effect it has not only on individual learning but also on the shifts in the power positions of domestic intellectual communities.

Glaser (1992, pp.515-6) undermines the rationalist approach by suggesting that intellectual communities have a vested interest in seeing uncertainty resolved in a particular way. A state's evaluation of a reassurance policy, therefore, will tend to be 'biased' if 'certain organisations are able to gain undue influence because of their power, prestige, bargaining skill, and/or public relations skill'. He adds that militaries and 'interest groups that would benefit from large investments in military capabilities' will impute malign intentions to the reassurance policy of an adversary. A cooperative state should, therefore, aim not necessarily to reassure the other side, as the traditional spiral model would suggest, but should pursue a policy that allows cooperative groups ('moderates') within the other state to marginalise those groups who benefit from competition ('hardliners'). The main question facing a state's security policy, therefore, as Glaser sees it, is this: under what conditions are offensive, competitive policies likely to shift the adversary's balance of domestic power favourably, and when are defensive, cooperative policies more likely to succeed?

In general, Glaser recommends that a cooperative state should usually pursue cooperative policies towards a state with moderates in power. Reciprocating their concessions or initiating a GRIT-type strategy would bolster their political standing by confirming their argument. It does not follow, however, that a competitive policy is suitable when hardliners are in power. The key issue is how that competitive policy will be interpreted within the adversary's debate. Thus, if the competitive policy is interpreted by moderates as a reaction to the hardline policies of their own government, it will tend to bolster their argument that the hardline approach is self-defeating. However, if it is interpreted by both moderates and hardliners not as a reaction, but as evidence of malign intent, hardline responses will gain support (Glaser, 1992, pp.521-5).

The success of a state's response, therefore, is dependent on the interpretation of the domestic politics of the target state. This emphasis on domestic politics recalls the Liberal response to the Neorealist criticism of the cooperation under anarchy thesis. Specifically, the interdependent and transnational nature of the respective debates highlights the potential for changing national interests so that they are pursued through cooperation not power competition. To argue that possibilities for interstate cooperation are immanent in transnational politics, however, does not mean the security dilemma is easily mitigated or transcended. If anything, the focus on domestic politics makes mitigation strategies more complex than those suggested by the offence-defence approach and game theorists. While it lacks the elegant parsimony of neorealism and neoliberalism, however, this approach is more realistic and, as chapter three demonstrates, empirically grounded.

To briefly summarise: the debate that characterises one state's security dilemma is influenced by competing interpretations of the balance of political influence among the competing opinions that characterise the other state's security dilemma. Advocates of deterrence policies have little faith that reassurance policies will be reciprocated because they see hardliners in political control of the other state. Those advocating reassurance policies would of course view the likelihood of reciprocation as greater because they see the political balance as reversed. Realists claim that the influence one state's military strategy has on the political debate of another is limited. A state cannot be certain that its strategy will have the intended effect and ultimately the security debate of another state is beyond the control of any outside influence. Self-help necessitates, they would therefore argue, that the defender be prepared for sudden shifts in the adversary's posture towards aggression. Worst case forecasting of this kind is a major obstacle to those advocating policies of reassurance. As is argued below, however, the power of this argument is, to a large extent, also dependent on the nature of an adversary's domestic political structure.

Transnationalism and the Change in Soviet Security Policy

In response to the neorealist claim that relative gains precluded long term cooperation between states, 'sophisticated versions of liberal theory' began to abandon the rationalist approach that took state's identities and interests as fixed. They acknowledged that institutions could, over time alter conceptions of interests and even constitute a different identity (Krasner, 1983). The agents of this process were transnational intellectual communities that worked to strengthen the domestic position of their respective partners to the point where the norms of the regime became embedded in the security discourse of both states and national interests converged around interstate cooperation.

To Joseph Nye (1987), while this process could not account for the overall superpower relationship (like Jervis he saw it in terms of a prudent approach to narrow definitions of self interest) it could explain what he called 'an incomplete mosaic of security regimes'. Furthermore, Emanuel Adler (1992) demonstrated how the idea of arms control that emerged within the American scientific community was disseminated among their Soviet counterparts through transnational fora such as the Pugwash Group. Both sides would then point to the existence of arms control lobbyists in both policymaking communities to support their advocacy of arms control. Both Nye and Alder argue that the test of an idea's influence is the extent to which it was institutionalised in domestic policy-making processes during the Cold War.

This emphasis on the institutional influence of ideas received additional attention after the failure of structural approaches to explain the radical change in Soviet interests and identity in the late 1980s. It is generally agreed that the change in Soviet policy during the Gorbachev era was decisive in ending the Cold War. Those accounts that focus on the role played by America's relative strength in prompting Soviet reforms, usually Realist explanations (Tara and Zeringue 1992; Waltz, 1993) or conservative histories (Gaddis, 1989; Winik, 1996), are contested on both empirical and theoretical grounds. These arguments are considered in detail in chapter three. It is sufficient to note here that such arguments are indeterminate. For example, Grunberg and Risse-Kappen (1995, p.111) note, these theories do not explain why 'these changes did not occur in the 1970s when [Soviet] decline was firmly on its way'. What Kjell Goldmann

(1995, p.88) calls 'sooner-or-later theories' can be neither confirmed nor falsified. They can tell us that change will happen but give no indication of the timing or nature of that change. An explanation that focuses only on material strength can tell us that the weakening state 'will fail to attain its current objectives, sooner or later'. They tell us something, but 'it is not much. We cannot say anything on this basis about the point where a state will give up a particular objective'.

This uncertainty as to how the Soviet Union would react to changes in the international environment was of course reflected in the political debate at the time. As Checkel (1997, p.91) notes structural explanations 'posit a logic and rationality that were not present in the increasingly tumultuous sociopolitical atmosphere of the USSR. This state of unrest, in which ideas, policies, and attacks came from all parts of the political spectrum, applied to the evolution of Soviet foreign policy as well'. To address the interdeterminacy of structural explanations Lebow amongst others argued for a focus on this 'irrational' process. An analyst of Soviet policy during this period, he concluded, 'must go outside the paradigm and look at the determining influence of domestic politics, belief systems, and learning' (Lebow, 1995 p.41).

At the domestic level, explanations have been advanced that focus on the change in generational leadership. Yet here too there is reason for scepticism. Checkel (1997, p.14) notes that although Gorbachev 'had clearly hinted that he was open to new ideas on international politics, there is no indication that he had developed a comprehensive conceptual or policy framework for foreign policy reform' when he came to power. Furthermore, the idea that Gorbachev would pursue reformist policies simply to assume power does not explain the radical policies he would later pursue, particularly as some interpreted them as heretical (Checkel, 1997, p.81). The indeterminacy of domestic as well as international-level explanations, therefore, has led to a focus on 'the interaction of international and domestic influences of state behaviour and *take the role of ideas - knowledge, values, and strategic concepts - seriously*' (Risse-Kappen, 1994, pp.185-186, emphasis added).

Why specifically in the mid-to-late 1980s did a radically different set of ideas inform Soviet policy and lead to security cooperation with the United States and ultimately the end of the Cold War? Jeffrey Checkel, has argued that the relative decline identified by Realist explanations created a crisis in security policy which effectively acted as a window of opportunity for 'policy entrepreneurs' to influence the policy discussions they had previously been exiled from. That policy vacuum was occupied by entrepreneurs who were part of a transnational intellectual community that was motivated in varying degrees by the principles of détente and common security (Herman, 1996, p.281). Thomas Risse-Kappen (1994) and Mathew Evangelista (1995) also note the influence of transnational coalitions on the end of the Cold War. Yet they qualify this point by arguing that the domestic political structure of a state mediated the influence of transnational ideas. These ideas influenced Soviet policy to a greater extent than American policy because of the centralised political structure of the former in comparison to the decentralised nature of the latter. In contrast to the West German response to New Thinking, where new ideas could influence policy because of the corporatist nature of the domestic structure, a coherent American response was hampered by the difficulties of building a political coalition in a pluralist system. The lack of positive American reciprocation in turn made it more difficult for Gorbachev to pursue New Thinking as the hardline criticism began to take on increasing political significance (Wohlforth, 1996 pp.14-18).

Checkel's analysis also qualifies the role played by transnational ideas. While his analysis acknowledges the influence of transnational agents, most of his analysis concerns debates specific to the Soviet Union. For example, the relationship between capitalism and war or socialism and peace had a logic seemingly independent from the actions of the U.S. Robert Herman (1996, pp.274-275) also notes that certain 'elements of New Thinking ... were indigenous, often the product of ongoing debate within the socialist bloc'. Thus while, Checkel, Herman, Risse-Kappen and Evangelista all agree that ideational factors played an important role, there is a difference of emphasis on their origins and the extent of their influence.

The important point here is not necessarily what this research means for our understanding of policy change in the Soviet Union, although they all advance greatly on early Realist attempts. The more significant point here is what these insights mean for our understanding of security regimes and the security dilemma. Specifically, it prompts one final step in recognising a definition of the security dilemma that holds immanent possibilities for its resolution.

Soviet Domestic Politics and America's Security Dilemma

The main conclusion of Risse-Kappen and Evangelista's research is that centralised domestic structures can give policy expression to new ideas as soon as they are adopted by politically significant actors. Once the political elite adopt a new set of ideas policy will change. Thus, outside observers viewing policy shifts in a state that has a centralised domestic structure can be more or less certain that policy has changed if it can demonstrate that the political elite has adopted new ideas. If those ideas are based on the spiral model it can be certain that a policy of reassurance will be reciprocated and not exploited. Yet that certainty will be limited to the short term or, more accurately, limited to the time that particular elite faction can maintain power. Soviet security policy changed very quickly, according to Risse-Kappen and Evangelista, because of the centralised political structure. In the case study they chose the shift took place from competitive to cooperative security policies. One can imply from their conclusions that a shift in the opposite direction could happen just as quickly if the centralised political structure was maintained.

It is this point, of course, that is central to the uncertainty that underpins the security dilemma. As noted above, Realists rule out the possibility of cooperation because of the fear of being duped by another state's defection. When dealing with a state that has a centralised political structure, the likelihood of defection is made easier because new ideas only have to convince the political elite rather than society as a whole. That is not to say that long term cooperation between decentralised and centralised structures cannot take place. However, it is likely that the Realists in a decentralised state will be politically strengthened because they can point to the suddenness with which the cooperative policy of a centralised state can be abandoned. Their political presence in the decentralised state will, of course, make it more difficult for those advocates of continued cooperation to maintain a policy coalition, which in turn may undermine the policy of cooperation in the centralised state.

The politics that determine which ideas are adopted by the political elite of a centralised state may be beyond the influence of transnational coalitions because of a relatively small number of access points. If this is the case then the decentralised state will have even less confidence in the prospects for long term cooperation. As Checkel and Herman note, ideas advocating cooperation influenced the Soviet leadership, but they were not necessarily the result of transnational influence. Indeed, because they were specific to Soviet ideology, transnational actors could not have affected the debate. Once again, the examples they use demonstrates a shift in Soviet ideology from a competitive view of the capitalist world, to one that saw capitalism as a potential partner rather than an aggressor. Because transnational actors cannot influence these issues and because the shift to a competitive view could just as easily happen, Realists would counsel a policy of caution.

Thomas Risse-Kappen suggests the reason why America did not fully reciprocate Soviet new thinking was because ideas of common security were 'rather alien to a political culture emphasising pluralist individualism at home and sharp zero-sum conflicts with ideological opponents abroad'. It is certainly true that American Realists emphasised the zero-sum character of the conflict with the Soviet Union.   The exceptionalism inherent in America's political culture and its willingness to elevate the opinions of the military reinforced this obstacle to the adoption of common security.

But as chapter three demonstrates, the political significance of American Realism in the late 1980s was reinforced by the uncertainty of Gorbachev's political position and his ability to permanently marginalise those Soviet institutions that had a vested interest in conflict.   This argument proved convenient for American institutions with similar interests and reinforced the cultural tendency that Risse-Kappen identifies. But until Soviet reform was considered irreversible it would be an argument that mobilised much political support.   Indeed, the only thing that would loosen the grip that Realism had on U.S. policy was the political defeat of the hardline institutions of the military, the KGB and the Communist Party in the Soviet Union.   Ultimately, American policy needed to see the decentralisation of political power within the Soviet Union.   Only then could it guarantee that cooperation would not be based on foundations that could be quickly undermined by new leaders whose power was unchecked by a more cooperative faction.

Resolving the Security Dilemma

The military dimension of the security dilemma, then, is identified as the political battle between those who see relations with another state in terms of the deterrence model, and those who see it in terms of the spiral model. If the outcome of the political debate is an approach that achieves a 'satisfactory solution' then debate will be marginalised[10].   Without politically significant criticism the policy maker will be confident that his or her policy has found a satisfactory solution.   Yet if a certain approach produces an 'unsatisfactory solution' a debate of political significance will continue.   This can take various forms, from an overt attack by political opponents (other intellectual communities) in the extended policymaking community, to the 'dissenting footnote' in an intelligence analysis or the 'leaking' of politically sensitive information that is meant to embarrass the government.

Movement between satisfactory and unsatisfactory solutions is caused by a combination of external events and internally inspired ideas[11]. The external events can create an unsatisfactory solution or as Checkel puts it 'a sense of crisis or uncertainty among elites' that then opens 'a window of opportunity' for policy entrepreneurs to jump through (Checkel, 1997, p.8). Yet an external event can be interpreted differently within the policymaking community. The political process of convincing policymakers that one view is more accurate than the other represents the dilemma of interpretation. The same process of convincing policymakers that the policy advocated will have the desired affect on the political process of the other state represents the dilemma of response.

The introduction of new 'knowledge' can upset a consensus that had formed around a satisfactory solution. The use of the term 'knowledge' as opposed to 'intelligence' is deliberate. While intelligence can be considered as knowledge, the term involves more than simply information about another state's intentions and capabilities. Knowledge includes anything that can influence a state's approach towards interpreting and responding to the security environment. For example, a revolution in military technology can make a previously considered satisfactory solution, unsatisfactory. The development of ballistic missile defence technology has for some analysts, made mutually assured destruction an unsatisfactory response to a nuclear armed opponent. 'New knowledge' may not be restricted to new military technology either. It can also include a change in social attitudes or a change in social relations that gives a voice to previously unheard opinions concerning the international situation.

A political consensus that has converged around a satisfactory solution is less likely to be temporary if a similar consensus exists in the other state. In other words, if both sides' understanding of their own national interest converges on an intersubjective understanding of the external situation then the relationship is likely to be stable. As Glaser points out, those seeking to reassure the other side should argue for policies that encourage and assist those advocating similar policies on the other side. This transnational cooperation at the level of sub-state intellectual communities is, in Glaser's analysis, limited to tacit understanding and signalling. Should that process lead both communities to gain decisive influence over the policy of their respective states, then their intersubjective understanding is reflected at the international level.

It is the nature of an intersubjective understanding, however, that it can change if one side party to that understanding alters its own subjective view. The subjective view of a state is, of course, a political concept that is more likely to change suddenly if political power within that state is easily captured. For this reason intersubjective understandings between centralised states, or between a decentralised state and a centralised state, will be weaker than those between decentralised states. Cooperation between centralised states may of course be more intense when there is a meeting of elite minds. However, it only takes the changing of a few minds for cooperation to end. Witness the sudden reversal of Sino-Soviet cooperation in the late 1950s and Sino-American confrontation in the early 1970s[12]. Among decentralised states cooperation may be less intense but more sustained as Realist doubters are balanced and sometimes defeated by Liberals who always manage to find points of influence in the domestic structure.

According to this argument then, the long term resolution of a security dilemma depends on intellectual communities that advocate cooperation maintaining a political presence and preferably political power within both states. As the recent work on the changes in Soviet foreign policy has illustrated, a transnational coalition will find it easier to implement its ideas within in a centralised state. It is further argued, however, that such a community will find it more difficult to maintain a permanent presence in the policy discourse of a centralised state than in one that is decentralised. This all-or-nothing scenario when dealing with a centralised state is unlikely to reassure other states. The Realist argument in those states will be strengthened by the prospect of a sudden reversal in policy and thus present a further political obstacle to the convergence of interstate expectations.

The side observing policy change will only be certain that a recent shift towards cooperation will outlast the transitional leadership if it is built on a broader political coalition[13]. Long term expectations of cooperation, therefore, are maintained if the intellectual community advocating cooperation holds a constant, if not necessarily a decisive influence on policy. Only then will either side be certain that an intellectual community advocating security competition cannot dominate policy. The extent of cooperation will be dependent on the political influence of, to use Glaser's terms, 'the moderates'. Even if they do not exercise decisive influence, however, their continued presence will dilute the influence that 'hardliners' have. This by itself mitigates the spiral dynamics that hardline policies have the potential to create.

The institutionalisation of the cooperative approach is, therefore, encouraged, though not guaranteed, by decentralising the domestic political structure. As is often pointed out, Hitler's ideas found expression and ultimately decisive influence in the decentralised structure of the

Weimar Republic. It is for this reason that the socio-political identity of the state, as well as its political structure is an important factor in permanently resolving the security dilemma. This issue is dealt with in chapter four.

Conclusion

The significance of redefining the security dilemma as a debate between competing intellectual communities goes beyond academic concerns for valid epistemology and coherent interpretive theory. It is in itself politically significant. It exposes the essentialist assumptions on which the traditional security dilemma is based and undermines the claim that it explains why states are forced to constantly compete for security. In doing so it reveals a practical possibility and strategy for security cooperation.

The traditional concept revolved around the problem of ascertaining the intentions of another state and unavoidably pursuing an inappropriate policy based on the subsequent misperception. This chapter has argued that the focus on a state's uncertainty, defined in terms of a debate between politically significant actors, is the only valid way of identifying a dilemma. Those who argue 'illusory incompatibility' is a necessary characteristic of the security dilemma make inappropriate claims to objectivity. Using the concepts of deterrence and spiral models as truth claims advocated by particular intellectual communities, however, allows one to identify the military dimension of the security dilemma. Moreover, the influence of these intellectual communities is best seen in terms of the consequence they have on the political debate that reflects the other state's security dilemma. By marginalising those who support policies of competition, and by embedding cooperative policies in *both* states, transnational politics can resolve the uncertainty within each state and transcend the self-fulfilling dynamics that spiral theorists identify. In effect, the political victory of transnational activists campaigning on behalf of common interests can move interstate relations beyond the security dilemma and towards a security community.

Notes

[1] For example, Collins writes 'It is important to note that it is not necessary for the state to be aware that its position is hopeless for this to be a dilemma. Indeed, unless the decision-makers were sensitive to the security dilemma, it is unlikely that continuing to accumulate arms will appear inappropriate' (Collins, 1996 p.14).

[2] For an example of this see Collins, 1996, pp.37-38. Collins contests Booth and Wheeler's claim that Germany faced a dilemma of response in 1924. Yet as evidence that a state, Germany, was certain about its response to France, he cites the opinion of an individual, Foreign Minister Gustav Streseman. He says '*Streseman* (emphasis added) was not faced with a dilemma of response' because he realised Germany's weakened position left it little room for manoeuvre. But the very fact that Streseman was defending his policy against political opponents who sought a more confrontational response towards France and the Versailles 'diktat', shows that *Germany* was uncertain and thus faced a dilemma of response.

[3] To Collins the existence of malign intent negates the possibility of a situation being labelled a security dilemma. It is argued here, however, that the intent of the state being observed will be politically contested by different opinions within the observer state. That does not mean the situation cannot be termed a dilemma. Rather it is a reflection that the state is uncertain. It is in a security dilemma. If a political consensus exists that can identify the other as aggressive then the state faces a security problem. As Collins points out (1996 p.32), Snyder confuses matters by labelling a similar situation as a security dilemma. He defines a security dilemma as 'a situation in which each state believed that its security required the insecurity of others' (1985 p.153). A state that requires the insecurity of another for its own security can only be regarded as a security problem. That does not mean the state does not face a dilemma of response. As is argued above, there may be different, equally unsatisfactory ways of responding to that particular state. For example it may be the case that some consider surrender a better option to fighting. If the decision to fight is made, a state or alliance may be confronted with another dilemma of response. During the Second World War, for instance, the western allies faced the dilemma of how best to respond to the Nazi threat. Was it best to open a second front in northern France as Stalin wished and the American military urged, or should the allies pursue a peripheral strategy as the British argued? (Feis, 1957).

[4] Ernst Haas (1980, p.390), for example notes that, '[a]wareness of newly understood causes of unwanted effects often results in the adoption of different, and more effective means to attain one's ends'.

[5] Political socialisation in this respect differs from that highlighted by constructivists like Wendt. The Neorealist view of socialisation emphasises punishment/reward for unacceptable/acceptable behaviour, a process which Herman and Legro note is more aptly described as simple adaptation (Herman, 1996, p.280 fn.25).

[6] 'Security dilemma theory' is often used interchangeably with 'offence-defense theory'. (Lynn-Jones, S.M. 1995, p.660). It is argued here, however, that offence-defense theorists take the identity of the state as given. Since the security dilemma is defined in terms of the uncertainty surrounding a state's behaviour and identity the practice of using offence-defense theory and security dilemma theory interchangeably should be abandoned. Again offence-defense theory should be considered as the argument of one intellectual community, not as a statement of fact.

[7] Others (Lynn-Jones, 1995; Van Evera, 1998; Glaser and Kaufmann, 1998) have added to Jervis's rather simplistic formula by adding factors such as geography and societal factors.

[8] Scott Sagan argues the demands of the alliance system compelled the offensive strategies that led to World War I (Sagan 1986; Sagan 1986/1987). On the other hand, Jack Snyder identifies the origins of offensive strategies in the ideology of military institutions and its relation to civilian policymakers (Snyder, 1984; Van Evera, 1984; Posen 1984; Kier, 1996).

[9] Jervis (1982 pp.357-378), for example, argued that the patterns of behaviour in superpower relations could not be considered the consequence of a security regime because

they were not 'far enough removed from immediate, narrow self-interest'. See also (Nye, 1987, p.373). For further discussion on the different prospects for economic and security regimes (see Lipson, 1993; Axelrod and Keohane, 1993).

[10] Collins claims that if a satisfactory solution can be found then it would be incorrect to label the situation a security dilemma. Yet he gives no indication as to how a state decides if a situation is satisfactory or not. Moreover, it would seem strange to tell a policymaker who had battled hard to implement a policy that turned out to be satisfactory, that s/he had not been involved in a security dilemma after all.

[11] Thus Robert Jervis writes that minds are changed when new opportunities and dangers can arise. But he also adds this can occur when new leaders can come to power and values shift (Jervis, 1982, p.168). Joseph Nye also notes that perceptions can change not only through cognitive learning and a normative evolution, but also following domestic shifts in power. He even suggests that 'Such political change may occur because of domestic issues largely unrelated to foreign policy' (Nye, 1987, p.378). Jeffrey Checkel, on the other hand, argues that such domestic level explanations for foreign policy change are incomplete. He suggests that even if 'preferences do change as a result of new knowledge, it is still important to ask who or what was the source of new knowledge and how this process occurred' (Checkel, 1997, p.14). He argues that changes in the international environment provides the stimulus for new ideas at the domestic level.

[12] It is often noted that the Sino-American détente could only happen because Nixon and Kissinger centralised American policy around themselves, conducted the diplomacy secretly and presented Congress and the public with a fait accompli. Moreover, Herman (1996, p.291) makes the point that the post-Vietnam decentralisation of America's war powers (e.g.War Powers Act) prompted liberal Americanists in the Soviet policymaking community to argue that American military interventions in the periphery would become anachronistic. This is turn contributed to the reinterpretation of the American threat that led to New Thinking.

[13] Gonzalez and Haggard (1998, p.299) note in their analysis of U.S.-Mexican relations 'states do not simply look at the policy pronouncements of their diplomatic interlocuters; they look through those pronouncements to the underlying institutional arrangements which determine the capacity to make credible commitments'.

References

Adler, E. (1992), 'The Emergence of Cooperation: national epistemic communities and the international evolution of the idea of arms control', *International Organization*, Vol.46, pp.101-146.

Axelrod, R. (1984), *The Evolution of Cooperation*, Basic Books, New York.

Axelrod, R. and Keohane, R.O. (1993), 'Achieving Cooperation Under Anarchy: Strategies and Institutions', in David A. Baldwin (ed.) *Neorealism and Neoliberalism. The Contemporary Debate*, Columbia University Press, New York, pp.85-115.

Booth, K. and Wheeler, N. (1992), 'The Security Dilemma', in Baylis, J. and Rengger, N. (eds.), *Dilemmas of World Politics: International Issues in a Changing World*, Clarendon Press, Oxford, pp.29-60.

Boserup, A. and Nield, R. (eds.) (1990), *The Foundations of Defensive Defense*, St. Martins Press, New York.

Butterfield, H. (1957), *History and Human Relations*, Collins, London.

Buzan, B. (1987), 'Common Security, Non-provocative Defence and the Future of Western Europe', *Review of International Studies*, Vol. 13, pp.265-279.

Checkel, J.T. (1997), *Ideas and International Political Change. Soviet/Russian Behaviour and the End of the Cold War*, Yale University Press, New Haven and London.

Collins, A. (1995), *The Security Dilemma and the End of the Cold War*, New York, Keele University Press.

Corwin, E.S. (1940), *The President: Office and Powers*, New York University Press, New York.

Cote, O. (1991), 'The Trident and the Triad: collecting the D-5 dividend', *International Security*, Vol.16, pp.117-145.

Etzioni, A. (1962), *The Hard Way to Peace: A New Strategy*, Collier Books, New York.

Evangelista, M. (1995), 'The Paradox of State Strength: Transnational Relations, Domestic Structures and Security Policy in Russia and the Soviet Union', *International Organization*, Vol.49 pp.1-38.

Feis, H. (1957), *Churchill, Roosevelt, Stalin: The War They Waged and the Peace They Sought*, Princeton University Press, Princeton.

Gaddis, J.L. (1989), 'Hanging Tough Paid Off', *Bulletin of Atomic Scientists*, Vol.45, pp.11-14.

Glaser, C.L. (1990), *Analyzing Strategic Nuclear Policy*, Princeton University Press, Princeton.

Glaser, C.L. (1992), 'Political Consequences of Military Strategy. Expanding and Refining the Spiral and Deterrence Models', *World Politics*, Vol.44, pp.497-538.

Glaser, C.L. and Kaufmann, C. (1998), 'What is the Offense-Defense Balance and Can We Measure It?', *International Security*, Vol.22, pp.44-82.

Goldmann, K. (1995), 'Bargaining, Power, Domestic Politics and Security Dilemmas: Soviet "New thinking" as Evidence', in Pierre Allan and Kjell Goldmann, *The End of the Cold War. Evaluating Theories of International Relations*, Kluwer Law, Dordecht, pp.82-103.

Gonzalez, G. and Haggard, S. (1998), 'The United States and Mexico: a pluralistic security community?', in Emanuel Adler and Michael Barnett, (eds.) *Security Communities*, Cambridge University Press, Cambridge, pp.295-332.

Gray, C. (1993), *Weapons Don't Make War: Policy, Strategy, and Military Technology*, University Press of Kansas, Lawrence, Kansas.

Grieco, J.M. (1993), 'Anarchy and the Limits of Cooperation: A Realist Critique of New Liberal Institutionalism', in D.A.Baldwin (ed.), *Neoliberalism and Neorealism: the contemporary debate*, Columbia University Press, New York, pp.116-140.

Grunberg, I. and Risse-Kappen, T. (1995), 'A Time of Reckoning? Theories of International relations and the End of the Cold War', in Pierre Allan and Kjell Goldmann, *The End of the Cold War. Evaluating Theories of International Relations*, Kluwer Law, Dordrecht, pp.104-146.

Haas, E. (1980), 'Why Collaborate? Issue-Linkage and International Regimes', *World Politics*, Vol.32 pp.357-405.

Herman, R.G. (1996), 'Identity, Norms, and National Security: The Soviet Foreign Policy Revolution and the End of the Cold War', in Peter J. Katzenstein (ed.) *The Culture of National Security. Norms and Identity in World Politics*, Columbia University Press, New York, pp.272-316.

Jervis, R. (1976), *Perception and Misperception in International Politics*, Princeton University Press, Princeton.

Jervis, R. (1978), 'Cooperation Under the Security Dilemma', *World Politics*, Vol.30, pp.167-214.

Jervis, R. (1982), 'Security Regimes', *International Organization*, Vol.36, pp.357-378.

Jervis, R. (1989), *The Meaning of the Nuclear Revolution. Statecraft and the Prospect of Armageddon*, Cornell University Press, Cornell.

Kier, E. (1996), 'Culture and French Military Doctrine Before World War II', in Peter J. Katzenstein (ed.), *The Culture of National Security. Norms and Identity in World Politics*, Columbia University Press, New York, pp.186-215.

Klein, B. (1994), *Strategic Studies and World Order*, Cambridge University Press, Cambridge.

Krasner, S. (ed.) (1983), *International Regimes*, Cornell University Press, Ithaca.

Lebow, R.N. (1995), 'The Long Peace, the End of the Cold War and the Failure of Realism', in Richard Ned Lebow and Thomas Risse-Kappen (eds.) *International Political Theory and the End of the Cold War*, Columbia University Press, New York, pp.23-55.

Lipson, C. (1993), 'International Cooperation in Economic and Security Affairs', in David A. Baldwin (ed.), *Neorealism and Neoliberalism. The Contemporary Debate*, Columbia University Press, New York, pp.60-84.

Lynn Jones, S.M. (1995), 'Offense-Defense Theory and its Critics', *Security Studies*, Vol.4, pp.660-691.

Nye, J.S. (1987), 'Nuclear Learning and U.S.-Soviet security regimes', *International Organization*, Vol.41, pp.371-402.

Osgood, C.E. (1962), *An Alternative to War and Surrender*, University of Illinois Press, Chicago.

Palme, O. (1982), *Common Security: a programme for disarmament*, Pan Books, London.

Posen, B.R. (1984), *The Sources of Military Doctrine: France, Britain and Germany Between the World Wars*, Cornell University Press, Ithaca.

Ralph, J. (1999), 'GRIT, Collins and the End of the Cold War', *Review of International Studies*, Vol.25, pp.721-725.

Ravenal, E.C. (1982), 'Counterforce and the Alliance: The Ultimate Connection', *International Security*, Vol.6, pp.26-43.

Risse-Kappen, T. (1994), 'Ideas do not float freely: transnational coalitions, domestic structures and the end of the Cold War', *International Organization*, Vol.48, pp.185-214.

Sagan, S.D. (1986), '1914 Revisited: Allies, Offense and Instability', *International Security*, Vol.11,pp.151-176.

Sagan, S.D. (1986/1987), 'Correspondence: The Origins of Offense and the Consequences of Counterforce', *International Security*, Vol.11, pp.193-198.

SIPRI (1985), *Policies for Common Security*, Taylor and Francis, London and Philadelphia.

Smoke, R. and Kortunov, A. (eds.) (1991), *Mutual Security: a new approach to Soviet-American Relations*, St.Martins Press, London.

Snyder, J. (1984), 'Civil-Military Relations and the Cult of the Offensive, 1914 and 1984', *International Security*, Vol.9, pp.93-146.

Snyder, J.L. (1985), 'Perception of the Security Dilemma in 1914', in Jervis, R., Ned Lebow, R. and Gross Stein, J. (eds.) *Psychology and Deterrence*, Johns Hopkins University Press, Baltimore.

Tara, R. and Zeringue, M. (1992), 'Grand Strategy in a Post-Bipolar World. Interpreting the Final Soviet Response', *Review of International Studies*, Vol.18, pp.335-375.

Van Evera, S. (1984), 'The Cult of the Offensive and the Origins of the First World War', *International Security*, Vol.9, pp.58-107.

Van Evera, S. (1998), 'Offense, Defense and the Causes of War', *International Security*, Vol.22, pp.5-43.

Waltz, K. (1993), 'The Emerging Structure of International Politics', *International Security*, Vol.18, pp.44-79.

Wendt, A. (1992), 'Anarchy is what states make of it: the social construction of power politics', *International Organization*, Vol.46, pp.391-426.

Windass, S. (ed.) (1985), *Avoiding Nuclear War: Common Security as a Strategy for the Defence of the West*, Brassey's, London.

Wiseman, G. (1989), *Common Security and non-provocative defence: alternative approaches to the security dilemma*, Peace Research Centre, Australian National University, Canberra.

Winik, J. (1996), *On the Brink. The Dramatic, Behind-the-Scenes Saga of the Reagan Era and the Men and Women Who Won the Cold War*, Simon and Schuster, New York.

Wohlforth, W.C. (1996), *Witnesses to the end of the Cold War*, Johns Hopkins University Press, Baltimore.

Wyn Jones, R. (1995), '"Messages in a Bottle"? Theory and Praxis in Critical Security Studies', *Contemporary Security Policy*, Vol.16, pp.299-319.

3 America's Cold War: the military dimension

Introduction

The security dilemma exists at the level of the state. It does not exist in the minds of statesmen or women, but in the political debate within the extended state. The previous chapter developed this in detail. This chapter uses this framework to interpret U.S. defence policy during the Cold War. The previous chapter also demonstrated the academic response to the development of military technology and introduced ways in which this influenced America's approach to its relations with the Soviet Union. The minimalist/maximalist distinction identified two politically significant intellectual communities in America's security discourse. This is mirrored by what Erik Beukel (1989) labelled nuclear/Soviet essentialists. Nuclear essentialists believed the nuclear revolution was embedded across both superpowers and that deterrence was stable. Soviet essentialists, on the other hand, argued that nuclear weapons had been integrated into a Soviet culture that continued to see military power as an extension of political ambition. Deterring the Soviet Union was infinitely more complex than nuclear essentialists supposed.

The previous chapter also demonstrated how uncertainty could be mitigated if shared norms of co-operation became embedded in the security discourse of each state. The intensity of that co-operation depended on the political influence of those intellectual communities advocating tension reduction. If such ideas are politically insignificant in one state then advocates of co-operation in another state will be increasingly marginalised in their own political environment. In this way transnational coalitions are almost always at work if only through tacit processes. The previous chapter suggested that this process of transnationalism could assist tension reduction by changing the structure of the security dilemma within states. In other words, transnational coalitions can encourage co-operation by seeking to marginalise the arguments of intellectual communities that have a vested interest in conflict and are therefore predisposed to see the other state in confrontational terms. This chapter demonstrates how the transnational activities of certain intellectual communities led to the process of arms control and détente based on the shared understanding of mutual vulnerability.

The previous chapter also suggested, however, that co-operation will be temporary if the norms are not embedded in the security discourse of the both states. The fate of détente illustrates this point perfectly. In effect tacit transnational coalitions were constructed between opponents of mutual vulnerability, particularly among those who had a vested interest in unilateral attempts to achieve national security, rather than bilateral or multilateral attempts to achieve international security[1]. While the U.S. military can be easily placed in this intellectual community, it drew on the support of those non-military advocates of strategic autarky who believed technology could preserve American exceptionalism and, like the Mayflower, deliver the American nation from the evil realities of the old world. Yet not all Americans were convinced of the effectiveness and necessity of the technology that these groups believed in. Nor were they willing to recognise the image of the Soviet Union that these groups disseminated to legitimise their military-technical response. Their opposition and the subsequent debate reflected America's security dilemma.

In the meantime transnational coalitions advocating common security emerged in reaction to the increased tension caused by the rise of militarism. Ultimately the military dimension to America's Cold War security dilemma was resolved only when Gorbachev's reforms, motivated by the ideas of this coalition, marginalised first the Soviet and then the American advocates of a military-technical solution. While complete nuclear disarmament was held back by a combination of arguments including commitments to allies, a political and financial commitment to the strategic modernisation programme and an almost blind-faith in the military point of view, the norm of mutual vulnerability was preserved and crisis stability was enhanced.

In contrast to the claims of conservatives, U.S.-Soviet co-operation on this basis was made possible by the ideas of common security and the political agency of those advocates on the political left. Certainly Soviet identity had to change before arms control re-established its influence in the American debate. But that had long been recognised by the transnational peace movements of the early 1980s. What they also recognised was the two-way process between disarmament and democratisation. Both the left and right agreed that disarmament would come with democratisation but only the left recognised that the reverse was also true. That is arms control and disarmament would assist the reform process in the Soviet Union and Eastern Europe by marginalising the concerns of traditionalists and creating a relatively secure environment for democratic movements to oppose totalitarian regimes. When international tension was high in the early 1980s there was little political space in which to protest. A point illustrated by the fate of such movements in Poland. When tensions were low and when disarmament reduced the danger that political disorder would escalate into unwanted and disproportionate violence, democracy and self-determination thrived. Where the peace movements recognised this in early 1980s, U.S. policy followed a decade later.

Détente

As chapter two suggested, the material realities of modern conflict began to change conceptions of the military's role. In articulating the social meaning of these realities an intellectual community emerged to explore the implications of Brodie's famous conclusion that the purpose of nuclear forces was to prevent wars rather than to win them (Brodie, 1946; 1959). For this group of defence intellectuals vulnerability became a reality, but it also became a means of preventing war[2]. The devastating power and penetrability of nuclear missiles made assured destruction inevitable and negated any political gain from military aggression. So long as either side had a credible retaliatory capacity that could deliver assured destruction and so long as that was clearly communicated to the potential adversary, then military aggression would be deterred. This position resolved the U.S. dilemma for most of the Eisenhower administration, which became aware of these ideas through the President's regular contacts with scientists and defence intellectuals (Adler, 1992, pp.117-118). Yet as the Soviets developed a nuclear capability to threaten the American homeland, the U.S. faced first a dilemma of interpretation and then a dilemma of response. At worst it signalled the incredibility of 'massive retaliation' and the potential for increased Soviet assertiveness. For others, the Soviet defence build-up was a reaction to its relative weakness. U.S. security was threatened no more than it had been before and in fact could benefit from an increasingly secure Soviet Union.

Despite Eisenhower's warnings of the distorting influence of a military-industrial complex on this debate, Senator Kennedy used the concerns of a missile gap and an inflexible nuclear strategy to attack the Republican handling of defence issues and to prove his anti-communist credentials. Once in office the administration increased flexibility by adopting a counterforce targeting policy and adding to America's strategic and conventional capability (Freedman, 1981, pp.228-239). Yet in due course, thinking across the Kennedy and Johnson administrations would resist the pressure to integrate nuclear weapons into a warfighting strategy and gradually embraced the growing arms control community. Defense Secretary McNamara willingly adopted the minimalist arguments of nuclear essentialists[3]. With America's commitment to the defence of South Vietnam a constant drain on resources, McNamara looked to hold down defence expenditure elsewhere. By arguing that the U.S. should exercise restraint in deploying strategic defences he was clearly identifying with the arms control ideas of crisis and arms race stability. By forgoing deployment the U.S. would not provoke the Soviets to build more offensive weapons in order to penetrate U.S. defences which in turn would ease the pressure for greater spending on America's offensive arsenal[4].

For security co-operation in terms of arms control to be secure, this minimalist thinking on crisis and arms race stability had to be embedded in both policymaking communities. While U.S. arms controllers had strong advocates in both the Johnson and Nixon administration, in the Soviet Union its influence was less secure. The minimalist position that led Khrushchev to push for test bans, despite a U.S. advantage, had not been received well by the Soviet military (Evangelista, 1999, pp.45-89). Their opposition to his restraint, in particular his preferred reliance on minimum nuclear deterrence at the expense of a large standing army, was exploited by Brezhnev who would rely on the armed forces for much of his power base[5]. The consolidation of a maximalist position under Brezhnev would be justified by hardliners with reference to Kennedy's build-up, NATO's gradual adoption of flexible response and its apparent emphasis on warfighting capability (Evangelista, 1999, pp.181-184). As for strategic defences the Soviet political leadership continued to follow the military lead. The causes of war were seen not as a technical matter but were considered a consequence of political aggression. Crisis instability was not their concern. Defending the Soviet Union against capitalist aggression was. Banning defences was considered both imprudent and an immoral denial of duty. Furthermore, it would not influence the arms race that was, in their eyes, driven by the capitalist military industrial complex (Evangelista, 1999, pp.135-138).

In the U.S., the arms control community had greater success in convincing the Johnson and then Nixon administration to hold back on deployment of defensive systems[6]. Despite the Soviet deployment of the Galosh system in 1964, a reciprocal response was deemed unsatisfactory. A political coalition across the Pentagon, the State Department, Congress and the White House exploited the public's leaning towards military restraint by supporting a policy of arms control rather than immediate deployment of a comprehensive system (Adler, 1992 pp.137-138). Yet that coalition would only hold if arms control delivered a strategic regime that could be credibly defended as stable in times of political crisis. Resolving uncertainty in favour of a cooperative policy, designed to guarantee crisis stability and to control the arms race, was contingent on the extent to which that kind of thinking was embedded in the Soviet approach to national security. McNamara's efforts to convince his Soviet counterparts of the logic of arms control by explaining arms-race and crisis stability fell on deaf ears. Yet despite this, and despite the political obstacles presented by wider superpower relations – the invasion of Czechoslovakia in August 1968 is often cited as a setback for moves towards arms control – a transnational coalition of arms controllers gradually convinced the Soviet leadership of the benefits of limiting strategic defenses.

Strategic, economic and technological factors have all been emphasised to explain why the Soviet leadership signed the ABM treaty. But as Matthew Evangelista's detailed analysis of the Soviet archives demonstrates, all these explanations are indeterminate. There was no consensus across the Soviet decision making community on the strategic, economic or technological implications of ABM technology. He presents strong circumstantial evidence that suggests the decisive arguments came from Soviet scientists who had themselves been convinced of the logic of banning ABMs by the transnational community of intellectuals that were members of groups such as Pugwash and the Soviet-American Disarmament Study Group (SADS) (Evangelista, 1999; Adler, 1992).

This was not the only influence of this transnational coalition. As well as convincing politically significant policymakers of the deterrence logic, its political strength in one state reassured doubters in the other that they would not be victims of a future defection. As Adler puts it:

> Although Soviet arms controllers were well aware of the ideological divisions in the U.S., they drew confidence from the fact that a strong group of arms control lobbyists existed in the United States and used this fact to persuade reluctant Soviet actors.... At the same time, once top Soviet leaders threw their weight in favour of arms control, they put pressure on the American policy game, helping to break the political impasse between

American ABM supporters and opponents (Adler, 1992, pp.137-138).

On this basis the ABM Treaty and SALT I that limited offensive capability became part of 'the incomplete mosaic' of partial superpower security regimes (Nye, 1987). These agreements sought to reinforce the shared understanding of crisis and arms race stability by institutionalising MAD. Yet the major weakness of the SALT regime was that the shared understanding was not hegemonic across both policymaking communities. To critics of the regime the Nixon administration was naïve to believe the Soviet Union accepted the logic of MAD. They pointed to the continuing support in the Soviet Union for strategic defences and emphasised the potential first-strike capability of the heavy Soviet ICBMs. Of course, one implication of Evangelista's analysis that the arguments of Soviet scientists were decisive in convincing the Soviet leadership to sign the ABM treaty, is that minimalist thinking was far from hegemonic in the Soviet security discourse. Evangelista does note, for example, that for several years after the signing of the ABM Treaty politically significant voices were still arguing the benefits of strategic defence.

As in the USSR, the idea of a nuclear revolution and its faith in the stability of mutual vulnerability, was not embedded in America's strategic culture. Arms control was far from a satisfactory solution. The military in particular were uncomfortable with the idea of national security being based on vulnerability rather than warfighting and damage limitation. In fact, actual targeting policy had not been influenced by declaratory changes to U.S. strategy. While defence intellectuals debated the specifics of crisis stability, the military would still prepare an operational doctrine for a wartime role which meant limiting the damage the Soviet Union could inflict on the United States (Friedberg, 1980; Ball 1982; Ball and Richelson, 1986). Without the defensive technology to intercept Soviet missiles, the military would demand more accurate offensive weapons that could disarm the Soviet force. Accuracy was easier to attain through land based missiles, but these themselves were vulnerable to similar weapons on the Soviet side. Despite this vulnerability and despite the potentially destabilising consequences of Multiple Independently targeted Reentry Vehicles (MIRVs)[7], the military continued to value these weapons and lobbied hard to maintain the land-based leg of the strategic triad and to increase its MIRV capability.

In fact limits on MIRVs had been deliberately left out of the SALT agreement because it was an American advantage. SALT I merely used launchers rather than warheads as the 'unit of account'. On the face of it the 1,618 ICBMs that the Soviets were allowed gave them an advantage over the 1,054 American.   Until that is one counted the number of warheads available to both sides across the strategic triad.   By choosing this formula and not limiting MIRVs, however, military interests presented opponents of détente with political ammunition.   Soviet ICBMs traditionally were capable of carrying a heavier 'payload'.   As such they could carry a greater number of warheads once the Soviets had acquired MIRV capability. It became the evidence cited by many Americans who believed the Soviets had the capacity to disarm America's retaliatory capability and would use that to their political advantage (Garthoff, 1985).

While the arguments of those in the military may have been based on a genuine assessment of Soviet capabilities and intentions, it does not escape the fact that their arguments legitimised the pursuit of certain narrowly defined interests.   As well as exaggerating Soviet capabilities they would advance a Soviet essentialist view of deterrence.   The counterforce capability supplied by MIRVs was not only considered necessary because of its capacity to limit damage should deterrence fail, it was considered necessary, according to this view, to make sure deterrence did not fail.   In other words, only by preparing to fight and, as extreme versions of this argument suggested, to win a controlled and limited nuclear war could a deterrence threat be made credible (Klein, 1994, pp.63-74; Kahn, 1960; Kahn 1962; Nitze, 1977; Gray and Payne, 1980).   What was the point, warfighters argued, of threatening massive retaliation if it was not in the country's military, political or moral interests?   The very fact that these questions were being asked, the argument continued, made the threat to retaliate incredible.   If the adversary thought retaliation was unlikely it may be encouraged to attack.   At the very least policymakers required limited nuclear options that made political and military sense.   The significance of this argument was recognised by the Nixon administration when it approved operational changes in 1974[8].

A Dilemma of Interpretation

While these arguments were propagated by those with a vested interest in a strong deterrence posture, their arguments took on an even greater significance in the late 1970s.   In particular, the window of vulnerability thesis argued that the Soviet military build-up of the 1960s and 1970s could be used to politically disadvantage the United States.   The Soviets could attack and destroy most U.S. ICBMs.

The US, stripped of its rapid-response counterforce capability, could retaliate only against industry and population centers, but to do so would bring down a similar attack on the US. Faced by grim alternatives, the President might decide that his best alternative was to opt for a political settlement on Soviet terms. Anticipation of this dilemma will, it is argued, embolden the Soviets and cause the United States to give way to Soviet pressures even in the absence of an attack (Johnson, 1983 p.962).

Nixon and Kissinger rejected such claims. For instance, in an outburst he would later come to regret, Kissinger rhetorically asked 'what, in the name of God, is strategic superiority? What is the significance of it, politically, militarily, operationally, at these levels of numbers? What do you do with it?' (Cahn, 1998, p.66). But many to the right of Kissinger recalled a golden age of strategic superiority, the political benefits it bought America and pointed in particular to the importance of the strategic balance on the outcome of the Cuban missile crisis[9]. Indeed, Kissinger himself had shown a willingness to engage in nuclear diplomacy by raising the alert status of strategic forces during the 1973 Middle East crisis[10]. This debate would not be resolved and continues to be contested (Lebow and Stein, 1998). Yet the significance of one side or the other had less to do with military or technological capabilities in the USSR than it did political developments in the U.S. intelligence community and the wider policymaking community.

During the 1970s the CIA had been attacked from the left for its covert activities. Yet it was from the right that its analytical performance had been questioned. After his time as Director of Central Intelligence (DCI), for instance, James Schlesinger testified that the CIA had developed an 'institutional bias' in favour of arms control (Cahn, 1998, p.72). Many considered that the CIA had overcompensated in adjusting to the lessons of the bomber and missile gaps of the 1950s when the intelligence community overestimated Soviet capabilities (Cahn, 1998, pp.108-109). Criticism also came from the Presidential Foreign Intelligence Advisory Board (PFIAB) that was dismissed by some as 'amateurish' but held enough significance for DCI William Colby to act on their concerns (Cahn, 1998, p.106). Colby, who had personally been heavily influenced by the window of vulnerability argument, took a number of initiatives that shifted influence away from the CIA. The Office of National Estimates was replaced by a system of National Intelligence Officers, which had the effect of creating an NIE drafting system 'that relied more heavily on the direct input of intelligence agencies other than the CIA' (Cahn, 1998, p.107; Freedman, 1977). As such the Defense Intelligence Agency (DIA), an agency that traditionally took a more pessimistic view on the USSR[11], was more involved in the process. The content of the NIEs themselves gradually reflected this bureaucratic shift.

Yet for some on the right the shift was insufficient. For instance, prominent members of PFIAB took the view that intelligence should call attention to the worst case scenario. In 1975, after consulting PFIAB through the NSC, the President directed 'a thorough critique of the new assessment by an independent entity' (Cahn, 1998, p.117). The 'competitive threat exercise' as it effectively became known, completely opened the assessment process. It emphasised views of the Soviet Union that opponents of détente believed were being repressed by the CIA's control of the estimating process. Yet the CIA rightly feared that the presence of an unqualified worst-case estimate would provide ammunition to support an unnecessary military build up. Those in the CIA who were sympathetic to the exercise have since admitted misunderstanding the intentions of 'those with a vested interest ...[who] saw a chance to... build sentiment for increased defence spending' (Cahn, 1998, p.138). It took the appointment of a new DCI, George Bush, whom many feared too high ranking a Republican to be impartial, before the exercise was confirmed.

Those working on the regular NIE (11-3/8-76) would be Team A, while the independent Team B would be made up of 'white males who shared an almost apoplectic animosity towards the Soviet Union'. Prominent members included Paul Nitze who had helped draft the Gaither Report (a significant cause of the missile gap), Professor Richard Pipes who had been a consultant to Senator Jackson who opposed détente and William Van Cleave, described as a 'hard-line ideologue' member of the SALT I negotiating team (Cahn, 1998, pp.141-152). Given this profile Team B's conclusions were not surprising. It attacked the CIA for underestimating the intensity and scope of the Soviet threat. Team A's estimate was far from complacent, for example it recognised the war-fighting doctrine and the immense capabilities of the Soviet military. However, it argued that the Soviet leadership could not anticipate being in a position whereby they 'could devastate the U.S. while preventing the U.S. from devastating the USSR'[12].

To Team B, the CIA's methodology was fundamentally flawed. As a result it misinterpreted the implications of Soviet doctrine. Team B attacked the NIEs 'tendency to view deterrence as an alternative to a warfighting capability rather than as complimentary to it'. The Soviet leadership was offensively minded and thus more likely to see the political and military advantages that strategic superiority offered their 'grand strategy'. Moreover, Team B universally favoured the worst-case interpretation of Soviet capabilities.   Where the evidence suggested otherwise it concluded that the U.S. could be adversely surprised.   'Within the ten year period of the National Estimate' the Report concluded, 'the Soviets may well expect to achieve a degree of military superiority which would permit a dramatically more aggressive military pursuit of their hegemonial objectives, including direct military challenges to western military interests, in the belief that such superior military force can be used to win a military contest at any level'[13].

Given the apparent lack of interest in the NIE process one should be careful not to overestimate the political consequence of the shifting emphasis of intelligence analysis (Cahn, 1998, p.92).   Yet the intelligence process did give some appearance of objectivity to political opponents of détente who would otherwise have been sidelined by the accusation of acting out of narrow self-interest.   This intelligence gained real political significance when its conclusions were publicised through leaks to the press.   Sensing the political mileage in these arguments, Team Bs conclusions were adopted by ambitious politicians eager to attack the administration's pursuit of détente.   Thus America's security dilemma in the late 1970s was a consequence not only of Soviet actions, but also of political shifts in the American security discourse.

The Dilemma Intensifies

Following the signing of SALT I, Senator Jackson had demanded that future agreements meet the criteria of numerical equivalence rather than a general agreement on the deterrence effects.   He also made sure the bureaucratic enthusiasm for arms control agreements was weakened by the appointment of Fred Ikle as ACDAs director and the purging of the SALT negotiating team (Cahn, 1998, pp.18-20).   In the mid-1970s, however, Jackson's arguments on SALT were marginal in the Democratic Party.   In the Republican Party, by contrast, President Ford's initial enthusiasm for arms control and détente waned after a politically bruising primary contest with Governor Ronald Reagan (Cahn, 1998, 60-62). With the Republican electoral chances more or less destroyed by the Watergate scandal, however, President Carter entered the White House.   In stark contrast to Jackson, Reagan and Ford's reading of détente, the Carter administration saw the Soviet leadership as susceptible to the incentives of greater co-operation with the West.   In terms of arms control the Carter administration would seek to act on the minimalist ideas of Paul Warnke who argued for a GRIT-type, exemplarist strategy.   The U.S., he argued, should be the first to step off the arms race treadmill (Warnke, 1975)[14]. This line of thinking was reflected in Carter's ambitious, but ultimately ill-fated March 1977 disarmament proposal.

Jackson's concerns with Nixon's pursuit of détente, were reinforced by an increasing number of voices who were even more concerned with President Carter's general approach. For example, Eugene Rostow, former Under Secretary of State and later head of ACDA during the Reagan administration, suggested that his views on Carter's appointments were unprintable.   The 'master' of the arms control game, Paul Nitze, characterised the administration's personnel as 'every softliner I can think of' (Sanders, 1983, p.191).   To coalesce and publicise their ideas and mobilise support for a military-technical response, Rostow, Nitze and others formed the Committee on the Present Danger (CPD).

This committee had exactly the same reading of Soviet intentions as Team B, which is not surprising considering many were members of both (Adler, 1992, p.110; Sanders, 1983, pp.162-4)[15]. They argued that Soviet intentions had not been changed by détente, nor would they change at the prospect of greater co-operation. It was still committed to revolutionary expansionism and would use its military advantage to secure that. What had changed was America's will to contain the Soviet Union through military means.   Given that the Soviets could not be trusted to keep agreements and given the imbalance of the SALT agreements, arms control was seen as appeasement[16]. To the CPD the Soviets maintained a Clausewitzian view of modern conflict.   War remained an extension of politics and even nuclear war could be fought and won (Pipes, 1977).   The fear amongst the CPD was not necessarily a bolt-from-the-blue attack, but the perception among America's allies that the American deterrent was incredible   thereby   increasing   the   argument   of   neutralists   and accommodationists.   The window had to be closed by a military build-up that closed the gaps in America's deterrence strategy.

Of course not all agreed with this interpretation of the Soviet 'threat' and would publicly defend the CIA's position.   While admitting that the Soviet military prepared to fight and win a nuclear war such plans were, they argued, more a response to the demands of Marxism-Leninist theory as well as a 'predictable reflection of the military role'. It was much less clear that the Soviet leadership believed that a nuclear war could be won 'in any meaningful sense'.   That leadership moreover, had already jettisoned doctrinal tenets relating to the inevitability of war between capitalism and socialism.   Even if the Soviet leadership had been inclined towards pursuing political ends through military force, it would not have seen as many vulnerabilities in the American position as the Committee for the Present Danger. Coordinating a first strike was only considered possible by those with a 'technocratic bias'. It was 'unlikely to be shared by the Soviets, who are attentive to the human and operational problems of modern warfare'. Political opponents of the CPD concluded that the Soviets would not 'bet their survival on an assumption that an American President would yield rather than retaliate against Soviet industry and population centers' with the large numbers of invulnerable, sea-based weapons (Johnson, 1983, pp.956-965).

Nonetheless the right's reading of Soviet intentions and capabilities became increasingly significant. It found support from an increasingly persuasive reading of Soviet behaviour in the Third World. The CPD wasted no opportunity to present Soviet 'adventurism' as a consequence of America's strategic weakness and evidence of Carter's naivete (Garthoff, 1985). The turning point, in terms of the American political debate, came with the Soviet invasion of Afghanistan in December 1979. Carter's own admission that the invasion changed his mind symbolised a much larger shift in the attitudes. Again opponents of this reading argued Soviet behaviour had less to do with the strategic balance and more to do with the specific regional context, in particular its concerns about the rise of Islamic fundamentalism. If Soviet military capabilities influenced Soviet behaviour it was their increased capacity for conventional force projection that was most relevant and not its strategic capability (Johnson, 1983, p.965). The election of President Reagan in November 1980, however, symbolised the successful propagation of the CPDs arguments.

The Dilemma of Response and America's Second Cold War

The shifts in attitudes towards the end of the Carter administration were accompanied by militarist responses. In seeming contradiction of his earlier emphasis on avoiding oversimplified approaches to a complex world, the 'Carter Doctrine' was an attempt to demonstrate America's resolve in the Gulf[17]. The decision to address concerns over NATO's deterrence by deploying Long-Range Theatre Nuclear Weapons (LRTNW) in Europe was also taken by the Carter administration. Furthermore, the Carter administration oversaw a change in strategic targeting that signalled a move in a warfighting direction. Instead of targeting Soviet recovery capability, under PD-59 America would target political and military assets, strategic military targets, and leadership targets. Secondly, it required the capability to fight a protracted nuclear conflict. This doctrinal shift towards maximalist thinking created political pressure to match intentions with capabilities. PD-59 almost doubled the number of targets needed to be covered if the Soviets were to be deterred and the need to endure and respond to first, second, even third strikes required increased investment in command and control. This investment was to be a major priority of the Reagan White House (Richelson, 1983).

Key appointments to the Reagan administration politically marginalised the arms control intellectual community that had been a permanent feature of the American security debate since the Kennedy administration. Positions were given to members of the CPD and security policy was directed towards finding a technical solution to the window of vulnerability[18]. Having dismissed SALTII as 'fatally flawed', arms control was relegated to an exercise in the management of public opinion (Johnson, 1983, p.958). The strategic arms talks, renamed Strategic arms reductions talks (START), and Intermediate Nuclear Force (INF) negotiations remained deadlocked until the Soviet walk-out in December 1983. The so-called 'zero-option', whereby the U.S. would not deploy Cruise and Pershing in return for the withdrawal of Soviet INF, was seen simply as a means of supporting western governments establish coalitions strong enough to support the deployment of INF (Haslam, 1989, pp.112-114)[19].

The defining feature of the Reagan defence policy was its refusal to accept mutual vulnerability. During the course of the first administration it set about restoring America's strategic autarky through a combination of offensive *and* defensive investments. The role of SDI will be discussed in detail below. The offensive build-up included a new MX missile, the introduction of the D-5 Sea Launched Ballistic Missile (SLBM) to Trident submarines, the upgrading of the Minuteman III missiles and the investment in the B-1 and B-2 bombers, all of which sought to address the perceived gap between strategic capabilities and the requirements of deterrence. National Security Decision Directive (NSDD) 13 reaffirmed the targeting policy of PD-59 and C3I links were also upgraded in order to support controlled counterattacks over a protracted period (Richelson, 1983, p.131; Garthoff, 1994, pp.36-42).

Yet the build-up faced opposition in Congress and the wider public for two reasons reflecting America's dilemma of response. Firstly, Congress refused to fund the MX programme until a deployment plan could be found that was not vulnerable to Soviet attack (Garthoff, 1994, pp.41-42). Secondly, some in Congress opposed the defence build-up because they feared provoking the Soviets and sought instead greater flexibility in the arms control negotiations. In light of Secretary Weinberger's argument that the U.S. had to be ready to 'prevail' in any conflict - that is end the conflict on terms favourable to the U.S. – they feared the administration was too insensitive to the dangers of Soviet misinterpretation[20]. For example, Senator Aucoin regularly defended the nuclear essentialist position and warned against creating a spiral of mistrust. In Congressional hearings he submitted to the Secretary of Defense that 'nuclear war cannot be won, neither side can prevail in a nuclear war, deterrence must be maintained, and that is why we need to look at procurement requests not from the standpoint of whether they deter but whether they provoke'. In response, both the Weinberger and his Chiefs identified Soviet aggression as the only reason deterrence could fail. General Vessey for instance stated that the Soviet leadership could only conclude that the U.S. was building a deterrence capability. 'He [the Soviet leader, Chernenko] knows as we do that first strike is not technology; first strike is a state of mind. He knows that we don't have that'[21].

How Vessey could be certain about knowing what Chernenko knew about America's 'state of mind' is unclear. Ultimately Vessey was making an argument to suit his political ends. While that argument managed to convince many politically significant actors at the time, retrospective accounts of Soviet concerns suggest Aucoin's approach may have been more appropriate. Politically significant constituencies in Soviet policy circles were, it seems, especially alarmed by Reagan's arms build-up and the accompanying rhetoric. So much so that Soviet intelligence services were put on alert to look for signs of Western preparations for war. In the context of this alert, known as RYAN (*Raketno-Yadernoye Napadenie* – 'Nuclear Missile Attack'), NATO conducted its annual Reforger exercises to test its theatre nuclear capability. Various accounts have suggested that Soviet intelligence interpreted the November 1983 Able Archer exercise as a cover for a NATO first strike and a nuclear alert was triggered[22]. Had NATO reacted to a Soviet alert the two alliances could have found themselves locked in a dynamic that could have easily spiralled to inadvertent nuclear war (Blair, 1993). While there is evidence to suggest the Soviet alert was a calculated disinformation exercise[23], Andrew and Gordievsky (1991, p.605) have written that during Able Archer 83 the world came close to the nuclear abyss, 'certainly closer than at any time since the Cuban missiles crisis of 1962'.

Robert Jervis (1982) has argued that the political pressure in favour of a security regime would be stronger if there was dramatic evidence that 'individualistic policies are leading to disaster'. He continues, '[o]f course the strongest possible evidence – an all out war – would render the project irrelevant. Perhaps a regime could be formed only in wake of a limited nuclear exchange or the accidental firing of a weapons'. There is a strong case to suggest that the arms control community in the U.S. gained political influence in the wake of the Cuban missile crisis. There is also evidence to suggest similar learning as a response to Able Archer. Andrew (1995, p.476, see also Fischer, 1997) claims the intelligence Gordievsky provided on RYAN and Able Archer 'left a profound impression on Reagan'. He even identifies November 1983 as the time when Reagan decided to tone down the rhetoric and set up a National Security Planning Group to open up dialogue with the Soviet Union.

The wider interpretation, however, is mixed. For example, two Special National Intelligence Estimates (SNIEs) of May and August 1984, the latter of which made extensive use of Gordievsky material, concluded that the Soviet alarm was part of a highly orchestrated deception campaign. It was intended to 'maintain an atmosphere of tension conducive to pressure by "peace" groups on Western governments; and, if possible, to undercut President Reagan's reelection prospects', elicit concessions in arms control negotiations, maintain ideological vigilance in Soviet society and strengthen cohesion within the Warsaw Pact[24].

Indeed, this mixed interpretation gained public expression in a way that suggests the administration was willing to use intelligence to suit whatever narrow political objective it had at the time. For example, Secretary Shultz suggested to the North Atlantic Assembly 'that talk about the increasing danger of war' was 'propaganda designed to intimidate. Deterrence has kept the peace, certainly in the NATO area'[25]. A year earlier, however, Shultz was willing to admit to a Disarmament Conference in Stockholm, that the administration's enthusiasm for a strong deterrence needed to be qualified. While not dismissing the lessons of the 1930s, he added 'we must never repeat the tragedy of 1914, when statesmen let technology drive decisions and when nations stumbled blindly into a disastrous war'[26].

Unfortunately for supporters of the latter position, the administration as whole, if not necessarily Shultz individually, was driven by the belief that a military-technical response could be found to resolve America's security dilemma. There were those in the administration who were willing to concede that America's defence policy could contribute to a spiral of mistrust and even inadvertent war. The irregularity of such statements and their significance relative to advocates of the strategic modernisation programme, however, made it easy to dismiss the administration's commitment to tension reduction.

The threat of inadvertence was not fully recognised by politically significant actors in the administration yet it was real for many serious commentators (Ned Lebow, 1985). While the Reagan administration paid lip service to tension reduction when it suited their political needs, as it did during the 1984 election campaign, those commentators would have to wait for Soviet New Thinking before seeing their recommendations acted on. In the meantime tension would remain high and valuable opportunities were missed so long as the U.S. sought its military-technical solution.

The Strategic Defence Initiative

The Strategic Defence Initiative (SDI) was partially a response to the window of vulnerability. If ways could not be found of addressing the vulnerability of the MX through various basing schemes then the U.S. would consider Ballistic Missile Defences (BMDs). This was by no means the only, nor indeed the primary, motivation behind SDI. It is argued here in fact that the Reagan administration had no single strategy of how to use SDI. Its conception was indeed a consequence of the Joint Chief's frustration with the MX basing problem. Its political birth, however, also required the seed of Presidential idealism which blatantly by-passed the national security bureaucracy. The President's March 1983 speech came as a complete surprise to Shultz and others (Winik, 1996, pp.315-315; Shultz, 1993, p.250-252). Indeed, the month prior to the announcement, Secretary of Defense, Weinberger, testified that the role of the U.S. military in space would 'remain essentially unchanged' over the next ten years[27].

Yet a number of directives had hinted at the deployment of Ballistic Missile Defence to solve MX vulnerability (Simpson, 1995, pp.123-124, pp.223-224). After a meeting with the Chiefs in February 1983, Admiral Watkins tapped into the President's own frustration with MAD by rhetorically asking 'wouldn't it be better to save lives than to avenge them?' (Nolan, 1989, pp.164-165). The Chiefs would live to regret provoking Reagan's idealism. Where they, supported by Defense Secretary Weinberger, saw BMD as a compliment to the counterforce capability of the strategic triad, Reagan saw it as an alternative. While official policy was 'to take every opportunity' to reduce a reliance on offensive nuclear weapons the President talked of making such weapons obsolete[28].

To others in the administration and Congress, SDI was an ill thought out attempt to resolve an imaginary problem. By threatening the ABM Treaty and the norm of mutual vulnerability, moreover, SDI risked provoking an even greater crisis with the Soviet Union. To Secretary of State, George Shultz and National Security Adviser, Robert McFarlane, dealing with SDI was a question of limiting the damage done to U.S.-

Soviet relations. They interpreted research into BMD not as an attempt to break out of the ABM Treaty. Rather, SDI was to be bargaining chip to force the Soviets to accept an American definition of crisis stability (Greenstein and Wohlforth, 1994, pp.10-11).

America's dilemma of response, then, had shifted focus. Rather than concerns about windows of vulnerability and warfighting postures, controversy surrounded the administration's interpretation of the ABM Treaty. During the course of this debate a number of developments strengthened the political position of the arms control community: the political consequences of the Scowcroft Commission; the change in the NSC staff that placed a new emphasis on dialogue; the development of the 'Strategic Concept' that sought to negotiate the role played by SDI; and finally, the marginalisation of Secretary of Defence, Caspar Weinberger.

The Scowcroft Commission

The results of the Scowcroft Commission, set up to 'rebuild a bipartisan consensus on strategic issues in co-operation with key members of the congressional armed services committee' (Fitzgerald, 2000, p.193), effectively dismissed the window of vulnerability argument. Furthermore, it identified a framework for future defence policy based on mutual vulnerability and crisis stability. The NIEs between 1976 and 1983 had maintained their cautious opposition to the more alarmist analysis of the CPD and the Reagan administration. For instance, NIE11-3/8-82 stated that the Soviets had not solved the technical problems of conducting nuclear war. As such they 'recognize that nuclear war is so destructive, and its course so uncertain, that they could not expect an outcome that was 'favourable' in any meaningful sense'[29]. This view was given political significance by the publication of Scowcroft's report. Scowcroft concluded that 'vulnerability is not so dominant a part of the overall problem so as to require other immediate steps. We believe the Soviets must have some uncertainties about their operational capabilities, notwithstanding whatever their test accuracies indicate to them'[30].

What the CPD had done for Team Bs analysis, the Scowcroft Commission now effectively did the same for the interpretation espoused by Team A and the CIA more generally. By setting up a Presidential commission independent of the normal policymaking process and investing it with the political weight of General Scowcroft, the administration was able to close the window of vulnerability without the military-technical solution that had been so elusive. Indeed the window was to close even further as future NIEs lowered their estimate of the accuracy of Soviet ICBMs[31]. While the DIA's footnotes to these estimates demonstrated continuing uncertainty within the intelligence community, of greater political significance were the public arguments provided by the Scowcroft Commission. They allowed the administration, now that it had no political need for it, to side-step the issue of ICBM vulnerability. Furthermore, the Commission was a powerful force in changing the administration's stance on arms control. Instead of being a means of cynically gaining public support for a warfighting posture and strategic autarky, arms control was to be integrated with a new force structure in a way that assured arms race and crisis stability.

Scowcroft's main concern was to reduce the incentive of either side to strike first in times of crisis. In those terms the record of SALT had been poor. While the shared understanding of mutual vulnerability was helped by the ABM Treaty, the failure to ban MIRVs had meant SALT in effect contributed to the unstable situation. The situation did not justify the window of vulnerability, yet the ratio of targets to warheads was developing in worrying direction.

Of course, the counterforce targeting policy of both sides was driving this dynamic, yet Scowcroft confined his recommendations to arms control and force structure. The U.S., he argued, should base the MX missiles in those silos that had been previously identified as vulnerable, but should also develop a single warhead ICBM (Midgetman). By only carrying one warhead the Soviets would have no incentive to target it (it took three warheads to guarantee a kill). Warheads should be the unit of account in arms control and the purpose of any negotiations should be crisis stability. Both sides, in other words, should move as close as possible to a target-to-warhead ratio of 1-to-1.

NSDD91 officially adopted Scowcroft's recommendations[32]. To act on those recommendations, however, the administration had to renew diplomatic dialogue with a view to starting strategic negotiations with the Soviets. That in turn was dependent on defining a role for SDI that was not inconsistent with the arms control norms that the Soviets stood by. Working with McFarlane, Paul Nitze, who had taken the title Special Adviser on Arms Control, outlined a compromise position that sought to integrate SDI, arms control and idea of crisis stability.

Presenting SDI

Nitze and McFarlane had always questioned the practicality of SDI. They believed the President had underestimated the technical difficulties and financial costs of his vision. Without being relatively cheaper, strategic defences would simply encourage an offensive arms build up[33]. Yet they also believed the President was 'fully dedicated to the idea of getting rid of ballistic missiles' (Wohlforth, 1996, p.40). Nitze's priority was to manage negotiations with the Soviets in a way that would lead to an agreed transition toward effective non-nuclear defences and the elimination of ballistic missiles. As Jervis pointed out, the strategic relationship between sides relying on defensive deterrence would mitigate the uncertainty that contributed to the security dilemma.   As Nitze put it, the 'strategic relationship could then be characterised as one of mutual assured security'[34].

Despite being adopted by the administration, the commitment to a negotiated transition varied[35]. To the Pentagon, the Soviets had violated the ABM Treaty with the construction of the Krasnoyarsk phased array radar. In response it recommended that the U.S. deploy strategic defences as soon as it was technologically feasible to do so. Thus while the State Department, National Security Council and politically significant actors outside the administration saw SDI as either a bargaining chip or as the end point of a negotiated transition[36], the Defence Department saw it as a supplement to a counterforce strategy that sought national autarky.

As a result of this split, the administration tentatively adopted a 'broad interpretation' of the ABM Treaty that allowed SDI testing but not, to the Pentagon's disappointment, early deployment. Coming at a time when the administration, despite strong Congressional opposition, broke the tacit acceptance of SALT II limits[37], this apparent disregard for arms control alarmed the Soviets and the NATO allies. SDI testing, however, was restricted by the political influence of the arms control community that was exercised through the Congressional powers of appropriation. Support for the ABM regime was strong in Congress and in due course it, along with the Soviet concessions on offensive forces, would resolve the American security dilemma in favour of a START and ABM regime based on mutual vulnerability and strategic stability. Getting to that position, however, required a change in attitude towards the Soviet Union, and ultimately a change of administration in the U.S.

Towards a Renewed Dialogue

The influence of those seeking to negotiate with the Soviet Union would steadily rise from 1983 on. An important victory for Shultz came with the appointment of Robert McFarlane as National Security Adviser instead of

Jeanne Kirkpatrick who had been the hardliner's choice. While Shultz initially favoured James Baker, it is fair to say that McFarlane provided more support for Shultz than Kirkpatrick would have and was therefore a good compromise for Shultz to make[38]. Indeed the advocacy of the NSC took on a different character with the appointment of career foreign service officer Jack Matlock. Matlock's vast experience of the USSR influenced a less essentialist view (Matlock, 1995, p.81)[39]. His influence in pushing the President towards increased dialogue with the Soviet Union is evident in the 16 January, 1984 speech which he wrote for Reagan. It is widely recognised as a turning point in the President's personal attitude (Garthoff, 1994, pp.142-145).

Indeed 1984 gradually saw a number of diplomatic initiatives to restore dialogue with the Soviet leadership. While some dismiss these moves as pandering to the electorate, such arguments cannot explain why the second Reagan administration continued the exploration of dialogue. While dialogue was pursued, however, the continued influence of Weinberger was a major obstacle to serious negotiation. His unshakeable dedication to the strategic modernisation programme and Reagan's strong personal commitment to him made compromise with the Soviets a politically arduous task. The frustration of those looking for clear signals from the administration is expressed clearly by McFarlane. He suggested to the recently re-elected Reagan that the 'oil and water' relationship of Shultz and Weinberger had to be resolved. Either the President take a more active policy role or he would have to start thinking about 'changing the configuration'. To the latter suggestion the President replied that both were his friends and he would fire neither. To the former he gave no indication to McFarlane of his priorities and said the NSA would simply have to work harder to balance the competing position of Shultz and Weinberger (McFarlane, 1994, pp.286-289). It is perhaps no coincidence that Reagan had six National Security Advisers in eight years. More importantly, the lack of leadership intensified America's security dilemma and, despite Reagan's professed intention to reduce tension, made it more difficult for transnational coalitions in favour of common security to gain political influence in the U.S.

Common Security, 'Peace through Strength' and Soviet Reform

The ideas of the Freeze movement in the U.S. only managed to penetrate certain parts of Congress and had a limited impact on U.S. arms control policy. While the administration did concern itself with 'negotiability', it was aimed at convincing the peace movements of its hard-line stance rather than convincing the Soviets that an agreement was in their mutual interest.   The apparent softening of tone during the run up to the presidential elections is the only evidence one can cite where the American public restrained the administration (Knopf, 1997).   While the ideas of crisis-stability and arms-control stability that were introduced to the national security bureaucracy in the 1960s managed to survive Reagan's onslaught, they were a long way from the ideas of common security identified in the previous chapter. Support for these ideas, however, was more significant across Europe. Yet even here right-wing supporters of a militarised response overcame the opposition of the peace movements. NATOs decision to deploy nuclear missiles in Europe went ahead in December 1983 despite the left wing opposition.

That the peace movements failed to influence the Reagan administration is not in doubt. Yet the right also claims that the end of the East-West military conflict, indeed the collapse of the Soviet Union itself, was a consequence of policies opposite to those advocated by the peace movements. The arms build up and the tough negotiating stance, 'peace through strength', is said to have led to the reversal of Soviet policy and ultimately its collapse.   It is argued here, however, that while events contributing to the end of the Cold War can be directly traced to this period, they do not support the right's claim that the U.S. military build up 'won' the Cold War.

The argument that the strategic modernisation programme was the straw that broke the back of Soviet militarism rests on the assumption that the Soviets tried, but ultimately failed to keep up with U.S. defence spending. Yet the impact of variations in the Soviet defence budget were small and 'the marginal impact on the Soviet economy was insignificant' (Evangelista, 1999, p.240; see also Oye, 1995; Chernoff, 1991). Indeed, Gorbachev's own assessment of the defence burden did not begin to effect policy until 1988 when 'the government's own contradictory and ill-conceived attempts at economic reform had done far more damage to the Soviet economy than whatever marginal increase in military spending Reagan's policies had occasioned' (Evangelista, 1999, pp.286-289). Even then Gorbachev had a hard time convincing the Soviet leadership of the need to scale down military spending.   The opposition of these traditionalists, Evangelista concludes, 'should make us cautious about assuming a straightforward relationship between high military spending and Gorbachev's foreign policy reforms' (Evangelista, 1999, p.258).

There were calls in the Soviet Union to respond with a defensive build-up to match SDI but they were marginal.   Given the fact that it was relatively cheaper to overwhelm SDI by adding to the SS-18 capability, advocates of an offensive build-up were of greater significance. Yet these too were marginal compared to the support for arms control and the ABM regime.   In fact the established arms control community in Moscow persuaded Soviet policymakers not to bankrupt the country by seeking to match the U.S. build up.   Rather, Soviet policy sought to bolster the transnational opponents of SDI through arms control and disarmament[40].

As will be shown below with reference to the Reykjavik summit, peace through strength cannot claim credit for what appeared to be unilateral Soviet concessions, because the U.S. was not following a coherent bargaining strategy. As in the 1950s, when the U.S. claimed Khrushchev's arms control concessions were a consequence American strength, the U.S. was unwilling to give up those systems that were regarded as bargaining chips (Evangelista, 1999, pp.112-113). That in part was a consequence of the fact that the strategic modernisation programme was a response to the perceived threat of Soviet strength and not a strategy to exploit Soviet weakness.

Even if an arms race and economic pressure on the Soviet Union was considered appropriate in some parts of the security bureaucracy, it was in no way considered established policy. For example, spokespersons from the State Department quite explicitly denied that the U.S. was waging economic warfare against the Soviet Union. 'We do not seek to cause the collapse of their economy' stated Undersecretary of State, Wallis. 'In fact we would not want that', he continued, 'that would be a dangerous development. We favour mutually beneficial economic relations where those relations are conducted on commercial terms and where advantages are mutual and balanced'[41]. Even if one was to dismiss this as rhetoric, it is hard to find evidence of a standard view on the probable Soviet response to economic warfare and the role played by SDI. Where some hardliners may have anticipated bankrupting the Soviet Union others did not foresee a radical departure from patterns of behaviour neither at the doctrinal level nor in terms of arms control or a crash offensive or defensive program[42].

The very fact that international influences are mediated by domestic politics would suggest that the American influence on Soviet reform was important but indeterminate. 'Peace through strength' and the strident rhetoric of the Reagan administration did cause hardliners in the Soviet Union to rethink the correlation of forces. Following the arguments of Charles Glaser, chapter two suggested that a hard-line response was appropriate when it undermined the arguments of hardliners in the other state and subsequently supported the political position of those advocating co-operation. Robert Patman has argued that the Reagan build up had this effect (Patman, 1999). The collapse of détente, a resurgent America and the war scares of the early 1980s contradicted the traditionalist prediction that a militarily strong Soviet Union would lead to compliant adversaries and international peace. 'By shaping circumstances that strengthened the position of 'system modernisers' in relation to conservative elements in the post-Brezhnev leadership' Patman concludes, 'the hard-line Reagan administration acted as a catalyst in promoting the early emergence of a comprehensive new Soviet foreign (and domestic) policy'.

Yet while peace through strength may have weakened the arguments of traditionalists it cannot account for the revolutionary policies that Gorbachev eventually adopted. It created a policy window for new ideas, but cannot explain why those ideas were as revolutionary as New Political Thinking (NPT). Indeed, none of the Soviet reformers viewed SDI or the U.S. strategic modernisation programme as helping their cause. Roald Sagdeev, former head of Soviet Space Research Institute maintained that SDI had 'absolutely zero influence' on the origins or course of Soviet reforms (Evangelista, 1999, pp.242-243).

Claims that the revolutionary changes were a direct response to peace through strength miss the fact that Gorbachev was elected to return policy to the status quo ante of the mid-1970s (Evangelista, 1999, p.252). Furthermore, when Gorbachev did eventually pursue revolutionary changes in the form of NPT it was not a response to U.S. behaviour nor simply a concession to the American agenda. It was a GRIT-type strategy that had learned not only the implications of détente's failure, but also important lessons of the Khrushchev period. In seeking to act on those lessons it did not capitulate to the American position, but adopted the ideas of common security and dragged the U.S. as far as it could toward that position.

Common Security: the origins of political significance

A consequence of the second Cold War was the increasing alarm across transnational civil society that the superpowers and their allies in governments across Europe were behaving irresponsibly. At the less radical end of this reaction, Soviet scientists revived the campaign for a Comprehensive Test Ban Treaty and, in an ironic reversal of transnational activity in the 1960s, sought to strengthen the arms control community in the United States (Evangelista, 1999, pp.233-245). Across Europe, civilian defence intellectuals on the left began to formulate alternative defence strategies that emphasised defensive technologies. Non-offensive defence was designed to lower the risk of war by removing the risk that military postures would be misperceived as aggressive.   As chapter two demonstrated, such strategies could be part of a GRIT-type strategy that sought to reassure the other side without making oneself vulnerable.

Others drew broader implications from the second Cold War. They linked what they saw as an increased threat of nuclear war not to gaps in deterrence but to growing gaps in democracy. As Mary Kaldor notes, these movements 'were concerned about the extent of power wielded by the state, the fact that politicians literally had the power to decide, without any consultation, about the fate of millions of people. Nuclear war was the ultimate barbarity. Nuclear weapons symbolised the lack of individual control not only over the conditions in which individuals live but life itself' (Kaldor, 1999, pp.198-199). In an influential pamphlet, *Protest and Survive*, E.P.Thompson (Thompson and Smith, 1980) argued that by increasing the interdependence between states, nuclear weapons had undermined national sovereignty and deformed the democratic process that depended on a responsive state. Security could only be attained by recognising the common fate of humanity and that recognition would only occur if the security apparatus of the state was democratised and made more responsive to transnational civil society.

The message of peace activists was made more urgent by the war scares of the early 1980s. Yet transnational civil society had received greatest encouragement during the period of East-West détente. The Helsinki Final Act signed by the 35 states of the Conference on Security and Co-operation in Europe in 1975, inspired independent social movements to make sure states complied with the human rights accords that they signed up to (Thomas, 1999). The influence of western policy on their activities is discussed in detail in chapter five, but it is worth noting here that these groups were, inspired, legitimised and to a certain extent protected by the link that détente and the Helsinki Final Act made between human rights and interstate trade and security co-operation. Its importance for this chapter is that these groups not only kept alive the idea of détente at the interstate level, their increased political significance highlighted the link between a state's political identity and the threat of nuclear war. They campaigned for nuclear disarmament *and* democratisation under the banner of common security. In so doing the peace movements also kept alive the vision of a security community beyond détente where a worthwhile peace and not simply coexistence could thrive.

It would be wrong to argue that these groups saw democracy only as a means of preventing war. Indeed Kaldor (1999, p.200) notes the intensity of the debate across these movements about the priority to be accorded to disarmament.   While those in the West tended to elevate the threat of nuclear war, those in the East tended to argue that 'totalitarianism was the cause of the nuclear arms race and democracy was the first priority, *even at the risk of nuclear war*'.   Yet gradually, Kaldor continues,   'the inseparability of peace and democracy and human rights, came to be mutually recognised'.   The dilemma for American foreign policy, of course, was to support these without provoking the Soviet Union.   This is discussed in chapter five, but it is clear that the peace movements saw democratisation and disarmament as inherently linked and mutually supporting.   Where New Political Thinking in the Soviet Union acted on this idea, U.S. policy saw this connection belatedly and reluctantly.   While it was eventually willing to disarm its conventional and tactical nuclear capability, special interests were resourceful enough to mobilise sufficient support to prevent the disarmament of its strategic nuclear forces.

Common Security: Soviet New Political Thinking

Ultimately the ideas of the peace and human rights transnational coalition were reflected in New Political Thinking. It would be wrong to argue all these ideas were reflected in a coherent foreign policy that Gorbachev gradually implemented. Given the political obstacles in his way it would be naïve to believe that a politically astute politician such as Gorbachev would have even contemplated such revolutionary reforms when entering the Kremlin.   But Gorbachev did take his general direction from the transnational peace movements who advocated common security, nuclear disarmament, non-offensive defence and ultimately democratisation. He would manufacture and seize opportunities to push Soviet foreign policy and its political identity in this direction. While the moves he occasionally made in order stay in power sometimes compromised his message, he would remain an agent of these ideas and in due course pay a heavy political price for that commitment.

Taking the advice of Evgenii Velikhov and other members of the transnational coalition of scientists campaigning for a test ban, one of Gorbachev's first moves was the politically risky unilateral moratorium on Soviet nuclear testing (Evangelista, 1999, pp.269-288). The most radical moves were inspired by his connection to the ideas and personnel of the Independent Commission on Disarmament and Security Issues or Palme Commission. As chapter two demonstrated, the conclusions of the Palme Commission clearly identified the Cold War in terms similar to Jervis's spiral model. Yet the Commission went further than Jervis's (and for that matter Paul Nitze's) emphasis on defensive weapons by advocating general and complete disarmament as the only way to escape the spiral. Nuclear weapons had highlighted the common fate of mankind and the need to find one's own security in the security of the other. 'International peace', Palme (1982, pp.138-139) concluded,

> must rest on a commitment to joint survival rather than the threat of mutual destruction. ... Unless they show mutual restraint and proper appreciation of the nuclear age...the pursuit of security can cause intensified competition and more tense political relations and, at the end of the day, a reduction in the security for all concerned.... There must be a partnership in the struggle against war itself....The Commission strongly supports the goal of general and complete disarmament.

Much of the work of this commission was done in the Brezhnev period at the time when many began questioning rationale for Soviet policy. Its influence on the direction of the Soviet rethink is clear. For example, Georgii Arbartov, who was a prominent member of the Commission and who would later be a key inspiration for Gorbachev's NPT, has stated that 'the work of the Palme Commission was a very important stage in my life and exerted a major influence on my understanding of politics and international relations' (Evangelista, 1999, p.161; Herman, 1996, pp.293-294). Aware of the crisis in Soviet foreign policy and psychologically open to new ideas, Gorbachev integrated what seemed to him a coherent philosophy into the Soviet approach to international relations (Gross Stein, 1994). For him this was not disavowing Marxism-Leninism, rather it was a refusal to live by 'ossified schemes and prescriptions valid everywhere and under all circumstances [which] is most definitely contrary to the essence and spirit of Marxism-Leninism'[43].

The arguments of the Palme Commission reinforced the lessons that Soviet reformers had taken from the Khrushchev period. If disarmament was to reduce tension it had to be comprehensive. Cuts to nuclear forces alone would be, and indeed were, interpreted as making the world safe for conventional war (Evangelista, 1999, p.290). Gorbachev again drew on the work of transnational peace activists and their supporters in the Soviet Union to inform his policy. They would integrate ideas of Western Social Democrats into Soviet military doctrine clearing the way for the unilateral reduction of 500,000 troops in December 1988. Andrei Kokoshin, for example, worked closely with Social Democrats and was instrumental both directly and indirectly, in the formulation of the Berlin Declaration of May 1987. This revolutionary declaration described Soviet military doctrine as 'subordinated to the task of preventing war, nuclear and conventional'. In the spirit of non-offensive defence it proposed the 'reduction in Europe of armed forces and conventional weapons to the level at which neither side, in guaranteeing its own defense, will have the means for sudden attack on another country or for the deployment of offensive operations in general' (Evangelista, 1999, pp.305-321)[44].

Yet cuts to conventional forces alone would be, as they were in the 1950s, willingly interpreted by hardliners in the west as a Soviet emphasis on nuclear warfighting. To Soviet reformers, even minimum nuclear deterrence, while being an improvement, was not ideal. Common security meant recognising a common identity that did not need the threat of nuclear holocaust to sustain it. Nuclear weapons had certainly highlighted a common *vulnerability*, but common *security* could only be attained by continuing to recognise a common identity even after nuclear disarmament. That would, as the more radical elements of the peace movements suggested, require a change in the balance of political power away from the militarist and exceptionalist conceptions of security. By setting a timetable for nuclear disarmament, and by democratising and then ultimately undermining the power of the CPSU, New Thinking did just that (Herman, 1996, p.282). As we shall see, however, the progress towards common security would be interrupted by the significance American identity attaches to militarist and exceptionalist conceptions of security.

Common Security: the initial American response

President Reagan's inability to appreciate Gorbachev's ideas is illustrated by the exchange they had at Geneva. Their common humanity, Reagan stated, would be easily recognised if they were threatened by 'other species, from another planet, outside this universe'. Gorbachev referred to this comment at the 27th CPSU Congress in February 1986. 'Isn't a nuclear disaster a more tangible danger than the landing of unknown extraterrestrials?...isn't all the experience accumulated by mankind enough to draw perfectly justified practical conclusions today, rather than wait until some other crisis breaks out?' (Oberdorfer, 1991, p.144; Wohlforth, 1996, p.97; Garthoff, 1994, p.310).

There were, however, elements of the administration's admittedly confused arms control policy that were not that far removed from Gorbachev's plan to abolish nuclear weapons announced in January 1986. The first public indication was the joint declaration that 'nuclear war could not be won and must never be fought', signed by Reagan and Gorbachev at the Geneva Summit of November 1985. While this was of immense political significance to reformers in the Soviet Union they would not have been aware of the extent to which Reagan's anti-nuclearism found expression in official U.S. policy other than from the vague statements accompanying SDI (Wohlforth, 1996, p.11). NSDD210 of February 1986, however, focused on 'promptly negotiating' an INF Treaty as an interim step and pursuing a 50% reduction in strategic forces as '*the first step toward the total elimination of nuclear weapons*'. Once the U.S. and Soviets had achieved such a reduction, it continued, 'we can envision subsequent steps which could involve the United Kingdom, France and the People's Republic of China so that all can move to zero nuclear weapons in a balanced stable manner'. Consistent with Nitze's 'strategic concept' the document made clear that 'the elimination of nuclear weapons would not obviate the need for defenses against such weapons, particularly to protect against cheating or breakout by any country'[45].

While the two sides were seemingly united in their understanding of the threat posed by nuclear weapons, therefore, the United States would draw different conclusions. It maintained the belief that a military-technical response was necessary given the aggressive identity of other states. While Nitze and others in the administration saw mutual reliance on defence as possible in the long run, and defined it as mutual assured survival, their continued faith in a military-technical solution was symbolic of a deep mistrust of other states that stemmed from a deeply embedded sense of exceptionalism. Nuclear weapons may have highlighted the interdependent nature of states but there was a strong American belief that this was only temporary. American technology could once more lead the American people from the security dilemmas of the old world. It was time, as Reagan put it, 'to put our survival back under our own control'[46].

Reagan's vision of SDI was symbolic of a view 180 degrees removed from Gorbachev's emphasis on common humanity and cooperative action to solve common problems. The U.S. President did not see SDI as part of the problem and by refusing to compromise in any strategic dialogue he demonstrated that the U.S. was unwilling to be part of the solution. Those who maintained control over policy believed it could and should separate itself from the world's problems regardless of the insecurities that created for other states. More directly it made it doubly difficult to convince Soviet hardliners to abandon reliance on offensive forces. They found it difficult to distinguish the role played by SDI in a transition to a more stable strategic relationship, from one that provided the U.S. with a first strike capacity. Particularly when significant voices in the U.S. and

Europe were arguing that SDI should compliment rather than replace offensive weapons.

Gorbachev's common security and Reagan's militarist exceptionalism clashed at the Reykjavik summit in October 1986. While NSDD210 spoke vaguely about eliminating nuclear weapons, Weinberger and Shultz had agreed on a more specific proposal to eliminate all ballistic missiles. Like Weinberger, the Chiefs accepted the proposal as a broad goal to be offered to Gorbachev in the abstract. As the Congressional Report on Reykjavik states, this 'failure on the part of the bureaucracy to take the President seriously would come back to haunt both the military and the President when it was reintroduced with specifics at Reykjavik'[47]. For at that summit, the U.S. delegation introduced Nitze's Strategic Concept. They proposed a 50 percent cut in strategic forces in five years, during which both sides would confine their research on defences to the laboratory. In a second five year period, both sides would eliminate ballistic missiles and widen the scope of defensive tests. At the end of the ten year period both sides would be free to deploy defences[48].

While the Soviets originally proposed confining defensive testing to the laboratory for 15 to 20 years, Gorbachev simultaneously compromised and raised the stakes. He agreed to a 10 year period after which both sides would begin negotiations of space based defences. He also proposed, however, that both sides eliminate all strategic nuclear weapons in the second five year period. While Reagan temporarily agreed to the complete abolition he reacted to the Soviet position on SDI 'as if he had been asked to toss his favourite child into an erupting volcano' (Matlock, 1995 p.97)[49]. Ultimately, the talks broke down with the U.S. proclaiming their right to withdraw from the ABM Treaty at any time. Despite the heated exchanges in the post-summit press conferences, Gorbachev did his best to emphasise the progress made. In stark contrast it seemed Reagan was more than willing to let arms control flounder as America continued to seek strategic autarky.   On return to the U.S. he offered the public the following alternatives: 'we can either bet on American technology to keep us safe, or on Soviet promises. And each has its own track record. I'll bet on American technology any time' (Garthoff, 1994, p.525).

Yet the advocates of the Strategic Concept in the administration were anxious not to let the agreement that was on offer at Reykjavik slip into history. While a relieved Joint Chiefs of Staff (JCS) renewed its opposition to nuclear disarmament, Shultz argued that MAD was part of the old way of thinking. Furthermore, as part of his challenge to 'wrap our minds around new interpretations and build new realities' he sought alternative ways of addressing the military's concern[50]. NSDD210, the document that seemingly matched Gorbachev's ambition for the elimination of all nuclear weapons, had identified the conventional imbalance as an obstacle to reciprocating Gorbachev's disarmament programme. Maintaining a credible counterforce deterrent was foremost in the Chief's mind. In response Shultz advocated raising the nuclear threshold by spending more on conventional forces as a way of accepting the ten year transition to a limited offensive nuclear capability. While accepting that conventional deterrence was more expensive than nuclear deterrence, Shultz believed the additional investment worthwhile in terms of strategic stability. 'You can't tell me', he challenged, 'that an economy that's already at $4.5 trillion and is moving toward 5, that we can't afford far more than $300 billion for our own defense and national security'[51].

Yet it was too much to pay. While Shultz was publicly advocating increased defence spending on conventional rather than nuclear forces, the President was reluctantly signing a National Defense Authorization Bill that had not fully appropriated the finance requested. If the administration was having trouble getting funds for its strategic modernisation programme it would have been virtually impossible getting even more spending on defence. One can draw two conclusions from this. First, if peace through strength had, as the administration claimed, forced Soviet concessions, the U.S. simply wasn't strong enough to cash in on those concessions[52]. A more convincing argument is that the initial spending on strategic modernisation was a wasted investment. It would have been better directed at raising the nuclear threshold and relaxing the reliance on nuclear weapons by strengthening NATOs conventional deterrence. If, as is argued above, Reagan's strategic modernisation programme had limited influence on Gorbachev's policies other than the negative one of strengthening his political opponents, it is safe to say that the defence build-up limited the American ability to positively reciprocate the "concessions" Gorbachev was more than willing to make.

Admiral Crowe's Security: American militarism and the post-Reykjavik follow-up

It can be argued that the political pressure from NATO allies forced the U.S. to abandon its Reykjavik position on ballistic missiles. By stating that 'we were prepared to go forward with it in any case', however, Nitze and Shultz suggest a greater commitment to the Strategic Concept than these arguments suggest (Wohlforth, 1996, p.117). Ultimately it was the Chiefs' opposition to the zero-ballistic missile proposal that won the day.

When Crowe spoke out against the proposal in the post-Summit NSC meeting, Reagan reportedly changed the subject and told the Admiral how much he liked the military. In light of Crowe's decision to resign rather than publicly defend the proposal he declared that the President's response was 'the most incredible thing in my life' (Crowe, 1993, pp.264-272). The Admiral's position was secure.

The post-Reykjavik directives acknowledged that 'present analytical tools' were unsatisfactory in resolving questions of security. In contrast to the civilian led revolution taking place in Soviet defence policy, however, U.S. policy maintained its faith in the ability of the military to deliver technical solutions. It concluded in a manner that was obviously designed to satisfy the ambitions of arms controllers while simultaneously addressing the wounded egos of a military that had been temporarily by-passed. '[U]ntil new methods adapted to the challenges and opportunities of this alternative future are fully developed, we will have to depend heavily on the experience, expertise, resourcefulness, creativity and judgement of our professional military and defense community'[53].

The decisive influence of the U.S. military was the key obstacle to a disarmament process that recognised nuclear war as a universal threat and acted on that common identity in a manner that ensured mutual security. By identifying the Soviet Union in essentialist terms as a state that could not be trusted, the military worked with the Pentagon and elements of the White House to make sure they dominated American security policy and influenced its defence budgets. The revolutionary change in Soviet identity would not be mirrored in the U.S. The American military would not dominate U.S. policy in the way the Soviet military had done in the past, yet neither would it surrender its influence on policy as the Soviet military ultimately did at the end of the Cold War. The Pentagon's view was far from hegemonic, however, and by the end of 1986 it had considerably less influence than it did at the start of the decade. Moreover, as Gorbachev's new thinking had greater influence on Soviet policy and unilaterally implemented a defensive posture, American hardliners were able to see those moves as concessions and thus felt justified in making their own concessions to the arms control agenda.

The nuclear arms control regime that eventually emerged, however, was far from the ideal of the Strategic Concept. In fact its basic foundation, mutual vulnerability, was the same as Reagan had rejected when entering office. Despite the claims of some, the INF Treaty did stabilise deterrence in Europe by reducing political tension and setting the precedent of on-site inspection to verify compliance[54]. Thanks mainly to a new Soviet approach that recognised the limited military value and the negative political effect of these weapons, the Treaty was signed before the end of the Reagan administration (Herman, 1996, p.69). Yet on every other indicator of stability the Reagan administration had nothing to show for its efforts. The ABM Treaty was still in place and no progress had been made towards a strategic agreement that addressed the concerns of the Scowcroft Commission.

It was Gorbachev's meeting with a high-profile member of the peace movements that provided the breakthrough for a new détente. In December 1986 Gorbachev met Andrei Sakharov, whom he had recently released from exile. Sakharov told the Soviet leader not to worry about Star Wars, predicting that the impracticable technology would eventually die on its own (Greenberg, 2000, p.142)[55]. Sakharov's prediction proved correct. During the remaining years of the Reagan administration funding restrictions and legislation locking the administration in to the narrow interpretation of the ABM Treaty kept testing limited. When Frank Carlucci took over from Weinberger as Secretary of Defense in 1988 the Pentagon adopted the Nitze criteria for strategic defence. Forced by further cuts to SDI funding, Carlucci argued that deployment would only go ahead if it was cost-effective relative to offensive missiles (Wohlforth, 1996, p.44, p.56).

In due course the Bush administration restricted the programme to researching the interception of limited strikes and made it clear that any results would benefit all[56]. Furthermore the Strategic Concept that involved radical cuts to offensive arsenals and the abolition of the strategic triad was forgotten. Ultimately it would take the collapse of the Soviet Union itself, before the American military was to compromise on its counterforce mission by abolishing the MIRV capability. The START I and II agreements, signed by the Bush administration, went much further in moving the relationship towards an MND regime. Yet they still fell short of the relationship envisaged by Gorbachev which recognised the reality of mutual insecurity and advocated nuclear disarmament as the only way of escaping it.

Ending America's Military Cold War

Gorbachev's philosophy was a long way from recognising liberalism as the ideological victor of the Cold War. Yet it did seek to transcend the Cold War by recognising the common values across East and West. It sought to integrate both sides into a single international community. Thus, while 'New Thinking' did not embrace 'the American way', indeed it directly opposed American militarism, *Glasnost, Perestroika* and *Democratization* did unleash support for the free market, civil and political rights and national self-determination.   On the face of it advocates of these ideas could have expected support from the United States.   Yet the potential disorder created by the implementation of these ideals and the possibility for violence was sufficient reason for Realists to urge caution.   The story of America's security policy at the end of the Cold War is that of a debate not between advocates of deterrence and spiral models, but between Realists and Liberals who argued over the normative implications of Gorbachev's reforms and the political movements it released.   This story is told in detail in chapter five.   As background to that chapter and as a conclusion to this, it is necessary to identify how American attitudes to arms control and its military forces slowly changed across the Reagan and Bush administration.

As Gorbachev's domestic reforms began to bite the U.S. policymaking community divided over their significance.   The intelligence community split along familiar lines.   While the CIA predicted that Gorbachev would continue to hold down defence spending and pursue arms control agreements, it did concede the possibility that 'new thinking' was simply an exercise in peredyshka (breathing space).   In other words a temporary relaxation of international tension was necessary to keep rising military budgets from choking off the reconstruction of the economy.   Where the CIA saw this as a 'bad news' scenario, the DIA argued that perestroika would simply result in an improved Soviet military and greater threat to the United States[57].   When the incoming Secretary of State, James Baker consulted leading Soviet specialists he found a split in the academic world too.   To Baker the debate between perestoika and peredyshka was beyond resolution.   Both 'views had analytic strengths and weakness' (Baker, 1995, p.69).   This debate would cast a shadow over most of Bush's foreign policy considerations.   As chapter five discusses in detail, whether one thought the glass half full or half empty, the policymaking community as a whole could not predict for certain the fate of Soviet reform (Baker, 1995 p.69; Beschloss and Talbott, 1993, pp.142-143; Evangelista, 1999)[58].   Given this uncertainty, Bush's decision to support Gorbachev as the best way of assuring democratic reform *and* international order was attacked by those who had reached different conclusions.

Essentially this debate and America's security dilemma, boiled down to perceptions of the political significance given to hard-line elements within the Soviet security discourse.   If Gorbachev's reforms could fundamentally change that and at the same time permanently elevate the significance of 'new thinkers' then 'the Soviet Union' would mean something completely different in the American discourse. In other words if Soviet identity was seen by politically significant voices in America's security discourse to be changing then the chances of U.S. disarmament would be enhanced. The Realist argument of guarding against a Soviet breakout (defection from a cooperative regime) would have less significance. Moreover, if Gorbachev's approach was also seen to be increasing individual freedoms for Soviet citizens, there would be less opposition to the disarmament agenda from Neoconservatives who linked the Soviet human rights record to arms control and trade. Soviet domestic practices, its system government and its political identity were inherently linked to the process of transcending the Cold War.

Of course, this was by no means an automatic process. America's political identity also mediated perceptions of Soviet identity. As the above discussion on U.S. defence policy illustrated, there are powerful intellectual communities who have a vested interest in international conflict and will peddle their 'theories' in order to further their narrowly defined interests. Despite Gorbachev's best efforts to marginalise their significance, they were resourceful enough to convince policymakers that complete nuclear disarmament was a threat to national security. Even when 'the Soviet Union' was confined to history, they elevated the significance of Russian and Chinese hardliners as well as the threat posed by rogue 'threshold' states. The point is that American political culture confers much political significance on those intellectual communities with vested interests in maintaining nuclear weapons and creating strategic defences. In doing so it sets a large obstacle to nuclear disarmament. By refusing to recognise the common threat of nuclear weapons it poses a significant barrier to the expansion of a security community. While those intellectual communities may be justified in their claim that the political identity of other states requires a retaliatory capability, it does not excuse a willingness to dismiss disarmament as utopian.

Gorbachev's disarmament programme was frustrated not only by the doubts about his ability to transform Soviet identity but also by a lack of political will among the nuclear powers. Yet his unilateral moves towards that goal did create political opportunities for the arms control community to influence American policy. As noted above, his unilateral moves to address the conventional imbalance in Europe were particularly significant. That imbalance had been highlighted by the U.S. military to reinforce its argument for a counterforce nuclear option. The Soviet move created intense pressure on the Bush administration to respond positively to Gorbachev's arms control agenda[59]. Yet Gorbachev's initiative had been pushed through the Soviet bureaucracy and delivered as a fait accompli to the military.   As Evangelista notes (1999, pp.315-319), the increasing centralisation of foreign policy power around new thinkers made this possible, yet it did not inspire confidence among sceptics in the U.S.

The uncertainty surrounding the political fate of Soviet reform, was reflected in the Bush administration. National Security Adviser, Brent Scowcroft, for instance, interpreted Gorbachev's 'peace offensive' as an exercise 'in making trouble within the western alliance'. The light at the end of the tunnel he suggested, may not be the end of the Cold War, but 'an on coming locomotive' (Beschloss and Talbott, 1993, pp.17-18). As the Polish regime conceded to Solidarity and the Soviets refused to intervene the President too reminded his audience at Boston University of his 'obligation to temper optimism with prudence'[60].   Non-offensive defence was far from embedded in Soviet policy, and to the conservative Bush administration further proof was needed of the impact of Gorbachev's reforms.

Yet as democratic revolutions spread across Eastern Europe the policy of 'status quo plus' seemingly lacked the ambition demanded by an increasingly confident liberal argument.   While recognising that containment was never an end in itself, National Security Directive (NSD) 23 was short on satisfactory responses.   When in May 1989 Bush announced his open skies proposal at Texas A&M University the influential editorials were invariably negative. After a five month long 'pause' and a national security review the president could only manage 'a stale proposal conceived by the CIA in the bitterest days of the Cold War'. He had 'pulled out of his hat not a live rabbit but a dead mouse' (Beschloss and Talbott, 1993, pp.70-71).

As chapter five demonstrates in detail, the domestic political pressure to positively reciprocate Gorbachev's unilateral disarmament was reinforced by the growing dispute in NATO on the modernisation of short-range lance missile or Follow-on-to-Lance (FOTL). Following the bad press Bush would begin to complain that the administration's proposals were 'too nuclear, too military' (Oberdorfer, 1991, p.349). Faced with a challenge to American leadership at the May NATO summit, and with a Secretary of State convinced that the hardline arguments of Thatcher were increasingly isolated in NATO, Bush chose to override his own hardliners in the military and proposed a 20 percent cut in U.S. and Soviet personnel in Europe. The decision on FOTL would be postponed while both sides negotiate their future status.

Heavily prompted as it was by Soviet actions, the arguments of the less hard-line NATO allies, and a general sense that the Bush administration was always one step behind revolutionary events, the U.S. approach to arms control did eventually evolve beyond the military obsessions with warfighting and strategic stability. Indeed the administration would openly admit the political rationale behind its conventional arms control proposal[61]. Secretary of State, Baker, for instance would tell Congress that U.S. policy was designed to 'help free the political reform process in Eastern Europe from the heavy weight of an excessive Soviet military presence. While we tend to see the Soviet forces as a potential invasion force, to millions in the East, the Soviets remain an occupation force'[62]. In other words, if reformers in Eastern Europe could witness the peaceful withdrawal of Soviet troops they would be encouraged to pursue the values that they and the U.S. held in common.

These proposals ultimately resulted in the Conventional Forces in Europe (CFE) Treaties. The Treaties themselves and the process leading up to them helped create a secure political space in which democratic revolution could be pursued, for the most part, peacefully. Of course, the CFE Treaty did not signal the end of the Cold War. Many dilemmas were created by the break up of the Warsaw Pact that could not be dealt with by focusing on military forces. These are discussed in detail in chapter five. Yet the main point to stress hear is that positive reciprocation of Gorbachev's disarmament programme assisted the peaceful political revolutions that ended the Cold War.

A similar logic guided U.S. arms control policy towards the potential disorder created by the political reform process in the Soviet Union. Gorbachev's reforms had unleashed a wave of nationalism in many of the 15 republics that made up the Soviet Union. As chapter five shows with specific reference to the Baltic independence movements, the political crisis this created posed a normative dilemma for America. This was again characterised by a debate between Realists who saw Moscow and Gorbachev as the key to international order, and Liberals who sought to encourage the process of democratic reform by offering early diplomatic recognition to the independence movements.

Gorbachev's efforts to forge compromise with the nationalists while preserving the Union led to the planned signing of a new Union Treaty in August 1991. Driven by a fear that their influence would be increasingly marginalised in the new Union, the 'Gang of Eight', a hard-line group headed by Vice-President, Gennady Yanayev, deposed Gorbachev as the Soviet leader rested in the Crimea. The initial American reaction exposed the tension between Realists and Liberals in the American policy community. Informed by Scowcroft's concern 'not to burn bridges' with the new leadership, Bush identified the coup as 'extra-constitutional'(Beschloss and Talbott, 1993, p.422). Others expressed frustration at the administration's unwillingness to condemn the hardliners in stronger terms. In fact, the attempt to avoid burning what these critics saw as imaginary bridges actually assisted the leaders of the coup legitimise their otherwise illegitimate actions (Matlock, 1995, pp.588-589). As it became clear that the coup was not as well organised as was initially expected and given the strong opposition mounted by Russian President Boris Yeltsin, the administration began to take a harder line.

The wider implications of this American dilemma are drawn out in chapter five. The point is here that the failure of the August coup, the nominal restoration of Gorbachev to power and the increasing political significance of the nationalist leaders, notably Yeltsin, changed the balance of opinion in America. No longer was the Realist concern of a hard-line backlash as salient as before. The hardliners were either dead, in jail or at the very least on the political margins. The primary concern facing the Bush administration was the potential disorder created by the probable break up of the Soviet Union. Intelligence on the command of nuclear weapons during the coup had been ambiguous and while there was little concern that a breakaway republic could use strategic nuclear weapons to blackmail an adversary, the U.S. was anxious as to the fate of Soviet tactical nuclear weapons[63].

Pressure to address this concern and advance on the START Treaty that had been signed just prior to the coup was also building in Congress. For example Senator Biden qualified his reluctance to offer financial support to Soviet reformers by arguing it was 'profoundly foolish too humiliate the reformers by expecting that they disarm unilaterally'. The United States, he said, 'should act without delay to explore every opportunity to further reduce the nuclear threat….no delay is warranted in answering the Gorbachev-Yeltsin call for wholesale reduction in nuclear weapons'[64]. Secretary Baker also writes that his staff were pushing for an increased emphasis on the dangers on accidental nuclear war (Baker, 1995, p.524)[65].

Strengthened by such arguments Bush ordered the Joint Chiefs to prepare a list of new disarmament measures. Once more this was against the more cautious advice from significant voices in the administration. On the 27th of September the President announced a series of unilateral arms control and disarmament measures. The U.S. would eliminate all ground force TNWs; remove non-strategic nuclear weapons from all U.S. naval ships and submarines, all U.S. strategic bombers would be taken off an alert posture and operational command systems would be consolidated in a manner that reduced the chances of error. While these measures clearly reinforced the moves towards crisis stability that the START process made, deterrence was not the only motivating factor.   As Director of ACDA, Ron Lehman explained, the initiative was designed 'to encourage advocates of reform who came to the fore during the trying days of the coup in Moscow both to accelerate democratisation and to enhance stability.... By proceeding with the elimination of ground-launched tactical nuclear arms now, we can reduce their potential for becoming a factor of instability in the Soviet Union in the years ahead'[66]. The Soviets reciprocated and went beyond the American initiative with an announcement on the 5th of October (Garthoff, 1994, pp.491-492).

The U.S. ended its Cold War with unilateral nuclear disarmament. Thanks to Gorbachev's 'New Thinking' and his faith in the ideas of the peace movements, the United States no longer faced a Soviet Union that could be interpreted as an expansionist adversary.   While prudence and a vested interest in confrontation delayed this reinterpretation, the persistence of Soviet reformers eventually changed the character of America's security dilemma.   As chapter five discusses in detail the new security dilemma revolved around the destabilising consequences of those reforms.   In essence it was a dilemma between order and justice.   The former emphasising détente with a cohesive USSR, the latter stressing the importance of democratic reform and national self-determination.   In pursuing the latter American foreign policy at the end of the Cold War found disarmament more useful than rearmament. Democratic reform had less risk of undermining international order if it did not have to contend with mass armies and nuclear weapons.   Although the conservatives claimed otherwise, this realisation was in contrast to the argument that 'hanging tough' paid off. Rather the events of 1989-1991 tend to prove the arguments of the peace movements of the early eighties. Democratisation was encouraged by the processes of arms control and disarmament.

Conclusion

America's security dilemma was influenced by its own domestic structure and its own identity.   Domestic structure gave political expression to a number of views on the Soviet Union.   Those views and the strategic prescriptions that arose from them were in turn mediated by the changes taking place in the Soviet domestic structure.   On the one hand, what Beukel calls Soviet essentialists saw little prospect for a successful reform of the Soviet Union and characterised it as an expansionist, revolutionary power that would seek and then use strategic superiority to coerce the U.S. into submission.   On the other hand there were nuclear essentialists who held that the Soviets were easily deterred by the mere presence of nuclear weapons. While not commenting on the prospects of political reform in the Soviet Union, they argued for a security policy that stabilised the strategic relationship around the norm of mutual vulnerability. Finally, as the consequences of Soviet reform became an issue in the U.S., the debate shifted. Realists argued that a strong U.S. force was needed as a hedge against a hard-line backlash, while Liberals tended to view the chances of reform in a more optimistic light and were more willing to encourage that process through U.S. disarmament. As the identity of Eastern Europe and the Soviet Union changed from communist aggressor, to democratic partner, a deterrence posture was increasingly inappropriate. Arms control policy was thus subtly redefined so that it fulfilled a political aim consistent with America's ideological goals, rather than simply a technical purpose of preserving the status quo.

Notes

[1] Evangelista (1999, p.40) uses the phrase tacit transnationalism to describe the group of Soviet scientists who never openly met with Western scientists, but were able 'to act on their moral convictions, and to do so in tacit concert with U.S. colleagues whom they had never met' by reading *Bulletin of the Atomic Scientists*. It is used here to identify a slightly different process. It would be incorrect to say opponents of mutual vulnerability collaborated, yet they did use the statements of the other to justify their arguments against security cooperation. In effect they inadvertently and tacitly supported each other in their respective domestic political battles.

[2] Adler (1992, pp.118-123) identifies the 1958 Surprise Attack Conference as the birthplace of 'the arms control epistemic community'. By 1960 with the publication of the *Daedulus* special issue, 'nuclear arms control came of age'.

[3] McNamara, who Adler (1992, pp.118-128) describes as 'an epistemic community's dream', headed the so called 'whizz kids', many of whom belonged to the arms control community. Roswell Gilpatrick, Paul Nitze, Henry Rowen and Charles Hitch filled key positions in the Pentagon. Appointments elsewhere in the administration and the creation of the Arms Control and Disarmament Agency (ACDA) helped create a network of relations between political elites and arms controllers. Moreover, ACDA meant 'arms control had become an irreversible factor in the domestic political game and a key consideration as agreements were negotiated and even as new weapons systems were contemplated'.

[4] McNamara's continuing advocacy of minimum nuclear deterrence suggests his membership of the arms control community was not simply a matter of political calculation.

[5] Khruschev's minimalism was motivated partly by economic constraints and partly by a desire to reduce international tension. It is important to note that the U.S. dismissed Khrushchev's troop reductions and disarmament proposals in terms of military expediency. Indeed, Khrushchev's shift to minimal nuclear deterrence provoked a nuclear arms buildup by the Kennedy administration, particularly as Khrushchev was forced to exaggerate the capabilities of Soviet strategic forces in order to sell minimalism to a domestic audience. Two lessons were drawn from the Khrushchev period: first, Soviet restraint had only encouraged the U.S. to seek superiority, hence Brezhnev's response to the American

buildup; second, Khrushchev's reliance on nuclear weapons had allowed American hardliners to ignore genuine efforts to reduce tension, hence Gorbachev's non-offensive defense *and* nuclear disarmament (Evangelista, 1999, pp.90-122).

[6] Opponents of this stance would not have found much political support in the intelligence community. Indeed, an intelligence memorandum of June 1967 underscored the fact that the Soviet Union had strong incentives to avoid the implications of an arms race. RR IM 67-36 Intelligence Memorandum, 'Soviet Military Policy in 1967: The Challenges and Issues', June 1967, *The Soviet Estimate: U.S. Analysis of the Soviet Union, 1947-1991*, (Washington, D.C.: The National Security Archive & Chadwyck-Healy Inc., 1995), no.00421

[7] By increasing the number of counterforce warheads relative to the number of targets, MIRV technology was clearly destabilising. The more force structures became MIRVed the greater the possibility of a successful first strike. The greater the possibility of a successful first strike, the greater the incentive for either side to strike first in a crisis. MIRV technology was clearly an obstacle to constructing a mutual understanding based on crisis stability.

[8] NSDM242 directed the development of limited nuclear options in order to increase the range of presidential options in the face of Soviet aggression (Ball and Richelson, 1986, p.74).

[9] See Committee for the Present Danger, *What is the Soviet Union Up To?* April 4, 1977, (Sanders, 1983 p.166). On this issue and the historiography of the crisis see Ned Lebow and Stein, 1994.

[10] The wider significance of this crisis was its influence on the powerful pro-Israeli lobby in the US. The handling of the crisis suggested U.S. and Soviet restraint in the name of superpower détente meant a restricted room for Israeli manoeuvre. Along with the issue of Jewish emigration the 1973 crisis contributed to the collapse of support for détente among this powerful lobby (Garthoff, 1985).

[11] For example, see DIA Report, 'Détente and Soviet Strategy, September 1975', *The Soviet Estimate: U.S. Analysis of the Soviet Union, 1947-1991*, (Washington, D.C.: The National Security Archive & Chadwyck-Healy Inc., 1995), no.00486.

[12] NIE 11-3/8-76, 'Soviet Forces for Intercontinental Attack Through the mid-1980s', December 1976, *The Soviet Estimate: U.S. Analysis of the Soviet Union, 1947-1991*, (Washington, D.C.: The National Security Archive & Chadwyck-Healy Inc., 1995), no.00502. Several dissenting footnotes demonstrated the compromise position taken by the NIE. The State Department believed the main motivation of the Soviet leadership was to avoid falling behind the U.S. While the Air Force characterised the Soviet build up as 'the most extensive peacetime war preparations in recorded history' and compared the strategic environment to the 1930s.

[13] Intelligence Community Experiment in Competitive Analysis, 'Soviet Strategic Objectives, An Alternative View, Report of Team "B"', December 1976, *The Soviet Estimate: U.S. Analysis of the Soviet Union, 1947-1991*, (Washington, D.C.: The National Security Archive & Chadwyck-Healy Inc., 1995), no.00501.

[14] Warnke became head of ACDA in the Carter administration. Carter was in no way impressed by Team B's analysis. Indeed one of his first acts was to abolish PFIAB which had originally inspired the competitive threat exercise (Cahn, 1998, p.180).

[15] Team B members Richard Pipes, Foy Kohler, Paul Nitze and William Van Cleave became founding board members of the CPD (Cahn, 1998, p.188).

[16] The Committee would have found support in Air Force intelligence which identified Soviet behaviour in terms of 'the most extensive peacetime war preparations in recorded

history' and identified détente in terms of 'a situation not unlike the mid-1930s, when the entire free world failed to appreciate the true nature of Nazi Germany's readily discernible preparations for was and conflict'. NIE 11-3/8-76, 'Soviet Forces for Intercontinental Attack Through the mid-1980s', December 1976, *The Soviet Estimate: U.S. Analysis of the Soviet Union, 1947-1991*, (Washington, D.C.: The National Security Archive & Chadwyck-Healy Inc., 1995), no.00502.

[17] The Carter Doctrine was a response to a number of issues including the Iranian Revolution (Melanson, 1996 pp.110-118). However, it would also have been a response to those who believed the Soviet invasion of Afghanistan was a precursor to the seizure of oil rich resources in the Gulf and a possible invasion of Iran. See DIA 20-80 Warning Intelligence Appraisal, 'USSR: A Military Option', February 1980, *The Soviet Estimate: U.S. Analysis of the Soviet Union, 1947-1991*, (Washington, D.C.: The National Security Archive & Chadwyck-Healy Inc., 1995), no.00532.

[18] For instance Director of CPD Eugene Rostow became head of ACDA.

[19] While the State Department sought an agreement on INF and feared creating the impression of a mere propaganda exercise, the White House and Pentagon persisted with the zero-option (Haig, Jr., 1984). See also Shultz, *Turmoil and Triumph* p.160.

[20] See also Weinberger's comments on 'horizontal escalation'. Where NATO strategy had traditionally been about limiting war, Weinberger argued that the alliance 'must be prepared to launch counteroffensives in other regions and try to exploit the aggressor's weaknesses wherever they exist'. Weinberger, 'The Defence Policy of the Reagan Administration', Address to the Council of Foreign Relations, New York, 17 June, 1981 (Garthoff, 1994 p.37).

[21] House Committee on Defence Appropriations FY85. 98th Congress, 1 March 1984. p.482; Questions were also raised concerning NATO's strategy of Follow-on-Forces-Attack (FOFA). In response NATO commanders argued FOFA was not about abandoning a defensive strategy, but an attempt to provide additional flexibility to Flexible Response by improving the alliance's conventional capability. See Theater Nuclear Warfare Issues. Senate Armed Services Committee, 98th Congress, 15 March 1983.

[22] Paul Stares (1991) writes that is unclear if 'Moscow ordered any concrete response', but Bruce Blair (1993) suggests that the Soviets increased the alert readiness of 'some unspecified portion of their nuclear command system and forces'. Don Oberdorfer (1991) states that 'Moscow placed on higher alert status about a dozen nuclear capable Soviet fighter aircraft stationed in forward bases in East Germany and Poland'. Garthoff (1994) also suggests that 'Soviet interceptor aircraft were observed by Western intelligence to have been placed on high alert. SNIE 11-10-84 also refers to the assumption of high alert status by Soviet air units in Germany and Poland. It adds, 'by confining heightened readiness to selected air units Moscow clearly revealed that it did not in fact think there was a possibility at this time of a NATO attack'.

[23] When asked about the incident, advisers close to Gorbachev seemed to confirm the less alarmist view. Chernayev suggests that there was 'no serious fear' in the highest echelon of government, while Tarasenko suggests contingency plans and staff manoeuvres were instituted around this time 'just to show Western intelligence that we were preparing for this sudden attack' (Wohlforth, 1996, pp.71-73).

[24] SNIE 11-10-84 'Implications of Recent Soviet Military-Political Activities', Washington, D.C., The National Security Archive.

[25] Address by the Secretary of State (Shultz) Before the North Atlantic Assembly, San Francisco, 14 October 1985. *American Foreign Policy. Current Documents 1985.* pp.100-108.

[26] Statement by the Secretary of State (Shultz) at the Opening Session of the Conference on Confiddence and Security Building Measures and Disarmament in Europe, Stockholm, 17 January 1984. *American Foreign Policy. Current Documents, 1984* pp.333-336. On the 1914 analogy see Emanuel Adler, 1992, p.109; Ned Lebow, 1985; Posen, 1982.

[27] Statement by the Secretary of Defense (Weinberger), 'Foundations of Defense policy', U.S. 98th Congress, House Committee, Defense Appropriations, FY84, 8 February, 1983, p.579.

[28] NSDD85 Eliminating the threat of ballistic missiles', (Simpson, 1995, p.233). 'Peace and National Security', Address by President Reagan, 23 March 1983, *American Foreign Policy. Current Documents 1983* pp.56-62.

[29] NIE 11-3/8-82, 'Soviet Capabilities for Strategic Nuclear Conflict, 1982-1992. National Intelligence Estimate. Volume I – Key Judgements and Summary', February 1983, *The Soviet Estimate: U.S. Analysis of the Soviet Union, 1947-1991*, (Washington, D.C.: The National Security Archive & Chadwyck-Healy Inc., 1995), 00568. For commentary on this estimate see William Wohlforth (eds.) *Witnesses to the End of the Cold War* (London: Johns Hopkins University Press, 1996) p.25.

[30] Statement by the Chairman of the President's Commission on Strategic Forces (Scowcroft), 11 April 1983. *American Foreign Policy. Current Documents 1983* pp.63-65.

[31] NIE11-3/8-83, 'Soviet capabilties for strategic nuclear conflict, 1983-1993. Volume I Key Judgements and Summary', 6 March 1984. *The Soviet Estimate: U.S. Analysis of the Soviet Union, 1947-1991*, (Washington, D.C.: The National Security Archive & Chadwyck-Healy Inc., 1995). See also Cahn *Killing Détente* p.146. In April 1989 the CIA admitted a 'tendency to substantially overestimate the rate of [Soviet] force modernization'. CIA 'Intelligence Forecasts of Soviet Intercontinental Attack Forces: An Evaluation of the Record. A Research Paper, April 1989', *The Soviet Estimate: U.S. Analysis of the Soviet Union, 1947-1991*, (Washington, D.C.: The National Security Archive & Chadwyck-Healy Inc., 1995), no.00601.

[32] NSDD91 Strategic Forces Modernization Program Change. 19 April 1983. Simpson *NSDs* pp.294-295.

[33] Address by the President's Assistant for National Security Affairs (McFarlane) Before the Overseas Writers Association, 7 March 1985. *American Foreign Policy. Current Documents 1985.* pp.47-51.

[34] Address by the President's and Secretary of State's Special Adviser on Arms Control Matters (Nitze) Before the World Affairs Council, Philadelphia, 20 February 1985. *American Foreign Policy. Current Documents 1985.* pp.76-80.

[35] NSDD172 Presenting the Strategic Defense Initiative, 30 May 1985 (Simpson, 1995, pp.535-548).

[36] President's Ford, Carter and Nixon all spoke of SDI as a bargaining chip. Their recommendations were reinforced when six former Secretaries of Defense called on the administration to avoid action that would undermine the ABM Treaty (Talbott, 1988, p.251; Garthoff, 1994, p.229).

[37] NSDD227 U.S. Interim Restraint Policy, 23 May 1986 (Simpson, 1995, pp.699-704).

[38] The departure of McFarlane in 1986 was a setback for those seeking greater cooperation. While he had contributed to the shift in policy his replacement, Admiral John Poindexter, was widely considered a more technocratic figure who usually remained neutral in policy disputes. As such Weinberger would gain greater access to Reagan than had been the case with McFarlane (Oberdorfer, 1991, p.48. Winik, 1996, pp.266-269).

[39] See also James H.Billington, 'With Russia: After Fifty Years', *Washington Post* November 1983, which provided an intellectual framework for the new approach of

engagement. A reading of Suzanne Massie's *Land of the Firebird: The Beauty of Old Russia* (Hearttree Press: 1980) and several meetings with its author is said to have further influenced the President's thinking in this direction (Garthoff, 1994, p.145).

[40] It is in this light that one should view the unilateral Anti-Satellite moratorium (ASAT) which was announced soon after the Star Wars speech. It was designed to strengthen Congressional opposition to SDI (Evangelista, 1999, pp.237-239). Encouraged by the transnational support for a test ban, this logic also motivated Gorbachev's nuclear test moratorium between August 1985 and February 1987. The need to resume testing and a willingness to negotiate on a Threshold (as opposed to a Comprehensive) Test Ban Treaty, however, undermined efforts by the transnational disarmament coalition to halt U.S. tests through legislation in Congress (Evangelista, 1999 pp.264-288).

[41] Address by the Under Secretary of State for Economic Affairs (Wallis) Before the American Society of Business Press Editors, Chicago, 20 June 1983, *American Foreign Policy, Current Documents, 1983*, pp.424-428.

[42] NIC M 83-10017, 'Possible Soviet Responses to the US Strategic Defense Initiative', 12 September 1983, *The Soviet Estimate: U.S. Analysis of the Soviet Union, 1947-1991*, (Washington, D.C.: The National Security Archive & Chadwyck-Healy Inc., 1995).

[43] Gorbachev's speech to the 27th Party Congress, February 1986 (Garthoff, 1994, p.260).

[44] It is argued that the increased defensive capacity that precision guided weapons gave NATO forced the Soviet Union to abandon its doctrinal reliance on the offensive. Yet such arguments are again indeterminate. For example, Evangelista argues that this conclusion was apparent to the Soviet military in 1975. Focusing on NATO actions alone cannot explain when and why the Soviets adopted a defensive doctrine (Evangelista, 1992, pp.292-293). For an excellent review of these debates on non-offensive defence see Frank and Gillette, 1992.

[45] NSDD210, 'Allied Consultations on the U.S. response to General Secretary Gorbachev's 14 January 1986 Arms Control Proposal', 4 February, 1986, Washington, D.C., The National Security Archive. Emphasis added.

[46] Statement by the President, Camp David, Maryland. 12 July 1986. *American Foreign Policy. Current Documents 1986.* pp.50-51.

[47] 'The Reykjavik Process: preparation for the Conduct of the Icelandic Summit and its Implications for Arms Control Policy', Report of the Defense Council of the Committee on Armed Services. House of Representatives. 99th Cong. 2nd Sess. (Washington: USPGO, 1987). See also Wohlforth, *Witnesses* p.176.

[48] NSDD249, 'Additional Instructions for the Current NST [Nuclear and Space talks] Negotiating Round', 29 October, 1986. The Ronald Reagan Library.

[49] Some Soviet accounts suggest the political leadership had been willing to compromise its position on SDI and that Chief of Staff, Akhromeyev was the only obstacle. Others, however, have suggested Gorbachev himself was committed to stopping SDI (Wohlforth, 1996, pp.179-181).

[50] Statement by the Secretary of State (Shultz), San Francisco, 31 October 1986. *American Foreign Policy. Current Documents. 1986.* pp.345-351.

[51] Statement by the Secretary of State, 17 October 1986. *American Foreign Policy. Current Documents 1986* pp.95-97.

[52] While the causal link between Gorbachev's disarmament policy and the US strategic modernisation programme is dubious there were those who argued the Reykjavik would have been the ultimate vindication of Reagan's first term defence policy. For example, the Congressional report on the summit stated that the 'agreement would have been the ultimate and conclusive refutation of the arguments of the European left that the INF build-up could

accomplish no good'. *Reykjavik and American Security.* Report of the Defense Policy Panel of the Committee on Armed Services House of Representatives. 99th Cong. 2nd Sess. February 1987. Committee Print No.26.

[53] NSDD250, 'Post –Reykjavik Follow-Up', The Ronald Reagan Library.

[54] Former Supreme Allied Commander for Europe, General Rogers argued that the removal of INF missiles would leave 'a significant gap in the spectrum of deterrence'. *The INF Treaty.* Report of the Senate Committee on Foreign Relations, 100th Cong. 2nd. Sess. 14 April, 1988. p.26. Such concerns, however, were of marginal significance. The Treaty was ratified by a vote of 93 to 5 (Garthoff, 1994 p.334).

[55] While Evangelista does not mention a meeting between Sakharov and Gorbachev, he does argue that the decision to delink SDI from arms control was heavily influenced by Sakharov and others in the transnational disarmament community. Among the ways Gorbachev became aware of their views on this issue was through KGB tapes of their conversation (Evangelista, 1999, pp.328-330; Herman, 1996, p.302).

[56] This was reflected in the name, Global Protection Against Limited Strikes (GPALS). While doubts continued over its compatibility with the ABM Treaty, congressional support for the Treaty remained strong. See *The SDI as it relates to the ABM Treaty.* Hearing before the Senate Congressional Committee on Foreign Relations 102nd Cong. 1st Sess. 24 April 1991.

[57] CIA, Office of Soviet Analysis, 'Gorbachev: Steering the USSR into the 1990s. An Intelligence Estimate', July 1987, *The Soviet Estimate: U.S. Analysis of the Soviet Union, 1947-1991,* (Washington, D.C.: The National Security Archive & Chadwyck-Healy Inc., 1995), no.00594; CIA, Office of Soviet Analysis, 'Soviet National Security Policy: Responses to the Changing Military and Economic Environment', June 1988, *The Soviet Estimate: U.S. Analysis of the Soviet Union, 1947-1991,* (Washington, D.C.: The National Security Archive & Chadwyck-Healy Inc., 1995), no.00598; Defense Research comment 82-87, 'Gorbachev: Soviet Economic Modernization and the Military', November 1987, *The Soviet Estimate: U.S. Analysis of the Soviet Union, 1947-1991,* (Washington, D.C.: The National Security Archive & Chadwyck-Healy Inc., 1995), no.00595.

[58] CIA, Office of Soviet Analysis, 'Gorbachev's Domestic Gambles and Instability in the USSR. An Intelligence Assessment', September 1989. *The Soviet Estimate: U.S. Analysis of the Soviet Union, 1947-1991,* (Washington, D.C.: The National Security Archive & Chadwyck-Healy Inc., 1995), no.00602.

[59] Having unsuccessfully tried to accelerate the multilateral negotiations by tabling a proposal to the American delegation at the Moscow Summit in June 1988, Gorbachev was forced make unilateral signals that were directed to Congress. According to Philip Karber, the numbers involved in Gorbachev's move corresponded to the proposal made by Senator Sam Nunn in March 1987. See Philip A. Karber, 'Soviet Implementation of the Gorbachev Unilateral Military reductions', in *Impact of Gorbachev's Reform Movement on the Soviet Military* Hearing Before the House Armed Services Committee, 100th Cong. 2nd Sess. (Washington D.C.: GPO, 1988). Furthermore Andrei Kokoshin invited Les Aspin, Chair of the House Armed Services Committee to a briefing on Soviet policy at is Institute in Moscow, a visit that was reciprocated when Kokoshin participated in hearings before Aspin's committee. Evangelista concludes that these contacts 'helped to counter the 'enemy image' of the hard-liners in both countries and made it easier for him [Kokoshin] to promote the transnational agenda of Soviet military reform' (Evangelista, 1999, pp.320).

[60] Address by President Bush, Boston, 21 May, 1989. *American Foreign Policy. Current Documents 1989.* pp.274-276.

[61] Although the May proposal necessarily required American leadership, the political rationale for disarmament had been identified at the North Atlantic Council almost a year earlier. See Statement Issued by the North Atlantic Council, Brussels, 3 March 1988. *American Foreign Policy. Current Documents 1988* pp.246-249.

[62] The Future of U.S.-Soviet Relations. Hearings Before the Senate Committee on Foreign Relations. 101st Cong. 1st Sess. 20 June 1989. p.912.

[63] During the coup U.S. intelligence had witnessed unusual activity around ICBM sites. Yet it was concluded that this behaviour, including a possible alert, was a precautionary measure to protect the ICBMs from any sabotage or hijack attempt on the part of the coup plotters or anyone else wishing to take advantage of the confused situation (Beschloss and Talbott, 1993, p.424; Baker, 1995, p.526).

[64] *Command and Control of Soviet Nuclear Weapons: Dangers and Opportunities Arising from the August Revolution*, Hearing Before the Senate Subcommittee on European Affairs of the Committee on Foreign Relations, 102nd Cong. 1st Sess. 24 September 1991, p.2.

[65] For an argument that the threat of inadvertence was an exaggerated but none the less important concerns see (Kramer, 1991, pp.94-97).

[66] Prepared Statement by the Director of the Arms Control and Disarmament Agency (Lehman), 7 November, 1991. *American Foreign Policy. Current Documents, 1991.* pp.70-74.

References

Adler, E. (1992), 'The emergence of cooperation: national epistemic communities and international evolution of the idea of nuclear arms control', *International Organization*, Vol.46, pp.101-146.

Andrew, C. (1995), *For the President's Eyes Only. Secret Intelligence and the American Presidency From Washington to Bush*, Harper Collins, London.

Andrew, C. and Gordievsky, O. (1991), *KGB. The Inside Story of its Operations From Lenin to Gorbachev*, Sceptre, London.

Baker III, J.A. (1995) (with Thomas M. Defrank), *The Politics of Diplomacy. Revolution, War and Peace, 1989-1992*, G.P.Putnam's Sons, New York.

Ball, D. (1982/3), 'U.S. Strategic Forces: How Would They Be Used?', *International Security*, Vol.7, pp.31-60.

Ball, D. and Richelson, J. (eds.) (1986), *Strategic Nuclear Targeting*, Cornell University Press, Ithaca.

Beukel, E. (1989), *American Perceptions of the Soviet Union and a Nuclear Adversary From Kennedy to Bush*, Pinter in association with Spiers, London.

Beschloss, M.R. and Talbott, S. (1993), *At the Highest Levels. The Inside Story of the End of the Cold War*, Little, Brown and Company, Boston, Toronto and London.

Blair, B. (1993), *The Logic of Accidental Nuclear War*, Brookings, Washington, D.C.

Brodie, B. (1946), 'Implications for Military Policy', in Bernard Brodie (ed.) *The Absolute Weapon: Atomic Power and World Order*, Harcourt and Company, New York, pp.70-107.

Brodie, B. (1959), *Strategy in the Missile Age*, Princeton University Press, Princeton.

Cahn, A.H. (1998), *Killing Détente. The Right Attacks the CIA*, Pennsylvania State University Press, Pennsylvania.

Chernoff, F. (1991), 'Ending the Cold War: The Soviet Retreat and the U.S. Military Build Up', *International Affairs*, Vol.67, pp.111-126.

Crowe, W.J. (1993) (with David Chanoff), *In the Line of Fire: from Washington to the Gulf, the Politics and battles of the New Military*, Simon and Schuster, New York.

Evangelista, M. (1999), *Unarmed Forces. The Transnational Movement and the End of the Cold War*, Cornell University Press, Ithaca and London.

Fischer, B.A. (1997), *The Reagan Reversal: Foreign Policy and the End of the Cold War*, University of Missouri Press, Columbia.

Fitzgerald, F. (2000), *Way Out There in the Blue. Reagan, Star Wars and the End of the Cold War*, Simon and Schuster, New York.

Frank, W.S. and Gillette, P.S. (1992), *Soviet Military Doctrine from Lenin to Gorbachev, 1915-1991*, Greenwood Press, London.

Freedman, L. (1981), *The Evolution of Nuclear Strategy*, Macmillan, London.

Friedberg, A.L. (1980), 'A History of U.S. Strategic "Doctrine" 1945 to 1980', *Journal of Strategic Studies*, Vol.3, pp.37-71.

Garthoff, R.L. (1985), *Détente and Confrontation. American-Soviet Relation from Nixon to Reagan*, Brookings, Washington, D.C.

Garthoff, R.L. (1994), *The Great Transition. American-Soviet Relations and the End of the Cold War*, Brookings, Washington, D.C.

Gray, C. and Payne, K. (1980), 'Victory is Possible', *Foreign Policy*, Vol.39, pp.14-27.

Greenberg, D.L. (2000), 'Review Essay: The Empire Strikes Out. Why Star Wars Did Not End the Cold War', *Foreign Affairs*, Vol.79, pp.136-143.

Greenstein, F.I. and Wohlforth, W.C. (eds.) (1994), *Retrospective on the End of the Cold War*, Center of International Studies, Monograph Series Number 6, Princeton University.

Gross Stein, J. (1994), 'Political Learning By Doing: Gorbachev as Uncommitted Thinker and Motivated Learner', *International Organization*, Vol.48, pp.155-183.

Haig, Jr. A. (1984), *Caveat: Realism, Reagan and Foreign Policy*, Macmillan, London.

Haslam, J. (1989), *The Soviet Union and the Politics of Nuclear Weapons in Europe, 1969-87: the problems of the SS-20*, Macmillan, Basingstoke.

Herman, R.G. (1996), 'Identity, Norms, and National Security: The Soviet Foreign Policy Revolution and the End of the Cold War', in Peter J. Katzenstein (ed.), *The Culture of National Security. Norms and Identity in World Politics*, Columbia University Press, New York, pp.271-356.

Jervis, R. (1982), 'Security Regimes', *International Organization*, Vol.36, pp.357-378.

Johnson, R.H. (1983), 'Periods of Peril. The Window of Vulnerability and Other Myths', *Foreign Affairs*, Vol.61, pp.950-970.

Kahn, H. (1960), *On Thermonuclear War*, Princeton University Press, Princeton.

Kahn, H. (1962), *Thinking About the Unthinkable*, Horizon Press, New York.

Kaldor, M. (1999), 'Transnational civil society', Tim Dunne and Nicholas J. Wheeler, (eds.), *Human Rights in Global Politics*, Cambridge University Press, Cambridge, pp.195-213.

Klein, B.S. (1994), *Strategic Studies and World Order. The Global Politics of Deterrence*, Cambridge University Press, Cambridge.

Knopf, J.W. (1997), 'The Nuclear Freeze Movement's Effect on Policy', in Thomas R. Rochon and David S. Meyer (eds.), *Coalitions and Political Movements. The Lessons of the Nuclear Freeze*, Lynne Rienner, Boulder, Colorado, pp.127-161.

Kramer, M. (1991), 'Warheads and Chaos. The Soviet Threat in Perspective', *The National Interest*, No.25, pp.94-97.

Lebow, R.N. (1985), 'The Soviet Offensive in Europe: The Schlieffen Plan Revisited?', *International Security*, Vol.9, pp.44-78.

Lebow, R.N. and Stein, J.G. (1994), *We All Lost the Cold War*, Princeton University Press, Princeton.

Lebow, R.N. and Stein, J. (1998), 'Nuclear Lessons of the Cold War', in Ken Booth (ed.), *Statecraft and Security. The Cold War and Beyond*, Cambridge University Press, Cambridge, pp.71-86.

Matlock, Jack F. (1995), *Autopsy of an Empire. The American Ambassador's Account of the Collapse of the Soviet Union*, Random House, New York.

McFarlane, R.C. (1994) (with Zofia Smardz), *Special Trust*, Cadell and Davies, New York.

Nitze, P. (1976/7), 'Deterring Our Deterrent', *Foreign Policy*, Vol.25, pp.195-210.

Nolan, J.E. (1989), *Guardians of the Arsenal. The Politics of Nuclear Strategy*, Basic Books, New York.

Oberdorfer, D. (1991), *The Turn, from the Cold War to a New Era: the United States and the Soviet Union, 1983-1990*, Simon and Schuster, New York.

Oye, K.A. (1995), 'Explaining the End of the Cold War: Morphological and Behavioural Adaptions to the Nuclear peace?', in Richard Ned Lebow and Thomas Risse-Kappen (eds.), *International Political Theory and the End of the Cold War*, Columbia University Press, New York, pp.57-83.

Palme, O. (1982), *Common Security: a programme for disarmament*, Pan Books, London.

Patman, R.G. (1999), 'Reagan, Gorbachev and the emergence of 'New Political Thinking', *Review of International Studies*, Vol.25, pp.571-601.

Pipes, R. (1977), 'Why the Soviet Union thinks it could fight and win a nuclear war', *Commentary*, Vol.64, pp.21-34.

Posen, B.R. (1982), 'Inadvertent Nuclear War? Escalation and NATO's Northern Flank', *International Security*, Vol.7, pp.28-45.

Richelson, J. (1983), 'PD-59, NSDD-13 and the Reagan Strategic Modernization Program', *Journal of Strategic Studies*, Vol.6, pp.125-146.

Sanders, J.W. (1983), *Peddlers of Crisis. The Committee on the Present Danger and the Politics of Containment*, South End Press, Boston, MA.

Shultz, G. (1993), *Turmoil and Triumph: My Years as Secretary of State*, Maxwell Macmillan International, New York.

Simpson, C. (1995), *National Security Directives of the Reagan and Bush Administrations. The Declassified History of U.S. Political and Military Policy, 1981-1991*, Westview Press, Oxford.

Stares, P. (1991), *Command Performance: the Neglected Dimension of European Security*, Brookings, Washington, D.C.

Talbott, S. (1988), *The Master of the Game: Paul Nitze and the Nuclear Peace*, Knopf, New York.

Thomas, D.S. (1999), 'The Helsinki Accords and Political Change in Eastern Europe', in Thomas Risse, Stephen C. Ropp and Kathryn Sikkink (eds.) *The Power of Human Rights. International Norms and Domestic Change*, Cambridge University Press, Cambridge, pp.205-233.

Thompson, E.P. and Smith, D. (eds.) (1980), *Protest and Survive*, Penguin, Harmondsworth.

Warnke, P. (1975), 'Apes on a Treadmill', *Foreign Policy*, Vol.18, pp.12-29.

Winik, J. (1996), *On the Brink: the Dramatic, Behind-the-Scenes Saga of the Reagan Era and the Men and Women Who Won the Cold War*, Simon and Schuster, New York.

Wohlforth, W. (ed.) (1996), *Witnesses to the End of the Cold War*, Johns Hopkins, Baltimore.

4 Security Communities and Normative Dilemmas

Introduction

Chapters two and three demonstrated theoretically and empirically how domestic political structure mediated the process of adopting and reciprocating GRIT-type policies. So long as the Soviet Union was seen as being totalitarian it would, according to politically significant opinions in America, be capable of aggression. In this sense America could not move beyond its security dilemma with the Soviet Union unless the latter decentralized and those institutions that threatened U.S. interests were on the political sideline. Until that happened, prudence would be a political ally of those intellectual communities in the U.S. discourse that had a vested interest in the Cold War. The political argument against disarmament would remain strong and the military would continue to heavily influence security policy.

While recognising the influence of domestic political structure on the nature of America's security dilemma, a more complete picture should also consider the identity of the intellectual communities competing for political significance. Where domestic structure highlights the institutional framework within which a state's identity is contested, the identity of the state itself is also made up of 'cognitive structures' that bloc or facilitate the adoption of new ideas (Adler and Barnett, 1998c, p.425). The United States was concerned less about the suddenness of a reversal, than it was about the political character of that reversal. In other words, it was the reversal of *liberal* reforms that was a potential threat to the U.S., its allies and its conception of world order. Of course, the centralized political system exaggerated America's concern because it feared being caught by surprise, but it wasn't the system per se that caused alarm. Rather it was the character of certain groups – the Communist Party, the Red Army and other groups deemed illiberal and undemocratic - that contested the right to represent and deploy the power of the Soviet state.

93

Of course, the Wilsonians in the U.S. security discourse argued that liberal democratic states were the foundations of a security community. Embedded liberalism was considered the foundation of a worthwhile and therefore enduring peace. Their reasoning and influence on U.S. Cold War policy is explored in greater detail in chapters five and six. The purpose of this chapter is to theoretically explore the role democracy and democracy promotion plays in the domestic and international politics of states so that they can move beyond the security dilemma. In so doing it sets a standard by which the following chapters can contribute to the critical assessment of America's role in the process of constructing a security community. Democracy and democracy promotion is considered central to that process, but America is not always committed to its democratic ideals, nor is American democracy always consistent with the values required of a security community.

Security Communities

Adler and Barnett (1998b) draw a distinction between tightly-coupled and loosely-coupled security communities. The dependable expectation of peaceful change exists across both kinds of communities. Yet in tightly-coupled communities that expectation rests on governance structures that rely 'not only on an understanding of their member states' behaviour in the international sphere but also on a reading of their domestic behaviour and arrangements'. In loosely-coupled communities by contrast, the expectation of peaceful change rests on intersubjective understandings among state leaders.

It is argued here, however, that without reassurance as to the domestic behaviour of member states, long term expectations of peaceful change simply cannot exist. If member states do not meet the basic needs of their citizens and fail to provide a means of peaceful conflict resolution it is more than likely that conflict will be securitized (Waever, 1995; 1998; Buzan, Waever and de Wilde, 1998). In other words, it could lead to an extreme political situation whereby the victims of unresponsive decision making feel justified in resorting to extraordinary means that break the normal political rules. For peaceful expectations of change to be absolute, securitization within the community has to be avoided and for this reason the domestic affairs of member states are central to the definition of a security community. What Adler and Barnett call tightly-coupled security communities are the only communities deserving the adjective security.

Indeed the text that first used the phrase 'security community' demanded much more than an understanding of peaceful change between states represented by elites. For Deutsch (1957, p.39, emphasis added) the integration of a security community rested on 'the ability to give messages from other political units adequate weight in the making of their own decisions, *to perceive the needs of the populations* and elites of other units, *and to respond to them adequately in terms of political or economic action*'. Furthermore, Deutsch (1957, p.50, emphasis added) notes that successful integration was based on 'widespread expectations of greater social or political equality, or of greater social or political rights or liberties, among important groups of the politically relevant strata - *and often among parts of the underlying populations* - in the political units concerned'. Put differently, Deutsch seemed to be arguing that the enduring peace characteristic of a security community is based on fulfilling the promise of greater social and political rights for the citizens of states. The absence of war is inextricably linked to those rights.

Where the community has failed to be responsive to the needs of its members - either because of insufficient administrative capabilities, the 'relative closure of the political elite', and/or 'the excessive delay in social, economic or political reforms which had been expected by the population' - a process of disintegration started. This process, according to Deutsch (1957, pp.59-65) is characterised by 'the rise of frustrated counter-elites among ethnic or cultural groups'. As Hurrell notes (1998, p.260) the absence of international wars is not a sufficient criteria for a Deutschian community. He writes:

> If, as Deutsch originally argued, security communities have to do with groups of *people*, as well as collectivities, integrated to the point that they will not fight each other, then it becomes impossible to hide behind the distinction between international wars and other forms of social conflict. ... [C]ontinued high levels of social conflict and the privatisation of violence provides a further reason for doubting the existence of even a loosely coupled security community.

Equally, Acharya's (1998) claim that the "Asian-way" based on non-interference and 'soft-authoritarianism' represent a possible path to security community has to be qualified. Indeed Acharya (1998, pp.215-216) notes the limitations of a community based on a common understanding among elites.

> The emergence of regional civil society in Southeast Asia opposing the official ASEAN regionalism on issues of human rights, environment and democracy attests, at the very least, to the dissatisfactions with, and incompleteness of, the community building enterprise led by the ASEAN elites.

To these human rights activists ASEAN is not a security institution but a security threat and by upholding the norms of ASEAN the member states cannot depend on expectations of peaceful change. ASEAN cannot be considered a security community.

Underlying the interest in transcending the security dilemma through loosely coupled security communities is the assumption that threats to individuals originate from outside rather than inside that community. By labeling loosely-integrated areas 'security' communities, it is taken for granted that peace between states translates into peace within and across states. As the ASEAN case demonstrates the norms around which states converge may foster peace between states, but they may also allow violent repression within states. In these circumstances, addressing the question of integration and security requires asking another question, security for whom? Adler and Barnett (1998c, p.427) recognise that the processes that foster intersubjective understanding between statist elite, may not necessarily be welcomed by everyone in the emerging security community. 'This elite-sponsored transnationalism', they write, 'is likely to be resisted by societal groups who perceive that they are being asked to transfer their loyalties to make political and economic sacrifices. Such resistance, if the European case is representative, can be destabilizing for the security community'.

The very fact that Adler and Barnett can foresee a process of destabilization and the fact that securitization is not unthinkable in such circumstances should be sufficient to negate the concept of an elite driven, loosely-coupled security community. If a "security community" between states is responsive only to particular interests within and across states, the neglected are likely to oppose those norms that perpetuate the intersubjective understandings between state elites. In other words, a community between statist elites is not worthy of the adjective 'security' until it responds to the needs *of all* within that community. It is no coincidence that domestic instability in the ASEAN region has placed limits on interstate cooperation. There is a constant risk, Acharya notes (1998, p.215) 'that regime change in a member state might alter its commitment to regional cooperation, especially if the new regime blames the ASEAN framework having condoned or supported the repressive policies of its predecessor'. For this reason, 'their remains a tendency among ASEAN members to engage in contingency-planning and war-oriented resource mobilization against each other' (Archarya, 1998, p.216). In this sense, true security communities cannot be constructed between states without regard for the affect their understandings have on domestic and transnational society. Moreover, common security must have as its referent object human security and not state security.

Common Security, the International and Democratic State

As was noted in the previous chapter, nuclear weapons highlighted the interdependent nature of state security. Advocates of common security and New Political Thinking drew the conclusion that states were increasingly unable to respond to the needs of their citizens through unilateral actions designed to achieve strategic autarky. These moves had failed and were ultimately counterproductive. To paraphrase Wendt, as the ability to meet these needs for security declined, so did the incentive to hang on to egoistic identities that generated such policies (Wendt, 1994). In the specific case of the Soviet Union, Gorbachev would seek *international* security because of the failed attempts by Brezhnev to achieve *national* security. Those who clung to the concept of 'state' or 'national security' could not rightly claim to speak for all the citizens of that state, because their efforts to guarantee security at the expense of other states simply perpetuated their insecurity. By continuing to pursue 'national security' these actors were at best naïve and at worst dishonestly pursuing selfish ends at the expense of those they had promised to protect.

For New Thinkers the only way to achieve security was to positively identify with the other 'such that the other is seen as a cognitive extension of the self rather than independent' (Wendt, 1994, p.386). Practically this translated into a policy of comprehensive disarmament. Just as it became unthinkable for Kohl to target the GDR with nuclear weapons in 1989, because it was culturally and soon to be legally regarded as an 'extension of the self', so Gorbachev's concept of 'a common European home' necessitated comprehensive disarmament.

New Thinking, in other words, sought to reform the particularist and exclusivist identities of the Superpowers. Their class-based and nation-state based identities were, in effect, to be replaced by what Wendt later called the 'international state'. The international state has both a duty and interest in the security of others. In an increasingly interdependent world the lives of individuals are, as New Thinkers recognised in the early 1980s, increasingly affected by states whose decisions they are powerless to influence. When democratic responsiveness breaks down in this way, the leaders of states have a duty not only to their citizens but also to convince their citizens of their duty to 'outsiders'. This is what Deutsch meant when he wrote that a security community rested on 'the ability to give messages from other political units adequate weight in the making of their own decisions' (Deutsch, 1957, p.39).

Citizens, including American citizens, were disenfranchised by the Cold War. They voted for leaders who ultimately had no control over the decisions of Soviet leaders. Through the concept of common security, New Thinking recognised the duty of states not only to their own citizens, but also to outsiders whose lives had been disenfranchised by the power of an interdependent state. The duty that interdependence highlighted, however, was far from an imposition. Rather, fulfilling that duty was ultimately in the interests of those to whom the state was directly responsible. To guarantee the security of outsiders was a duty, but it was also in the interests of states. That was the radical, but ultimately true meaning of common security. The particular and universal became fused. The citizens of the U.S. were, to Soviet New Thinkers, an extended responsibility of the Soviet leaders and vice-versa.

The above critique of the concept of a 'security community' is deploying the same logic. One cannot be truly secure until the concept of war is unthinkable and one can depend on expectations of peaceful change. But one cannot claim to live in a security community until that community responds to the basic needs of all and has a peaceful mechanism to resolve clashing aspirations. The fusion of duty and interest therefore does not only exist at the level of the state. It is rational for self-interested individuals to see others as an extension of the self. The interdependent fate of individuals not only imposes a duty on one to consider the consequence of their actions on the other, but making sure the needs of others are met discourages the process of securitization. As noted above, true security can only be attained in a security community and that is only possible when securitization is unthinkable. Individuals have a particular interest in seeing that the needs of others are met universally.

Common security, therefore, is not limited to removing the military causes of mutual vulnerability. It is about promoting a system of governance that reduces the need to take up arms. Individuals are motivated to do this when their voice is ignored, or, to paraphrase Deutsch, when their 'messages' are not given adequate weight by the community. To avoid this kind of securitization, an extended community needs to listen and respond to the voices of all, a formulation that recalls a Habermasian definition of democracy. For Habermas, a legitimate community could only be established 'through a mode of dialogue in which human beings strive to reach agreement. Participants aim to be guided by nothing other than the force of the better argument and agree that norms cannot be valid unless they command the consent of everyone who stands to be affected by them' (Linklater, 1996, p.286).

The political and cultural outcome of any dialogue based on these foundations is open. The legitimising power of the discourse, however, comes not from the outcome, but from the process of trying to include everyone in that dialogue. As Linklater notes (1996, p.293), the political significance of discourse ethics comes from the exposure of the 'gulf between actual social practices and discourse ethics....In addition to setting out the formal conditions which have to be satisfied before open dialogue can exist, discourse ethics invites the critique of structures and beliefs which obstruct open dialogue'.

On this basis, discourse ethics is critical of '"forms of life based on domination, violence and systematic inequality" which prevent full participation and therefore supportive of moves to equalise power' (Linklater, 1996, pp.293-294, quoting Cohen, 1990). Linklater (1998) builds on this by arguing that legitimate extensions of political community must involve provision for political and socio-economic rights as well as respect for morally insignificant difference. The standard by which the use of power and 'internationalising' process should be judged in relation to processes that reinforce nationalist, statist or local responses, therefore, is its power to include a greater number of individuals in a dialogue on their future.

Defined in these terms democratisation is central to the construction of a security community. Yet for reasons highlighted, the democratisation of the state, while important is also insufficient. Holding one's own state to account is pointless if the state cannot influence the issues that affect the lives of its citizens, whether it be the decision to use nuclear weapons or decisions that influence the global economy and environment. As noted this imposes a cosmopolitan duty on the power holders who can influence those decisions. A failure to recognise that duty, despite the proven link to particular interests, increases the chances of securitization. It is imperative, therefore, that those who hold power be bought to account through the practice of cosmopolitan democracy.

A full discussion of cosmopolitan democracy is beyond the scope of this book (see Held 1995). Yet it is important to note the required balance between regional and international responses to individual needs and aspirations. Promoting democracy at the state level and getting the balance right between national and international governance creates its own dilemmas. These are explored empirically in Chapters five and six. Before defining these new security dilemmas, it is worth considering how others have attempted to redefine the security dilemma.

Societal Security Dilemma

The idea of extending conceptions of the self is by definition a threat to previous definitions of the self. The claim of New Thinkers that one can only realise Soviet security in the context of American security was seen by Soviet traditionalists as a threat to the USSR. That internationalisation can pose a threat to communities where the idea of common security is not embedded, recalls the Copenhagen School's concept of societal security. While recognising the social contingency of society, the Copenhagen School nevertheless argue that it can be identified as a 'strong infrastructure of norms, values and institutions' that exists separately of the state, particular social groups and individuals. They see national identity as 'the most important of large-scale social and political identity'. Unlike 'ideological, sexual, environmental, occupational, political, sporting, class and hobbyist' identities, only national identity is 'robust enough in construction, and comprehensive enough in its following, but also broad enough in the quality of identity it carries, to enable it to compete with the territorial state as a political organizing principle'. With society defined in these terms, the Copenhagen School concludes that 'societal security concerns the ability of a society to persist in its essential character under changing conditions and possible threats' (Waever, 1993, pp.20-24).

From this perspective, the internationalisation of a state is not seen as a process that necessarily leads to the construction of a worthwhile and therefore enduring order. Rather the 'powerful inflows of language, style, culture and values' are seen as a threat to 'the ability of local cultures to reproduce themselves'(Buzan, 1993, p.42). In this sense, a threat to society is not necessarily the same as a military threat to occupy the territory it considers its 'homeland'. Societies can feel threatened by the interplay of ideas and communication, and/or by migration. What is more, the state that nominally speaks for that society can be an agent of these ideas.

In an attempt to draw an 'analogy with international politics' the Copenhagen School suggest that the tensions over migration, identity and territory can be seen as a 'societal security dilemma'. 'This would imply' Buzan notes (1993, pp.46):

that societies can experience processes in which perceptions of 'the others' develop into mutually reinforcing 'enemy-pictures' leading to the same kind of negative dialectics as with the security dilemma between states. Societal security dilemmas might explain why some processes of social conflict seem to acquire a dynamic of their own.

Buzan's definition of the societal security dilemma reveals the same flaws and the same practical dangers as Collins' definition of the traditional security dilemma. Identifying it in terms of 'mutually reinforcing 'enemy-images'' or 'negative dialectics' confuses cause and effect. The spiral of mistrust implied here is a possible consequence of actions being made under conditions of uncertainty. Conditions that can only be identified by a political debate on what the society stands for and whether that stand is threatened by internationalisation. As noted in chapter two, an academic observer cannot escape the political consequences of their analysis. In the same manner by which academic observers become part of a political debate that helps constitute a state's interests, so commentators of society, regardless of their claim to objectivity, become part of the political process that helps constitute that society. Like deterrence and spiral theorists claimed objectivity but simply became part of the political dispute that signified the state's security dilemma, so analysts of national and international society will help constitute the societal security dilemma.

The danger of missing this point is the reification of society and the acceptance of 'negative dialectics' between societies as an immutable fact. On the other hand, to recognise the political process by which threats to society are interpreted is to realise the immanent possibility of transcending the dilemma. As Adler and Barnett note, not all will welcome internationalisation. The implication of that statement of course is that some will welcome such a process. The societal security dilemma is therefore reflected in the political battle between contradictory interpretations of the threats and opportunities presented by internationalisation. Creating a common identity in a way that transcends the suspicion of the other rests, of course, with the political marginalisation of those who resist internationalisation. The key to that, as noted above, is to make sure internationalisation creates security and opportunity for all and does not merely respond to the needs of some at the expense of others. Internationalisation without democratisation is resolving the uncertainty of states simply to see it manifest itself in relations between groups within and across states. As such, the new internationalist identity of states cannot be guaranteed[1], and even if it could the focus of conflict would simply shift from the inter- to the intra-state level.

So that academic observation reveals these possibilities it is necessary not to reify states, societies or any other communities, by using traditional concepts (like the traditional security dilemma) that takes their identities as fixed. It is impossible to identify a threat to a society, or to claim a society has misperceived a situation as a threat, without taking a normative stance on that society. This point is illustrated by John McSweeney's attack (1996) on the Copenhagen School's concept of societal security. McSweeney asks 'who speaks for society?' For him 'society' is less structured than the Copenhagen School suggests. His individualism, as opposed to their collectivism, sees society more as an ongoing process of negotiation, affirmation and reproduction. 'Collective identity', he notes, is not "out there", waiting to be discovered. 'What is "out there" is an identity discourse on the part of political leaders, intellectuals and countless others, who engage in the process of constructing, negotiating and affirming a response to the demand...for a collective image'. He would thus give greater political significance to the 'ideological, sexual, environmental, occupational, political, sporting, class and hobbyist' groups that the Copenhagen School felt able to dismiss when talking about society and its security.

McSweeney's fear is that the objectivism of the Copenhagen School has the potential to reify structures that pose an epistemic barrier to the formation of a collective identity[2]. Booth (1995) also warns against 'blackboxing' cultures in the same way as Realists blackboxed states for the sake of theoretical parsimony. Not only is it empirically wrong, in that it 'plays down multiple identities and overlooks transcultural ties and sympathies', it is also normatively misguided as it 'plays into the hands of the powerful'. By making local culture the referent object of security Booth argues that communitarianism effectively takes a snapshot of an ongoing exercise in power and turns it into 'a timeless definition of the human condition'. Moreover, by accepting that the local actors appointed by that process are and will for ever be the only authentic representatives of that culture, communitarianism effectively colludes in the repression of voices that had no say in that process. As Booth puts it 'culture can be torture, and "authenticity" the means of maintaining oppressive power structures'.

In this sense the focus on societal security and societal security dilemmas normatively fails the process of constructing a true security community. By potentially reifying 'society' it legitimises the claims of the elite, usually the most powerful in society, to speak on behalf of that society regardless of whether or not they are responsive to the needs and aspirations of others. It can politically legitimise the loosely-coupled communities that rest on intersubjective understandings among elites while they continue to repress the weak. By limiting their goals to inter-state order, the concept of a loosely-coupled security community allows statist elites to claim their duties are fulfilled even when there are victims of the peace they enjoy. For reasons already noted, this is insufficient to be regarded as a security community.

It was argued in chapter one, then, that the decentralisation of political authority was required to assure a defensive state that the cooperative intentions of the other would not suffer a quick reversal. To the extent that liberal democracy guarantees a slow and transparent process of change, liberal democratic states are more likely to cooperate knowing that any change of the other's intentions will come with much warning. In this chapter the obstacle to the creation of security communities where war is unthinkable comes not from other states but from systems of governance that are unresponsive to the needs and aspirations of individuals. Certain individuals of course may be denied the right to pursue certain aspirations because they are inconsistent with the rights of others. The process of deciding such restrictions is a potential source of securitization, but one that is limited if the process is legitimised through democratic practice. The foundations of such practice are legitimised by Habermasian discourse ethics. This requires an approach to security that seeks the best way to promote liberal *and* social democracy at the national *and* international level. Only when this allows all voices a guaranteed contribution to the social process that constructs society can its members expect change to be gradual and peaceful.

The Security Dilemma Redefined

As noted above the 'state', 'society' and 'community' should not be viewed in essentialist terms, nor should they, if movement is to be made towards extending a security community, be made objects of security. Yet as the Copenhagen School and others point out, the political significance of these institutions can present seemingly immovable obstacles to the promotion of democracy. Worse still they can mobilize power that could, if provoked, undermine the order between different social groups that pluralists see as the best possible situation. As Bull wrote (1995, quoted in Wheeler, 1992, p.470)

> [I]f international society were really to treat human justice as primary and co-existence [of states] as secondary ... then a situation in which there is no agreement as to what human rights are or in what hierarchy of priorities they should be arranged, the result could only be to undermine international order.

Statecraft that puts the individual at the center of its concerns risks undermining an international order that is not necessarily perfect in terms of democratic responsiveness and long term security but is nonetheless the best possible order at that particular time. The distribution of power amongst competing conceptions of rights and good governance may preclude a state's promotion of democracy. In such situations those speaking on behalf of the state are often confronted with 'agonizing decisions' (Wight, 1966, quoted by Wheeler, 1996, p.124) or 'terrible choices' (Bull, 1984, Quoted by Wheeler, 1996, p.124). They may find themselves, according to Jackson (1996), caught in a 'normative dilemma'.

Given this situation the statesperson's primary responsibility according to Jackson (1996; 1999, pp.139-174) is to either to the national interest or inter-state order[3]. Yet he also recognises the political force of arguments that suggest statesmen or women are responsible to humanitarian interests based on cosmopolitan conceptions of rights and solidarist conceptions of order. He writes: 'If these foregoing criteria and the precepts they give rise to are operative norms and not merely academic speculations', in other words, if these conceptions of responsibility become politically significant in a state's security discourse, 'it becomes clear that we should expect normative dilemmas and conflicts to be a feature of contemporary international relations' (Jackson, 1996, p.118).

Jackson's point that state's are sometimes pressured to act on wider conceptions of duty and interests than those seen by Realists or pluralists is also evident in Bull's work. Bull was unwilling to prioritise interstate order over individual justice. He suggested (1995, quoted by Wheeler, 1992, p.470) that '...the question of order *versus* justice will always be considered by the parties concerned in relation to the merits of a particular case'. The first aspect of the normative security dilemma, then, is the uncertainty as to when the opportunity to advance democracy presents itself in a manner that will not compromise national or international interests. This does not mean national or international interests are valued more highly than solidarist concerns for democracy promotion. Rather it is recognition of the fact that neglecting all concern for national and international interests can mobilise opposition against a policy of democracy promotion.

'Politics as an art' writes Tony Smith (1995, p.107) in the context of America's policy of promoting democracy:

> requires the desirable in terms of the possible. The dilemma of leadership is to decide when it is weakness to fail to exploit the inevitable ambiguities, and therefore possibilities, of the historical moment, and when it is foolhardy to attempt to overcome immovable constraints set by a combination of forces past and present. Since options are always open to some extent, greatness requires creating opportunities and taking risks within the limits set by history.

In the context of this chapter, the dilemma Smith identifies is reflected in the uncertainty faced by a state that seeks to support the forces of internationalisation and democratisation in a transitional state in order to integrate that state into a security community. As observed above, the forces of internationalisation and democratisation may not be welcomed by all within the transitional state or society creating a political debate and a security dilemma. The normative dilemma of the state promoting internationalisation and democratisation is reflected in the debate on how best to exploit the fluidity of the political situation in the transitional state.

A state's normative security dilemma is thus dynamically related to the political process of the transitional state and the intensity of its dilemma. As with the traditional security dilemma, it faces a dilemma of interpretation. How intense is the transitional state's dilemma and how significant are the forces of internationalisation and democratisation? Dependent on this question is the nature of a state's dilemma of response. Would political intervention further the political aims of democratic internationalists and thus assist the process of expanding the integrated security community? Of course, if it is perceived that there is little possibility of the transitional state's dilemma being resolved in favour of the internationalist and democratic perspective then it will affect the other state's normative response. Should that state risk relations with the transitional state by supporting internationalists and democrats if they have little chance of affecting a transition in their favour? This may be dependent on an assessment of what is at stake in the relationship between the states involved. If the stakes are high, if for example a breakdown in relations could lead to the breakdown of international order then it may be prudent for the state to abandon its support of democratic internationalists and postpone its aims of expanding a security community.

The political process of a state's normative dilemma is also influenced by factors internal to that state. A foreign policy debate that is dominated by pluralist conceptions of order and a relativist conception of rights and duties is unlikely to be concerned with opportunities for advancing democracy as a means of integrating others into a security community. Regardless of the political opportunities presented by a process of reform in a transitional state, a debate of this character is likely to prioritise relations with elites and be extra-sensitive to the costs of undermining their position. Conversely a debate that is dominated by a solidarist conception of order and a cosmopolitan conception of rights and duties is likely to seize on an opportunity to advance democracy and extend the security community. It would be more willing to bear potential costs to international order if a more democratic and enduring order was possible. One can identify the state's normative dilemma when both sides of this debate hold politically significant positions in the state's security discourse.

The Responsibility of Internationalist and Democratic State

In the position adopted by Bull, where the possibility of advancing good governance should be taken on a case by case basis, prudence can be considered a moral virtue. If, after 'due care and attention to the situation in hand' (Jackson, 1996, p.126) responsible statesmen decide the cause of democracy would be setback by the consequences of an interventionist policy, then reneging on promises to promote good governance are justified. There are those however, who take a skeptical look at a state's claim that its non-interventionist stance is based on prudence and is therefore normatively justified. Wheeler (1992, p.480) separates John Vincent's work from Hedley Bull's on these grounds. He notes that Vincent, writing with Peter Wilson (1993), 'expressed reservations with a "morality of states" which requires that "we have to act *as if* other states are legitimate, not because they *are* legitimate [in their upholding of conceptions of the good] but because to do otherwise would lead to chaos"'.

Like Vincent, Booth (1994) is anxious not to excuse "selfish" behaviour, that which benefits an individual at the expense of the wider community, by allowing a justification based on prudence. Yet he also recognises the limits of action based on a duty to a wider community. When prudence is "self-interested", that is when it does not necessarily exclude the interests of other, it is according to Booth, justified. In certain contexts, then, the national interest is an important part of sustaining a commitment to the international interest, which while not being perfect has a normative value in itself. Specifically, if a commitment to humanitarian responsibilities and solidarist interests bear such a cost to narrower conceptions of the national interest it may provoke a reaction against all forms of internationalist commitment. In other words the limited but nonetheless worthwhile commitment to an international order based on democratic and internationalist states may be undermined by a retreat into an egoistic approach based on even narrower conceptions of self-interest.

The significance of this point is made clear in subsequent chapters. For example, it is an unfortunate feature of the contemporary global community (though some would deny the existence of such a thing) that the multilateral practices on which the security community of liberal states rests is dependent on the satisfaction not of the needs of the powerful but on the satisfaction of their desires. This double standard is perpetuated by concerns that efforts to remedy it will be met not by greater solidarity but by myopic egoism. In other words, should solidarist policies in aid of the weak not carry the support of the powerful, the powerful may become disillusioned with the system that produced those policies and withdraw its support from the present order that is unsatisfactory but not the worst scenario imaginable. Specifically, an unwillingness to bear the short term costs of encouraging democracy elsewhere not only means opportunities are lost but also jeopardises policies needed to sustain the democratic security community that presently exists.

To put such a glaring injustice in terms of a dilemma that could be used by statesmen and women as an excuse for not acting on behalf of a wider ethical community is regrettable. Yet it is a reality that those looking to the modern state as an agent of change must face. The intention here is not to excuse statesmen and women, it is simply to understand the limits of contemporary statecraft. In fact the consequence of this argument for heads of state is less a source of consolation than an undressing of their belief that they can affect progressive change. As the following chapter notes, President Bush's contribution to the 1989 revolutions was remarkable for what he didn't do rather than what he did.

Changing the Structure of the Dilemma: transnational civil society

Where universalist conceptions of rights and duties lack political significance practical action on behalf of such an agenda is often faced with difficult decisions. Yet to leave it at that is to indulge the tyranny of statism and presentism (Booth, 1999). By claiming that a pluralist community, based on different conceptions of rights is the best possible international community, we fail to recognise the historical and political contingency of those rights. In answering the question are rights universal, Booth (1999, pp.35-36) replies that it is simply too soon to say. 'The argument is not that a strong universal rights culture will happen, only that there are no grounds – historically or anthropologically – for saying that it will not.' Communitarianism that leads to relativism or an ideology that uncritically celebrates the state only offers 'snap shots' of this historical process. By recognising the openness of social potential one should recognise that communities and their values are open to construction, reconstruction and deconstruction.

Self-other relationships that presently exist have not always been nor will always be like they presently stand. The self can come to see the other as an extension of the self. The North-Atlantic security community is only a recent construction and, as is argued in the following chapter, it defines itself not against an other, but in terms of values that an other can adopt and become part of that community (Risse-Kappen, 1996). Those presently outside that community may be the subjects of the security dilemma, but they are also the subjects of social processes that can potentially change interests and identities so that they become part of rather than separate from the security community. The security dilemma can be transcended if social processes can foster a common identity across states.

Expanding on the normative aspect of the security dilemma, Robert Jackson suggests that there is 'an underlying normative pluralism which statesmen cannot escape from'. Yet by his own logic this is not the case. The key phrase in Jackson's argument of converting normative pluralism into a normative dilemma is 'operative norms'. To repeat, Jackson argues that if the different conceptions of rights, order and responsibility 'are operative norms and not merely academic speculations it becomes clear that we should expect normative dilemmas and conflicts to be a feature of contemporary international relations'. What turns an academic speculation into an operative norm, however, is political activism within society. Without political support statesmen and women will not wish, nor be able, to act in certain ways. Normative pluralism at the level of the state is, in other words, contingent on social processes across society.

Political support or opposition from below can change the structure of a state's dilemma. If support for democrats within the society of a transitional state forces non-democratic movements to be politically marginalised then it eases the normative dilemma of the established democratic state that is looking to promote its values. Because its intervention on the side of democracy has more chance of success Realists are less likely to oppose a policy of democracy promotion. Moreover, if the transnational coalition that supports democratisation is as strong in the established state as it is in the transitional state, then a policy of democracy promotion is likely to gain much support.

The point is that the decisive work in transcending the security dilemma, both in its traditional and normative character is done at the level of transnational civil society. The political significance of those values that recognise the interdependent nature of security and the duties that they imply is particularly important. Thus as Booth puts it, the best hope for progressive change 'will be global social movements committed to world order values such as non-violence, economic justice, environmental sustainability, good governance and human rights' (Booth, 1998, p.349).

This point was noted by, amongst others, Hedley Bull who recognised that interstate relations was only one level on which inter- or trans-national politics was practiced. For Bull the role of the state was simply to provide order in which more solidarist conceptions of justice could develop. He argued that both superpowers were acting irresponsibly at the beginning of the 1980s (Bull, 1980). The role of U.S. foreign policy at the end of that decade is examined in chapter five. It argues that the policy of the Bush administration toward the collapse of the Soviet empire was prudent in a manner that not only maintained order but also encouraged democratic reform. As chapter three demonstrated, however, this was a consequence not of American rearmament but of multilateral disarmament, heavily prompted as it was by Gorbachev. The cautious approach to supporting agents of democracy and recognising their claims to self determination (with perhaps the exception of Germany where the U.S. risked good relations with the USSR in order to pursue German self-determination), combined with a sensitivity to the political position of New Thinkers in Moscow vis-à-vis the traditional hardliners, reflected an awareness of America's responsibility in maintaining international order. Importantly it maintained that order in a manner that allowed democratic and internationalist forces across transnational civil society to pursue their political programmes in relative security. Not all will agree with this conclusion and indeed it was contested at the time.

Conclusion

The purpose of this chapter has been to identify pathways for transcending the uncertainty of the security dilemma and creating a security community. In so doing it has further refined the definition of the security dilemma and set standards by which one can assess normative statecraft. Chapter two emphasised the need to see the security dilemma in terms of a political debate rather than as an objective description of a particular situation. Chapter three demonstrated how this approach can inform our understanding of how the military confrontation between the United States and Soviet Union was wound down. Ultimately that military conflict was contingent on the political reform process in Soviet Union. Under Gorbachev that process involved both internationalisation and democratisation and because both these processes were contested it is fair to say that the Soviet Union faced a security dilemma. This dilemma did not revolve around the issue of NATO's military intentions, rather it was an issue of Soviet identity in relation to the 'West'. To the extent that traditional Soviet identity helped constitute America's security dilemma, assisting the processes of Soviet internationalisation and democratisation was a matter of national and international security for the United States. America's security dilemma took on a distinctly normative character. The threat came not from the Warsaw Pact's military intentions, rather there was a danger that the opportunity to promote the foundations of a wider security community would be missed. The security dilemma, then, is a normative dilemma.

But then it always has been. The problem with traditional definitions of the security dilemma is that they have mistakenly believed 'national security' is an objective starting point for an analysis that can escape normative judgement. By taking the state as the referent object of security these so-called 'objective' analyses are making normative assumptions. They assume the state is worth defending without examining its political identity, what it stands for and what it does for or to individuals. In other words the traditional security dilemma of chapters two and three is not different to the normative security dilemma of this chapter, they simply have different starting points. The security dilemma is a normative dilemma. Certainly the security dilemma discussed in chapters two and three took the state as the referent object, but only to the extent that the state stood for certain political values. Indeed an important and often overlooked part of America's security dilemma was the view that the policies used to interpret and respond to the 'Soviet threat' were undermining the democratic values that the United States stood for. This national uncertainty was reflected in many ways including the opposition movements to the Vietnam War and in the numerous court cases bought against secrecy laws.

The point is that a security policy should not be about defending states per se, but about political values that the state may or may not uphold.

Once this is realised the dilemma of promoting democracy is no different to that of defending democratic states. America faced a security dilemma in the late 1980s not only because the opportunity of enduring security presented itself and it was in America's particular interests to see it consolidated, but also because the values it supposedly stood for were at stake. As Risse-Kappen's (1996) work on democratic communities demonstrates, democracies can see each other as extensions of the self. Some representatives of democracies see duties not only to their own electoral constituencies, but to the principle of democracy itself and to the wider community of democrats.

Ultimately the state's response to threats or opportunities is determined and articulated by the statesmen and women. But the political pressure that constitutes the state's dilemma is contingent on society as a whole. It has been argued here that the structure of the dilemma facing a state can be changed and can be ultimately transcended by the spread of transnational civil society. By promoting internationalist, inclusive, democratic values civil society does two things: firstly it strengthens the arguments of those in democratic states that a policy that seeks to promote democracy will find fertile soil. Conversely it weakens the Realist-Pluralist argument that democracy promotion is unlikely to succeed and the national interest is best preserved by cooperating with statist elites despite their repression of individuals. Secondly, it provides hope that the securitization of unresponsive regimes will not necessarily be violent. What the 1989 revolutions across Eastern Europe for the most part showed, was that the political strength of transnational civil society held open the prospect of responsive internationalist states that could be integrated into a wider security community (Chiltern, 1994; Kaldor, 1999; Thomas, 1999).

The final aim of this chapter was to draw attention to the fact that the state and the international system provides a context for, and even a direct influence on, the development of civil society. At this point the assessment of America's role in constructing security communities finds its standards. Firstly chapter three noted the rise of democratic civil society in response to the 'irresponsible' behaviour of the Reagan administration in its attitude towards the Soviet Union. In fact it is argued in the following chapter that these policies inspired democratic movements to react against American defence policy. Moreover, when American policy severed cooperative links with the Soviet Union, Communist regimes could easily ignore the human rights issues that had assumed such a high profile during the Carter presidency. The repression of *Solidarity* in 1981 was perhaps no coincidence. It is further argued that the Bush administration's renewed emphasis on détente at the state level and a prudent commitment to democratic principles, casts American policy in a more responsible light. This combination gave civil society across Eastern Europe a relatively secure political space in which to operate.

Notes

[1] As Wendt notes, '[t]he vulnerabilities that accompany interdependence may generate perceived threats to self-control, and rising similarity may generate fears that the state has no raison d'etre if it is not different to other states. States may respond to these systemic processes, in other words, by redoubling their efforts to defend egoistic identities'. Wendt, (1994, p.390)

[2] McSweeney fears that by reifying society, in the way traditional Realists reified the state, methodological collectivism limits the possibilities of political action. As Buzan and Waever note in their reply to McSweeney (1997, pp.241-250), their notion of societal security applies to those identities that have, following the process McSweeney emphasizes, 'become socially sedimented'. Identities they argue, 'can petrify and become relatively constant elements to be reckoned with'. Their debate with McSweeney, is therefore, a matter of emphasis. Both sides agree that society is socially constructed and the process by which societies identify threats is political.

[3] Jackson argues that the morality of both positions depends upon the assumption that states are 'valuable places where the good life, if not always realised fully, is nevertheless a definite possibility' (Jackson, 1990, pp.266-7).

References

Acharya, A. (1998), 'Collective identity and conflict management in Southeast Asia', in E.Adler and M.Barnett, *Security Communities*, Cambridge University Press, Cambridge, pp.198-227.

Adler, E. and Barnett, M. (1998a), 'Security Communities in theoretical perspective', in E.Adler and M.Barnett, *Security Communities*, Cambridge University Press, Cambridge, pp.3-28.

Adler, E. and Barnett, M. (1998b), 'A Framework for the study of security communities', in E.Adler and M.Barnett, *Security Communities*, Cambridge University Press, Cambridge, pp.29-65.

Adler, E. and Barnett, M. (1998c), 'Studying Security Communities in theory, comparison and history', in E.Adler and M.Barnett, *Security Communities*, Cambridge University Press, Cambridge, pp.413-441.

Booth, K. (1994), 'Military Intervention: Duty and Prudence', in L.Freedman (ed.) *Military Intervention in European Conflicts*, Blackwell, Oxford, pp.56-75.

Booth, K. (1995), 'Human Wrongs in International Relations', *International Affairs*, Vol.71, pp.103-126.

Booth, K. (1998), 'Conclusion: security within global transformation?', in Ken Booth (ed.), *Statecraft and Security. The Cold War and Beyond*, Cambridge University Press, Cambridge, pp.338-355.

Booth, K. (1999), 'Three Tyrannies', in Tim Dunne and Nicholas Wheeler, *Human Rights in Global Politics*, Cambridge University Press, Cambridge, pp.31-70.

Bull, H. (1980), 'The great irresponsibles? The United States, the Soviet Union and world order', *International Journal*, Vol.35, pp.437-447.

Bull, H. (1984), *Justice in International Relations*, The Hagey Lectures, University of Waterloo, Ontario.

Buzan, B. (1993), 'Societal security, state security and internationalisation', in Ole Waever, Barry Buzan, Morten Kelstrup and Pierre Lemaitre, *Identity, Migration and the New Security Agenda in Europe*, Pinter Publishers Ltd, London, pp.41-88.

Buzan, B. and Waever, O. (1997), 'Slippery? Contradictory? Sociologically untenable? The Copenhagen school replies', *Review of International Studies*, Vol.23, pp.241-250.

Buzan, B., Waever, O. and de Wilde, J. (1998), *Security. A New Framework for Analysis*, Lynne Rienner, Boulder, Colorado.

Chiltern, P. (1994), 'Mechanics of Change: Social Movements, Transnational Coalition and the Transformation Processes in Eastern Europe', *Democratization*, Vol.1, pp.151-181.

Cohen, J. (1990), 'Discourse Ethics and Civil Society', in D.Rasmussen (ed.), *Universalism vs Communitarianism*, MIT Press, Cambridge, MA., pp.83-105.

Deutsch, K.W. et.al. (1957), *Political Community in the North Atlantic Area. International Organization in the Light of Historical Experience*, Princeton University Press, Princeton.

Held, D. (1995), *Democracy and Global Order. From the Modern State to Cosmopolitan Governance*, Polity Press, Oxford.

Hurrell, A. (1998), 'An emerging security community in South America?', in E. Adler and M.Barnett, *Security Communities*, Cambridge University Press, Cambridge, pp.228-264.

Jackson, R. (1990), 'Martin Wight, International Theory and the Good Life', *Millennium: Journal of International Studies*, Vol.19, pp.261-272.

Jackson, R. (1996), 'The Political Theory of International Society', in Ken Booth and Steve Smith (eds.), *International Relations Theory Today*, Polity Press, Oxford, pp.110-128.

Jackson, R. and Sorensen, G. (1999), *Introduction to International Relations*, Oxford University Press, Oxford.

Kaldor, M. (1999), 'Transnational Civil Society', in Tim Dunne and Nicholas Wheeler, *Human Rights in Global Politics*, Cambridge University Press, Cambridge, pp.195-213.

Linklater, A. (1996), 'The achievements of critical theory', in M.Zalewski, K.Booth and S.Smith (eds.), *After Positivism*, Cambridge University Press, Cambridge, pp.279-298.

Linklater, A. (1998), *The Transformation of Political Community. Ethical Foundations of the Post-Westphalian Era*, Polity Press, Oxford.

McSweeney, B. (1996), 'Identity and security: Buzan and the Copenhagen School', *Review of International Studies*, Vol.22, pp.81-94.

Risse-Kappen, T. (1996), 'Collective Identity in a Democratic Community: The Case of NATO', in Peter J. Katzenstein (ed.), *The Culture of National Security. Norms and Identity in World Politics*, Columbia University Press, New York, pp.357-399.

Smith, T. (1995), *America's Mission. The United States and the Worldwide Struggle for Democracy in the Twentieth Century*, Princeton University Press, Princeton.

Thomas, D.C. (1999), 'The Helsinki accords, and political change in Eastern Europe', in Thomas Risse-Kappen, Stephen C. Ropp and Kathryn Sikkink, *The Power of Human Rights. International Norms and Domestic Change*, Cambridge University Press, Cambridge, pp.205-333.

Vincent, R.J. and Wilson, P. (1993), 'Beyond Non-Intervention', in Ian Forbes and Mark Hoffman (eds.), *Political Theory, International Relations and the Ethics of Intervention*, St.Martins, New York, pp.122-132.

Waever, O. (1993), 'Societal Security: the concept', in Ole Waever, Barry Buzan, Morten Kelstrup and Pierre Lemaitre, *Identity, Migration and the New Security Agenda in Europe*, Pinter Publishers Ltd, London, pp.20-24.

Waever, O. (1995), 'Securitization and Desecuritization', in Lipschutz, R.D. (ed.) *On Security*, Columbia University Press, New York, pp.46-86.

Waever, O. (1998), 'Insecurity, security and asecurity in the West European non-war community', in E.Adler and M.Barnett, *Security Communities*, Cambridge University Press, Cambridge, pp.228-264.

Wendt, A. (1994), 'Collective Identity Formation and the International State', *American Political Science Review*, Vol.88, pp.384-396.

Wheeler, N.J. (1992), 'Pluralist or Solidarist Conceptions of International Society: Bull and Vincent on Humanitarian Intervention', *Millennium: Journal of International Studies*, Vol.21, pp.463-487.

Wheeler, N.J. (1996), 'Guardian Angel or Global Gangster: a Review of the Ethical Claims of International Society', *Political Studies*, Vol.44, pp.123-135.

Wight, M. (1966), 'Western values in International Relations', in H.Butterfield and M.Wight (eds.), *Diplomatic Investigations*, Allen and Unwin, London, pp.89-131.

5 America's Cold War: the political dimension

Introduction

A security community is based on a common identity that sustains dependable expectations of peaceful change and thus makes war unthinkable. When political units see each other as extensions of themselves it is irrational for them to prepare for war against each other and threats to the other are seen as threats to themselves. Extending a security community involves 'the ability to give messages from other political units adequate weight' in a manner that guarantees the peaceful resolution of conflict. Chapter four argued that peace is only guaranteed if the community responds to the basic needs of all individuals. The 'political units' of a security community can be states, nations or societies, but only to the extent that they meet the basic needs of the individual. An individual observer has no right to proclaim a security community if the political units of that 'community' deny other individuals their basic needs. Where such needs are denied, where individuals are excluded from a dialogue on their future, any assertion of a security community does more to highlight the security and privilege of the observer than it does the objectivity of their analysis. Without common security there can be no objective identification of a security community. A security community does not exist except when it takes into account the voices of all.

The next two chapters examine the role America plays in constructing a security community. The record is mixed. As a 'reluctant, open and penetrated' state (Deudney and Ikenberry, 1999), American hegemony has reassured other political units and provided channels through which messages of those units have gained political significance. This decentralised political system, moreover, has given expression to a liberal intellectual community that sees 'outsiders' as political extensions of America, and has therefore felt protective of their identity and the principles they share. This community has worked hard to define

America's national interest in terms of a wider international and humanitarian interest. Through international organisations based on multilateral decision-making and diffuse reciprocity, liberals have worked to construct institutions that facilitate international dialogue. They have also sought to persuade American exceptionalists that a compromise to that dialogue would benefit Americans.

Liberals have been politically successful when the link between the particular and the universal has been easily illustrated. This has been the case in the international institutions that these next two chapters focus on. This chapter focuses on the political dimension of the NATO alliance, while the next focuses on the economic dimension of the Bretton Woods institutions. Where American interests have been clearly identified with a stable European continent or an open international trading system, liberals have had little trouble in getting Realists to support those institutions that provide the basis for cooperation. Clearly, a united NATO was central to the Realist aim of balancing the power of the Soviet Union. Countering the Soviet threat, however, was not the only, nor indeed the primary aim of NATO. As this chapter demonstrates, the Wilsonian motive behind America's European policy contributed to the creation of an organisation that would, through the practice of multilateralism, make sure the voices of other political units were heard and long-term order was based on consensus.

America's Cold War security dilemma was reflected in the tension between the two sides of this coalition. On the one hand, liberals argued that the multilateral practices of NATO were most important for the security of Europe and that compromise with the allies was essential even if one thought that undermined the most appropriate policy towards the Soviet Union. On the other hand, Realists argued that the relationship with the Soviet Union, whether it be defined in terms of a deterrence or spiral model was of utmost importance. They were less willing to preserve the multilateral practices of the security community if it meant complicating the relationship with the Soviet Union.

Clearly by extending their conception of America to embrace NATO, liberals were introducing into alliance politics the same dilemmas that America itself confronted when faced with the Soviet threat. America's European policy faced the same question as did narrower conceptions of 'national' security. Should the U.S. compromise those principles that liberals believed preserved democracy and peace and set a good example for others to follow for the sake of pursuing a policy that Realists claimed was necessary to deter the Soviet Union? Of course, in the U.S. this dilemma was reflected in the debates over secrecy, covert operations and the centralisation of foreign policy around the White House. Reaching its greatest intensity in the mid-to-late 1970s this security dilemma was reflected in the liberal opposition to the Nixon White House and the practices of the CIA. Liberals argued that the threat to the U.S. came from an undemocratic reaction to an exaggerated Soviet threat. Whereas Realists like Nixon and prominent members of the Reagan administration interpreted the threat to American values in terms of the Soviet rather than the American state. The Iran-Contra scandal was, of course, a clear indication of America's security dilemma.

This chapter concentrates on the dilemma American policy faced in seeking to preserve and extend the principles that underpinned the transatlantic security community based around NATO. While this dilemma was at its most intense at the end of the Cold War, it had always been present since NATOs formation. This chapter focuses on the Wilsonian principles of self-determination and non-discrimination as the basis for the transatlantic security community and shows how the defence of those principles was sometimes opposed by Realists who believed they should have been compromised in order to deter or negotiate with the Soviet Union. First it is necessary to examine the claim that American hegemony and the Wilsonian principles it promotes provide sound building blocks for the transatlantic community.

NATO as a Liberal Democratic Community

Liberal theorists seeking to explain why NATO persists after the collapse of the Soviet threat have viewed the alliance as an expression of a democratic community rather than simply a defensive alliance[1]. In contrast to Realist accounts of its founding, several commentators have argued that NATO remains 'for as well as against something'[2]. In other words, when that which it was against (the Soviet Union) disappeared, NATO was still required to fulfil an important security function, the multilateral management of security relations between democratic states in a manner that made war unthinkable. In short, it remained an important institution in protecting the norms that underpinned the transatlantic security community.

NATO obviously fulfilled the Realist role of a collective defence organisation. Yet according to Liberal accounts, this was not its only, nor indeed its primary purpose. Thomas Risse-Kappen for instance, notes that the USSR was not considered an offensive military threat to Western Europe during the late 1940s. Rather the main threat was considered to be the Soviet ability to politically exploit the economic weakness of post-war Europe (Risse-Kappen, 1996, p.361). This line of argument is also pursued by John Ikenberry and Steve Weber who note that faith in the principle of collective security was not easily abandoned by American liberals. Weber (1993) for instance, demonstrates that the U.S. repeatedly turned its back on European requests for bilateral alliances. Ikenberry also notes that NATO's collective defence functions were located within the U.N. Charter and were thus consistent with Wilson and Roosevelt's liberalism rather than a response to the perceived failure of those approaches (Ikenberry, 1989; Deudney and Ikenberry, 1999).

Mary Hampton's work (1996) clearly demonstrates the 'hybrid' nature of NATO's identity. She also argues that U.S. policy was less concerned with the Soviet military threat than it was with establishing a trans-Atlantic community that included a peaceful Germany. She writes:

> while it is true that the emergence of the Soviet threat galvanised American foreign policy and the Western community in a way that the initial expression of the Wilsonian impulse did not, it is not true that the threat created the drive for Western unity and German rehabilitation.

As the alliance evolved in this context it adopted the dual identity of a collective defence pact and a 'Wilsonian collective security community' (Hampton, 1996, p.7).

According to Hampton, the motivating influence for this policy was historical analogy. As chapter three showed, the Munich analogy inspired or attempted to legitimise the arguments of those who advocated a strong deterrence posture. In opposition to that intellectual community were those who utilised the 1914 analogy. They advocated a policy that was sensitive to legitimate Soviet security concerns. They argued that the policies of their political opponents provoked the Soviet Union and simply created the problems they purported to solve. Chapter three followed this debate as a way of articulating the military dimension of America's security dilemma. Hampton's work, however, clearly shows that a different historical analogy inspired the intellectual community that she labels Wilsonians. The main historical lesson for this community was not 1938 or 1914, but 1919 and the Versailles Peace Treaty. What she calls the 'Versailles remedial ... reflected the widespread belief of American policymakers that Germany must not be treated as harshly after World War II as it had been at Versailles in 1919' (Hampton, 1996, p.1).

To integrate post-war Germany into a community American policy was careful not to make the same mistakes in 1919 and treat Germany separately to its other allies. Rather it would support democracy and Germany's right to national self-determination even if, as is argued below, that risked relations with other states. The principle of non-discrimination was non-negotiable. The right to democratic self-determination would apply to Germany as it would to all states within the community that post-war Wilsonians envisioned. Beyond that, however, the manner in which those principles were defended was open for discussion. As Hampton notes, the 'emphasis on consultation, consensus, parliamentary procedure and cooperation among freely associated partners would heavily inform the future direction and the positioning of states'. In other words, the interests and identities of the states in NATO began to change such that their relationships became infused with 'political obligation and diffuse reciprocity'(Hampton, 1996, p.21). In effect, liberals across NATO began to see member states as extensions of each other. Thus Risse-Kappen (1996, pp.176) writes that the 'U.S. membership in an alliance of democratic states shaped the process by which American decision makers struggled over the definition of American interests and preferences'. He concludes (1996, p.181) that NATO membership 'affected the identity of American actors in the sense that "we" in whose name the President decided incorporated the European allies'.

The Versailles analogy, however, was not embedded across the U.S. security bureaucracy. The Wilsonian view of security was generally institutionalised in the State Department (Hampton, 1996, p.8). Its unwillingness to exaggerate Soviet military capabilities combined with a bias towards arms control and Wilsonianism, suggests that liberalism was more or less embedded within the State Department. This does not mean the Wilsonian attitude towards NATO did not find expression in other parts of the American discourse. As Hampton notes many policymakers considered Realist in their attitude towards the Soviet Union were strongly committed to Wilsonian principles, particularly in relation to Germany. Yet when relations with NATO clashed with a proposed policy towards the Soviet Union, Wilsonians who supported NATO consensus as an end in itself were often opposed by American Realists who held a more particularist conception of security.

Convincing American Realists of the importance of consensus was in essence the role played by what Hampton identifies as the 'Versailles remedial'. The lesson of Versailles was not the only factor motivating American liberals. Amongst committed liberals there was a genuine belief that America should defend democracy and self-determination wherever it was threatened because that was America's purpose. The lesson of Versailles, however, allowed liberals to argue convincingly that defending these principles was not only in America's ideological interest but also in its particular material interests. The history of the inter-war years had provided a clear link between the violation of Wilsonian principles and the rise of military revisionism in Europe. It was clear to Wilsonians that America's security depended on the observance of democracy, self-determination and non-discrimination. The lesson of Versailles made their task of convincing American Realists a lot easier.

Yet there was a tension in liberal advocacy. On the one hand liberals were more inclined seek cooperation with the Soviet Union based on the view that the U.S.-Soviet relationship reflected a spiral of mistrust. On the other hand, some were less than willing to compromise on the principles that underpinned their efforts to construct a security community across Western Europe and North America. Two issues in particular complicated U.S.-Soviet relations by limiting the concessions American liberals were willing to make. Supporting the German right to national self-determination implied tacit support for the West German policy of reunification. Such a stance, as Hampton notes, was inherently revisionist (Hampton, 1996, pp.41-42). A fact that those who view the Cold War as an unrefined security dilemma, that is a case of illusory incompatibility, tend to overlook.

The liberal approach to integrating Germany into a security community by respecting its right to self-determination meant that the early post-war efforts to cooperate with the Soviets on this issue collapsed. U.S. policy it seemed, faced a dilemma: drop support for reunification in order to cooperate with the Soviet Union at the risk of losing West German support for the transatlantic community, or maintain West German confidence by retaining a commitment to reunification at the risk of provoking the Soviet Union. Hampton argues that this dilemma was, for the most part, resolved in favour of the latter course of action. Only during the Kennedy administration did U.S. policy seem to favour détente with the Soviet Union over West German concerns. America's concern to retain West Germany's commitment to the transatlantic security community was a factor that informed the political process that constituted the security dilemma posed by the Soviet Union.

A similar question was posed by the issue of nuclear weapons and the principle of non- discrimination. As Hampton notes (1996, pp.55-56), these two issues were linked in that 'Bonn had agreed not to produce nuclear weapons on West German soil and not to pursue reunification on its own provided that the Allies take collective responsibility for achieving eventual German reunification'. There was, however, a separate issue involved here. The principles of the transatlantic community meant West Germany being treated as an equal and not being singled out for particular arms control arrangements. Ruling out nuclear weapons for West Germany when Britain and France responded to their own concerns regarding NATO strategy by acquiring their own national force would cause a crisis within NATO. At the same time, allowing proliferation throughout NATO would contradict any American moves towards détente with the Soviet Union. Hampton notes (1996 pp.52-57) that the American stance on the Multilateral Force (MLF) issue of the early 1960s was motivated primarily by its desire to make sure West German attitudes were firmly embedded in NATO policy. Thus despite clear evidence that the Kennedy and Johnson administrations wanted nuclear agreements with the Soviet Union it continued to jeopardise these ambitions by refusing to drop the MLF issue. Again America's priority was not relations with the Soviet Union, but managing NATO in a manner that preserved the norms of a Wilsonian security community.

The conviction with which the U.S. pursued this priority suggests the trade off between NATO unity and relations with the Soviet Union did not pose a dilemma for America. The consensus opinion prioritised NATO unity over relations with the Soviet Union. But there clearly was a trade off and the U.S. did sometimes pursue policies towards the USSR that risked upsetting good relations within the transatlantic community. Risse-Kappen (1996) notes that Kennedy's stance during the Cuban missile crisis was motivated by a common identity across NATO, while Hampton (1996) makes much of Kennedy's disregard for European opinions relative to particular American concerns. The debate that addressed these priorities is reflective of an American security dilemma.

America's dilemma is clearly of a different emphasis to that identified in chapters two and three. Yet it is worthy of the label security dilemma, because the issue was fundamentally the same. Principles were at stake that American liberals regarded as essential to peace both at home and abroad. As such the territorial distinction became blurred. The dilemma was posed when policies guided by those principles provoked the Soviet Union and jeopardised movement towards U.S.-Soviet détente. How this dilemma was expressed at the end of the Cold War is explored in more detail below.

The Benefits of American Hegemony

Clearly hegemony based solely on coercion is likely to be securitized as the Soviet experience in Eastern Europe demonstrated (Gaddis, 1998, pp.26-84). Chapter four argued that the long term stability of a community is more likely if the norms that underpin it are adopted consensually across the whole of the community. Gramsci identified the active consent of others as central to the exercise of hegemony. Hegemony, in effect, is consensus based on the political superstructure of a coherent social order that is only protected and not created by the 'armour of coercion' that material superiority allows (Robinson, 1999, pp.20-25; Wyn Jones, p.311). Ikenberry and Kupchan (1990, p.283) also recognise this 'more subtle component of hegemonic power'. 'Acquiescence', they argue, 'is the result of the socialisation of leaders in secondary nations. Elites in secondary states buy into and internalise norms that are articulated by the hegemon and therefore pursue policies consistent with the hegemon's notion of international order'. It is important to note that this process of socialisation is a two way process. While not strictly symmetrical, the give and take of this process helps legitimate the adoption of a normative order.

As noted above, Liberal commentators have argued that the institutions of American hegemony, including NATO, have contributed to such a process through the practice of multilateralism. Ruggie (1993, p.11) defines multilateralism as

> an institutional form that coordinates relations among three or more states on the basis of generalised principles which specify appropriate conduct for a class of actions, *without regard to the particularistic interests of the parties* or the strategic exigencies that may exist in any specific occurrence.

Strict adherence to those principles ensures that voices of all members of the community are listened to and the institutions that embody cooperation are 'robust and adaptive' (Ruggie, 1993, p.35). Those institutions themselves become the ends of policy and not simply the means of ensuring a united front against the Soviet threat. 'NATO was', to repeat, 'for as well as against something'.

While multilateralism is not dependent on the existence of a hegemon, it has been encouraged by the existence of *American* hegemony. In other words the character of a hegemon has a significant influence on the long term prospects of the community. Recent histories of NATO decision making have, in contrast to Realist predictions, revealed how smaller powers, notably West Germany and the U.K., wielded a rather unexpected influence (Risse-Kappen, 1995). American sensitivity to the Versailles remedial can partly explain West German influence. Yet while this emphasis on the historical conditioning of certain parts of the American elite is not misplaced it fails to capture other aspects of American hegemony that assists the process of consensus building and legitimation.

Deudney and Ikenberry (1999, p.185), for instance, note that the distinctive features of the American state have assisted the legitimisation of its hegemony. The transparent nature of its political process means 'secondary powers' are not subject to surprises, while the decentralised structure provides numerous points of access and increased opportunity to exert influence. This system encourages the creation of transnational relations which act 'as vehicles by which subordinate actors in the system represent their interests to the hegemonic power and the vehicle through which consensus between the hegemon and lesser powers are achieved'. According to this Liberal perspective, transnational relations can address the concerns that were expressed in chapter four. Transnational processes, conclude Deudney and Ikenberry, 'endow the relations with a degree of acceptability in the eyes of subordinate powers. This in turn reduces the tendency of the subordinate powers to resist and, correspondingly, diminishes the need for the hegemon to exercise coercion'. This reinforces the point made in chapters two and three that the decentralisation of power is fundamental to a process that transcends the uncertainty of the security dilemma.

America's constitutional tradition is, according to Liberals, another feature of its identity that allows it to act as a progressive force in the construction a stable order with the characteristics of a security community. Central to their argument is the idea that the benefits of liberal constitutionalism are externalised in a manner that applies to relations between as well as within states. Multilateral institutions, in other words, limit the "returns to power" in the same way that constitutional law limits the power of governments. The most powerful cannot dominate the community so long as the constitutional or mulitlateral decision making procedures are observed. In this way citizens consider their governments as legitimate and at the international level weaker states are reassured and do not resort to balancing or security competition (Ikenberry, 1999). Maintaining those procedures themselves become the ends of security policy.

Smaller powers were further reassured at the prospect of American hegemony by the reluctance of the isolationist tradition. The fact that it was *liberals* who dragged American power into European affairs suggested that its internationalism was benign. Combined with the openness and penetrated character of its political system these factors contributed to the consensual manner in which American hegemony was practised. The American empire was, and to a large extent remains, 'an empire by invitation' (Lundestad, 1990, p.54).

Yet it is the creation of a transnational civil society within the political framework of this international arrangement that is the foundation of the western security community. Deudney and Ikenberry (1999, p.194) write that the 'cumulative weight of these international homogenizing and interacting forces has been to create an increasingly common identity and culture – a powerful sense that 'we' constitutes more than a traditional community of the nation-state'. This is language that closely approximates Deutsch's security community and would suggest American hegemony facilitates moves in that direction.

Yet these Liberal commentaries overestimate the extent to which the 'distinctively American' liberal consensus is, and can be, embedded in other communities. Central to Deudney and Ikenberry's (1999, pp.192-193) optimism is the claim that a 'common civic identity is intimately associated with capitalism, and its business and commodity cultures'. Yet free market capitalism that is 'distinctively American' cannot, nor has it been, the foundation of the transatlantic security community. As chapter six argues, liberalism became embedded across Western Europe because capitalism was tempered by states that could intervene in the marketplace in order to respond to the needs of those alienated by market force and to meet the aspirations of those seeking social justice. The concern expressed in chapter six is that American hegemony needs to compromise its faith in free market capitalism if it is firstly to stop liberalism becoming disembedded, and if it is to extend the successful post-war transatlantic security community.

The Wilsonian principles advocated by Liberals of the Roosevelt and Truman administrations were central to the construction of the transatlantic security community that emerged around NATO. Moreover, as the concluding sections of this chapter demonstrate, they were central to the peaceful resolution of the Cold War and the continued integration of that community. American foreign policy, however, has not always been committed to the pursuit of these principles. Wilsonian arguments are opposed by a Realist argument that warns of the potential costs to international order if a policy to promote liberal democracy is pursued imprudently.

It would be naïve to assert those as the only obstacles. As chapter three demonstrated in the context of the military dimension and chapter six will demonstrate in the context of the economic dimension, the 'Wilsonian impulse' is restrained by special interests that control foreign policy and use it to pursue particular interests that jeopardise the creation of a security community. Their political significance is undeniably an important obstacle to the maintenance and extension of a security community.

Yet the sophisticated Realism that applies prudence in a way that is not inadvertently allied to these special interests can be normatively justified. While international order may be unsatisfactory in that it accommodates undemocratic regimes, it nonetheless sustains principles that emancipate many from immediate insecurity. Long-term security rests on universal emancipation, but imprudent actions to achieve that goal can make situations worse. The road to hell, Realists are fond of reminding liberal idealists, is paved with good intentions. This argument does not legitimise the particular interests that also oppose a Liberal foreign policy. Rather it points to the potentially self-defeating consequences of certain policies and legitimises on the grounds of prudence those policies that would otherwise be considered hypocritical.

High Stakes and No Alternatives: democracy promotion during the Cold War

Tony Smith (1994, p.107) nicely summarises this dilemma when he writes that

> politics as an art requires the desirable in terms of the possible. The dilemma of leadership is to decide when it is weakness to fail to exploit the inevitable ambiguities, and therefore possibilities, of the historical moment, and when it is foolhardy to attempt to overcome immovable constraints set by a combination of forces past and present. Since options are always open to some extent, greatness requires creating opportunities and taking risks within the limits set by history.

In seeking to promote democracy and possibly extend a security community, America's dilemma revolved around these 'inevitable ambiguities' and 'possibilities, of the historical moment'.

The answers to two sets of questions influenced the way America resolved this dilemma. Firstly, were the forces of democratic change of sufficient strength for the U.S. to be able to offer decisive support? What was the likelihood that a U.S. intervention would be able to influence the politics of a transitional state in a democratic direction? Secondly, if the forces of democracy were not strong, should the U.S. risk undermining relations with the likely victors of the transition and in so doing create international tension between the two states? More to the point, should the U.S. risk undermining a friendly but undemocratic regime by supporting the forces of democracy, if that instability is exploited by an undemocratic *and* unfriendly regime? This dilemma was clearly articulated by President Kennedy when considering U.S. policy towards the Dominican Republic after the death of the long-time dictator Rafael Trujillo. 'There are three possibilities in descending order of preference', he is reported to have said. '[A] decent democratic regime, a continuation of the Trujillo regime, or a Castro regime. We ought to aim at the first, but we really can't renounce the second until we are sure we can avoid the third' (Smith, 1994, p.226).

Here the constraint on U.S. policy was the relative weakness of democratic forces in the Dominican Republic. Yet the risks of democracy promotion were increased by the Cold War context. Undermining the unsatisfactory but nonetheless tolerable (in terms of U.S. particular interests) Trujillo regime would not have been risky had it not been for U.S. perceptions that the other alternative, 'a Castro regime', would have weakened U.S. policy towards the Soviet Union. The U.S. dilemma, therefore, revolved around estimates of the likelihood of instability and the significance of that particular case in terms of the Cold War.

This perception of threat and opportunity was influenced by the preconceptions of special interests. Realists who elevated policy towards the Soviet Union above all other considerations argued that it was in America's interest to support non-democratic anti-Soviet regimes. Roosevelt for instance recognised that Somoza of Nicaragua was a 'Son of a bitch, but' he quickly added, 'at least he's our son of a bitch'. Realists argued, of course, that success in the geopolitical conflict against the Soviet Union was a precondition of long-term security based on a liberal world order. Their argument collapses, however, when it becomes clear that the Soviet threat was wilfully exaggerated. Not only was support for authoritarian regimes a dubious way to fight communist tyranny (a point explored in detail below) but exaggerating the Soviet threat in order to legitimise such policies and then, under that banner of anti-Sovietism, pursue interests at the expense of the local population, was totally unjustified. As critics of U.S. policy have noted, democratic reform movements that challenged the particular interests of U.S. capital, were labelled communist and the forces of the American state were mobilised against them (Chomsky, 1992; Gills, Rocamora and Wilson, 1993).

American commercial interests, in other words, corrupted the normative justification for Realist policies. It may have been prudent not to fully support democratic movements all the time, but when support for authoritarian regimes was motivated by the particular interests of a militarist and/or capitalist elite and not the long term interests of democrats, Realist policies contradicted the aim of constructing a security community.

Yet Realism has not been completely dominant in its control of American foreign policy. Liberal ideas on democracy and foreign policy began to gain political significance following the disaster in South East Asia and public dissatisfaction with the continued Realism of the Nixon Doctrine that indirectly assisted pro-American regimes in place of direct intervention (Litwak, 1984). President Carter's emphasis on human rights and a North-South dialogue was a response that sought to make a clearer link between support for democracy and American interests. By supporting dictatorships and dismissing genuine social reform programmes as Kremlin-inspired plots, American Realism was, according to Carter, swimming against the tide of post-colonial history. In effect American Realism was simply driving the repressed into the hands of the Soviet Union. In the name of anti-communism, American policy was in fact contributing to communism's appeal in the Third World.

Informed by the work of the Trilateral Commission, Carter sought to redress the process by instituting a 'dialogue' with the South (Melanson, 1996, pp.95-110). By understanding and responding to the needs of individuals across the South U.S. policy would contribute to the mobilisation of those who wanted to be integrated into the West rather than the East. The central focus for that dialogue would be human rights and Carter made sure of its significance in political discourse by establishing a human rights bureau in the State Department[3]. The U.S., furthermore, would cut its support to human rights violators regardless of their loyalty in the geopolitical battle with the Soviet Union.

Where Realists saw little scope for democracy promotion, therefore, Carter was more willing to take chances. He was, as Smith notes (1994, p.244), more willing

> to push obstinate authoritarians to reform even at the risk of damaging other American interests that might be involved, and so to attack the premises of realistic thinking with its weary resignation to the SOB's of this world. While not oblivious to the counsels of prudence, Carter was far less persuaded than liberals since FDR's time had been that the limits of American power and

the seriousness of the East-West struggle dictated a go-slow approach to authoritarian allies who were faithful in their opposition to Soviet expansion.

If Carter challenged Realism's dominance, his philosophy and his view of the Soviet Union was far from hegemonic across the national security policymaking community. Indeed when the Somoza regime in Nicaragua was overthrown in 1979, Realists in the United States blamed Carter's human rights diplomacy. With increasing Soviet influence in the Third World, the political significance of the Realist criticism increased and Carter's eventual concession to their recommendations made him seem naïve. As chapter two demonstrated in the context of the strategic balance, Carter's apparent weakness was exploited by neoconservatives who eventually gained control of foreign policy through the election of Reagan to the White House. Realism was to reassert itself through the Reagan Doctrine which promised to assist 'freedom fighters' in their opposition to Soviet backed communists. While Reagan's supporters (Kirkpatrick, 1982) sought to justify its support of authoritarian regimes on ideological grounds – they were more likely to reform than pro-Soviet totalitarian regimes, and only tolerated rather than committed human rights abuses – the driving force behind Reagan's policy was the geopolitical battle with the Soviet Union.

The record of Carter's policy, however, should not be dismissed as naïve simply because it failed to maintain control on U.S. foreign policy. Indeed the fatuous logic of the Reagan Doctrine and the motivation to expose its brutal consequences stems in part from Carter's willingness to emphasise human rights. More significantly, Carter's influence on the development of democracy is less negative than neoconservative critics had it at the time. Firstly, the anti-American nature of the Third World revolutions in the late 1970s was less a consequence of the withdrawal of U.S. aid than it was the result of previous American support for right-wing dictatorships. As Steinmetz (1994) notes, the nature of the Sandinista regime in Nicaragua was influenced less by Carter's policy than it was the long history of what they considered to be American imperialism. If there had been an opportunity to influence the nature of the transition it was in 1973-1974 when the Somoza regime was weak and the opposition movement was still moderate. Yet the Realism informing U.S. policy at that time meant the Nixon administration was unwilling to take the risks involved in ditching Somoza. Indeed Steinmetz argues that the pro-Soviet nature of the Sandinistas was not decided until the Realist policies of the

Reagan administration sought to overthrow their regime. Only then were the Sandinista's driven to adopt a pro-Soviet stance.

This argument redeems Carter's policy somewhat, but only by stressing the limited opportunities for successful human rights diplomacy. A stronger defence of Carter's record arises out his influence on East European democratic reform. As noted, Carter linked technical and economic assistance for other states to their human rights practices. In the mid-to-late 1970s, the Communist regimes of Eastern Europe, including the Soviet Union, were almost desperate to gain this kind of support from the United States. Carter's emphasis on arms control and disarmament predisposed him towards détente, but the influence of interstate cooperation went beyond mitigating the military dimension of the security dilemma. By linking human rights to arms control and trade the Carter administration turned interstate cooperation into a lever for democratic reform. Even if this link was tacit, East European and Soviet leaders were conscious that their human rights record would influence their chances of cooperation with the U.S.

Carter's emphasis on human rights combined with the political movements that emerged across Eastern Europe following the signing of the Helsinki Final Act, contributed to the processes that undermined Communist control. For as long as the United States was concerned about human rights and was simultaneously willing to cooperate at the interstate level, those in the East that had an interest in cooperation with the West would pressure Communist governments across Eastern Europe to make tactical concessions to human rights activists. For example, Daniel Thomas (1999, p.226) cites the example of a Charter 77 activist in Czechoslovakia who 'was actually told by his secret police "tail" that the Interior Ministry was prepared to arrest the entire Charter 77 leadership, but was being restrained by the Foreign Ministry'. In effect the combination of interstate cooperation and concern for human rights provided protection for human rights activists on the ground across Eastern Europe.

That protection, however, was only as strong as the incentives given to East European governments to make concessions to the human rights agenda. If Communist governments had nothing to gain in terms of trade or arms control, why would they be concerned about what the U.S. thought of their human rights record? It is testament to the disingenuous nature of the neoconservative critique that forced Carter to abandon his emphasis on human rights that it failed to recognise this link. It is counterfactual to argue that the imposition of martial law in Poland in the early 1980s could have been prevented by maintaining the link made by Carter, yet it is clear that the Reagan administration was powerless to stop it. By breaking the link between interstate cooperation and human rights activism, the Reagan administration's human rights rhetoric was reduced to political insignificance across Eastern Europe.

It is totally misplaced to suggest the revolutions of 1989 were a consequence of Reagan's human rights and peace through strength agenda. Ironically, the accusations of naïve idealism that were levelled at Carter's policies are perhaps more accurate when directed at Reagan's human rights rhetoric. By demonstrating a seriousness about human rights and by linking human rights records to the prospect of interstate cooperation, Carter's policies had a concrete influence on the ground. By combining human rights rhetoric with a confrontational stance, Reagan's policies had little influence on the ground and possibly made the situation worse for human rights activists. Reaganite Realists would of course claim that peace through strength was a response to the so-called window of vulnerability that the administration deemed necessary. That maybe so, but as chapter three argued peace through strength was largely based on a myth that mobilised support for policies that suited the particular interests of those with a vested interest in confrontation. In terms of promoting democracy, extending the security community and guaranteeing America's long term interests, it was a policy that had many costs.

Human rights activism survived the early 1980s despite and not because of the policies of the Reagan administration. Promoting democracy in Eastern Europe, as chapter three also argued, was facilitated by the process of interstate cooperation and disarmament. By resolving the American dilemma in these terms, the Bush administration had to overcome the opposition of the military. Yet military opinion was not the only constraint on the Bush administration. As the democratic movements across Eastern Europe became increasingly significant the U.S. faced several dilemmas. When seeking to legitimise the democratic revolutions and integrate the new regimes into the transatlantic security community, U.S. policy was in danger of provoking Soviet traditionalists in a way that jeopardised the reform process. The final sections of this chapter demonstrate how the administration resolved that dilemma. Its conclusions reinforce the main point made here: the Cold War ended with the U.S. pursuing a policy based on cooperation with the Soviet state *and* a commitment to the liberal principles that underpinned the western security community.

"Backing-off principles" to back Gorbachev?

The understated way in which the Bush administration greeted the events of 1989 and in particular the collapse of the Berlin Wall has led one commentator to label the President a 'reluctant revolutionary'. 'The inherent drama of the Bush administration', writes Harvey Sicherman, (1999, p.301) was 'the attempt by an evolutionary to grapple with the revolutionary'. Certainly the failure to capture the moment in presidential rhetoric was symptomatic of the difficulties Bush had in following the style set by President Reagan. And while Bush's refusal as he put it to 'dance up and down on the wall' may have been the response of a 'natural' conservative, its political position was strengthened by those, particularly within the administration, who saw such prudent Realism as a satisfactory response to the unfolding uncertainty.

As chapter three demonstrated, following the initial security review the Bush administration was less uncertain as to Gorbachev's intentions. Rather it's main concern revolved around his ability to implement them. The intelligence and policymaking communities, it seems, were divided between the "glass half-empty" opinion that saw Gorbachev's reforms as likely to fail[4], and the "glass half-full" view that was more optimistic. It is clear, however, that the major players within the administration saw Gorbachev as the most likely Soviet leader to cooperate on American terms. Certainly after Baker's meeting with Shevardnadze at Jackson Hole in October and the President's meeting with Gorbachev at Malta in December 1989, the administration had dropped the idea of 'testing' Gorbachev in favour of cooperating with him on points of mutual advantage (Baker, 1995, pp.144-152). As noted below, when democracy began to take hold in the republics and an unelected Gorbachev clung to the CPSU as a vanguard for reform, many in the U.S. began to question Bush's commitment to Gorbachev. Yet in 1989 and 1990 at least, it seems the Bush administration decided to work with Gorbachev because there seemed no democratic alternative that could offer and deliver the concessions to America's vision of international order in the way Gorbachev could.

While Gorbachev's political fortunes would ultimately be determined by domestic events, the American administration was sensitive to the influence U.S. statements and actions had on Kremlin politics. For example, the Office of Soviet Analysis (SOVA) in the CIA was sceptical of Gorbachev's chances but pointed to ways in which the U.S. could help. It argued that:

foreign policy achievements that allow him to justify further cuts in military spending on the basis of a reduction in external threat would give him more room for manoeuvre. Western actions that could be presented by his opponents as attempts to "take advantage" of Soviet internal instability could hurt Gorbachev[5].

The dilemma for the Bush administration in trying to consolidate the European security community was, as the President himself put it, 'figuring out exactly where the line was and what was likely to be seen by the Soviets as provocative' (Bush and Scowcroft, 1998, p.40). Thus on his trip to Eastern Europe in the summer of 1989 Bush wanted to be seen as supporting 'freedom and democracy...in a way that would not make us appear gloating over'. While the President, as he put it, refused to 'back-off my principles because it offended Gorbachev', he was aware that 'hot rhetoric would needlessly antagonise the militant elements within the Soviet Union and the Pact, and might cause them to rise up against these changes and perhaps against their perpetrator, Gorbachev' (Bush and Scowcroft, 1998, p.115).

There were, however, limits to the Bush administration's willingness to compromise with Gorbachev in a manner that gave him foreign policy successes and boosted his political standing. While reviewing policy, the administration's consultations with Henry Kissinger had leaked to the press. True to his Realist philosophy, Kissinger had proposed doing a deal with the Soviet Union over the political fate of Eastern Europe. The liberals in the State Department were strongly opposed to such a policy. Negotiating with the Soviets in this way would in the eyes of Assistant Secretary Rozanne Ridgeway, simply legitimise the Soviet presence there. The public rejection of the Kissinger plan by Secretary of State James Baker was symbolic[6]. Thanks to political activism across transnational civil society, Eastern Europe was democratising. The U.S. could assist this process by doing nothing that would either legitimise the Soviet empire or alarm Soviet traditionalists so that they felt insecure without the empire (Beschloss and Talbott, 1993 pp.19-20; Matlock, 1995, pp.190-192).

In fact it was the logic of maintaining and expanding the NATO security community that took priority in the Bush administration. As is demonstrated below, on certain issues such as SNF modernisation and conventional arms control, management of NATO and support for Gorbachev's political standing worked in the same direction. On the issue of German reunification, however, the two seemed diametrically opposed. When this became clear, the U.S. worked hard to soften the blow for

Gorbachev, but ultimately it refused to compromise on the issue of a united Germany being allowed to exercise its sovereign right to NATO membership.

NATO Unity and Arms Control

Chapter two demonstrated how American arms control policy was motivated by the political objective of removing Soviet troops from Eastern Europe in order to reassure the people of that region that it was relatively safe to support their revolutions. This rationale led many politically significant actors, notably Scowcroft, to support the May 1989 initiative. Yet the character and certainly the timing of that proposal can also be explained in terms of the American response to a developing crisis within NATO. This crisis had been prompted by the impending obsolescence of the Lance missile. The issue had been politicised not only by Gorbachev's unilateral concessions that began to remove Soviet conventional superiority, but also by Chancellor Kohl's increasing opposition to a Follow-on-to-Lance (FOTL). Such weapons, of course, were designed to destroy the eastern part of the country that he would soon be governing. In the context of a united Germany, such weapons made no sense at all. The initial American position, however, supported strongly by Britain, was that abandoning modernisation would lead to a nuclear-free Europe and thus undermine NATO's strategy that had, according to them, guaranteed post-war European peace.

The NATO dilemma was a familiar one: how best to respond to the Soviet threat without undermining the principles that had guaranteed peace in the transatlantic community. Ultimately, Bush's May 1989 CFE proposal was a response to the latter priority. Chapter three demonstrated its role in reciprocating Gorbachev's disarmament initiatives and giving the political space for democracy to flourish across Eastern Europe. These were worthy goals, they were however secondary to the role the May 1989 proposal played in preserving NATO unity. It was designed primarily to ease NATO's crisis by addressing the conventional imbalance and thus eliminating the need for a short range nuclear capability. The American conversion to arms control rather than modernisation began with Baker's first tour of Europe as Secretary of State. He put it to Norwegian Prime Minister Gro Brundtland, that modernisation was a matter of demonstrating resolve. Brundtland simply replied "What does 'showing resolve' mean in terms of our specific agenda". Baker goes on: 'Both she and the Danish Foreign Minister Ufe Elleman Jensen, argued that this debate over a weapons system really had nothing to do with military requirements, but it had everything to do with politics - and their politics were distinctly not Britain's'. Further support for this approach was given by Dutch Foreign Minister Hans Van Den Broek, who, according to Baker, said 'We talk too much about modernisation which just creates problems for Germany and not enough about what we actually need'. Baker left Europe agreeing with Broek that the May 1989 NATO summit needed an arms control plan. President Bush too came under pressure to resolve the developing crisis. President Mitterand of France had urged Bush at the Kennebunkport meeting in May 1989, to rescue NATO from the 'poisonous debate' on FOTL. 'Under Mitterand's influence', Beschloss and Talbott (1993, p.77) write that 'Bush's focus shifted from the reasons for doing less in CFE, which were military, to the reasons for doing more, which were diplomatic and political'. In their memoirs Bush and Scowcroft (1998, p.77) claim they reached this conclusion before Mitterand's visit. Yet it is clear that Mitterand supported their effort to 'find a way to help Helmut Kohl without letting NATO drift'.

The chosen tactic to head off an alliance split over the nuclear issue was to seize the initiative at the conventional level (Bush and Scowcroft, 1998, p.65). The May 1989 CFE proposal was combined with a NATO decision to enter into negotiations to achieve the partial reduction of American and Soviet land based nuclear forces to equal and verifiable levels. A decision on FOTL was postponed to 1992[7]. The crisis passed, dialogue had produced consensus and ultimately the issue was overtaken by events. The important point here, is that NATO unity was the main priority in the arms control proposal. Strategic imperatives were clearly low down its list of priorities and were, as the opposition by the military suggested, reasons for not acting[8]. America's arms control policy was motivated by the twin political motives of liberating Eastern Europe and managing the western security community. Eventually, America's proposal, guided by the non-British European opinion, united NATO in a manner that also reinforced Gorbachev's political standing. This was not the case when considering the issue of German reunification.

German Reunification

With the collapse of the Warsaw Pact provoking doubts about the long term legitimacy of NATO[9], the administration was quick to reinforce the centrality of the alliance to its vision of post-Cold War Europe. In fact, following his meeting at Malta with Gorbachev, Bush spoke to his NATO allies and argued 'the alliance was established...to provide the basis for precisely the extraordinary evolution which is occurring in Eastern Europe today....The task before us is to consolidate the fruits of the peaceful revolution and provide architecture for continued peaceful change' (Bush and Scowcroft, 1998, p.200). "New Atlanticism", as this policy became known, was a clear expression of the Wilsonian impulse[10]. Some Soviets, Gorbachev included, also recognised the stabilising influence America's presence had on the continent. Yet the political opposition to this view was of greater significance in Moscow than it was in Washington. That opposition was strongest when it became clear that American policy sought to integrate a united Germany in NATO. While American liberals were motivated by the idea of consolidating and extending the liberal security community, that was not how Soviet traditionalists saw it.

Here we clearly see in practice the dilemmas that chapter four articulated in theory. A policy designed to extend a security community created a security dilemma for those outside that community as a politically significant group remained unconvinced of its rationale and felt threatened by the move. Specifically, while New Thinkers in the Soviet Union were comfortable with the idea of a united Germany in NATO and in fact preferred it to a neutral and possibly nuclear Germany, "traditionalists" saw it as a threat to Soviet security. The intensity of the traditionalist opposition on this issue clearly identifies Soviet uncertainty and the Soviet security dilemma.

The inverse of this was an America dilemma that sought the most appropriate way to exploit the political opportunities without undermining an established order. Specifically it revolved around the issue of how best to integrate Germany into the democratic community institutionalised by NATO without strengthening the traditionalist position in the Soviet Union, undermining the prospect of inter-state cooperation and risking the process of democratisation there[11]. The other solution of course, was either to deny Germany's right to reunify as it wished or allow reunification to take place and reform the European security framework so that NATO was either disbanded or at least not strengthened by a united Germany. Both these alternatives were unsatisfactory to America, of course, because they undermined the liberal norms that had helped construct the security community across Western Europe.

Yet as German actions on both sides of the border in late 1989 and early 1990 increased the prospect of early reunification, the proposals put forward for the international arrangements seemed unable to avoid such a trade-off. A neutral Germany within a regional arrangement that downgraded NATO and invested hopes for security in a pan-European organisation seemed to be the preferred Soviet plan. While American policymakers often had recourse to the Helsinki principles on several occasions they generally dismissed the CSCE as either a 'talking shop' or as an institution providing collective security that, like the League of Nations or United Nations 'was, in the end, no security at all' (Bush and Scowcroft, 1998, p.249). They certainly had no intention of privileging the CSCE over NATO.

Other proposals sought to impose conditions on a united Germany such as its alliance affiliation or its level of arms and therefore evoked the parallels with the Versailles Treaty that the American administration was at pains to avoid. Given the strength of the traditionalist thinking on this issue, Soviet policy had no sympathy for German self-determination. In light of the emotion aroused by Soviet-German history it was, as the most enlightened of New Thinkers noted, 'useless to appeal to forgiveness or to argue that every nation has the right to self-determination'(Shevardnadze, 1991, p.132). If Germany was to reunify it would do so under conditions *imposed* by the four wartime powers. To Wilsonian opinion in the Bush administration the Soviet position unduly punished Germans and risked sowing the seeds of future resentment[12]. Brent Scowcroft was strongest on this issue. His inclination was to allow Germany to reunify without any outside interference whatsoever (Rice and Zelikow, 1995, p.226)[13]. The Soviet Union, however, was not the only state in Europe nervous at the prospect of a united Germany. Both the British and French governments expressed reservations and were keen to at least maintain influence in the process. Sensitive to the allies' concerns, and increasingly sensitive to the precarious position of Soviet new thinkers, U.S. policy never adopted Scowcroft's extreme. It proposed the 2-plus-4 forum for dealing with unification making sure that the 2 preceded the 4 as a symbol that the two Germany's were the primary actors in determining their own fate.

Once in the negotiations, however, the U.S. opposed any proposal that sought to decide Germany's alliance membership or single it out for a particular arms control status. The U.S. supported Chancellor Kohl's position that Germany would give promises about future troop strength but would not be subject to these assurances until all other countries in Europe had also placed limits on their troops. In this way 'singularity' was avoided and Germany's right to determine it own security was protected. A similar strategy was adopted towards the issue of external alliances. While the administration preferred to see a united Germany in NATO, they clearly could not force it to be part of an alliance if it was also to abide by the principles of a community. Again the tactic was to trust Kohl's ability to convince his policymaking community that being a member of NATO was in Germany's best interests and hope that the New Thinker's commitment to self-determination prevailed in Soviet Union.

The 'Wilsonian Impulse' that Hampton identifies as central to the transatlantic security community created in the post-war period clearly motivated the Bush administration as it managed the transition to the post-Cold War period. The danger of course was that pursuing its ideological agenda in this manner risked losing the possibility of integrating the Soviet Union into the liberal democratic security community. Both Gorbachev and Shevardnadze knew their position and their reforms were in danger if they were seen to sell out traditional Soviet interests. A growing conservative opposition led by Politburo member Yegor Ligachev had watched the outer-empire crumble and were making a stand on the issue of Germany, portraying the issue as another "Munich" (Rice and Zelikow, pp.179-180). Influenced by this opinion, Soviet government directives for Shevardnaze would describe the inclusion of a unified Germany in NATO as 'unacceptable to us'[14] and in response Shevardnadze's position at the 2-plus-4 meetings would harden (Bush and Scowcroft, 1998, pp.269-270).

Yet despite this political pressure from conservatives both Shevardnadze and Gorbachev were ultimately unable to resist the logic of the American position that a united Germany be allowed to choose its own alliance. The breakthrough it seems came at the June 1990 Washington summit when Gorbachev agreed that under the Helsinki principles a united Germany had the right to join whatever alliance it wished[15]. The political costs imposed by such a concession were symbolised by the consternation Gorbachev's actions caused among the Soviet delegation in Washington. While Gorbachev felt comfortable with the concession, Shevardnadze at first refused to be associated with it, even contradicting Gorbachev in front of the American delegation (Bush and Scowcroft, 1998, pp.282-3). While fundamentally believing in Germany's right, Shevardnadze's opposition was motivated by two factors. At the personal level he felt as if he was being cast as the scapegoat in order to protect Gorbachev from the heavy criticism that would inevitably come from such a move[16]. Yet as he explains in his memoirs, NATO was considered a military alliance which posed a security threat to the Soviet Union. His firm stance on the issue was motivated not by a desire to deny Germany its sovereign rights, but by the need to convince Western states that NATO had to be transformed if the Soviet Union was to allow German membership (Shevardnadze, 1991, p.138).

The Bush administration had been sensitive to the dangers of portraying the issue in terms of winners and losers. Indeed reforming NATO was central to the idea of allowing the Soviet Union to save face as it conceded to the U.S. agenda. It had been part of a nine point reassurance plan that was designed initially to convince Gorbachev to allow Germany to unite and then to ease his task of convincing traditionalists to back his policy (Bush and Scowcroft, 1998, pp.273-274). The American task in softening the political opposition in the Soviet Union was guided by Shevardnadze. At the June 1990 Berlin 2+4 meeting, for example, Shevardnadze explained in private that the tough Soviet stance was 'window dressing' and not necessarily a reversal of Gorbachev's Washington position. He conveyed to Baker the importance of positive public steps at the forthcoming NATO meeting in London (Baker, 1995, pp.256-257). Acting on this advice NATO responded with a declaration that seemingly gave Gorbachev the political ammunition needed to pass his concessions through the Party Congress that was meeting almost simultaneously (Bush and Scowcroft, 1998, p.293). Shevardnadze notes that 'without the decisions passed by the NATO Council in London, membership would have been unacceptable to us' (Shevardnadze, 1991, p.145; Rice and Zelikow, 1995, pp.343-344, p.472). Gorbachev's close adviser, Anatolii Chernayev goes even further, suggesting that the London summit even averted a coup attempt against Gorbachev in 1990 (Rice and Zelikow, 1995, p.332).

Thus by being sensitive to Soviet domestic politics and effectively forming a transnational coalition with Soviet New Thinkers that helped guide the process of reciprocation, the U.S. seemingly transcended its dilemma. Germany's right to self determination was protected, the western security community was strengthened and the reformist position in Moscow was seemingly in tact. German reunification, however, despite being handled carefully by the Bush administration was a bitter pill for Soviet conservatives to swallow. From 1989, Chernayev notes, Gorbachev's relations with the military began to deteriorate (Wohlforth, 1996, p.85). While avoiding a coup in 1990, the Soviet leader would not be so fortunate in 1991. German reunification contributed to that process. As such, Bush's relentless support for German ambitions despite the costs to Gorbachev is somewhat at odds with accounts that suggest the president's commitment to Gorbachev's political standing came at the expense of America's ideological agenda. That conclusion should be reversed. Indeed, one may even compare the American stance to that of a determined player in a game of diplomatic chicken. While it valued the prospect of a constructive relationship with a democratic USSR and saw Gorbachev's leadership as the vehicle for securing that, it was willing to risk that goal in order to demonstrate its resolve on the issue of German self determination.

Ultimately American diplomacy allowed Gorbachev to concede to the U.S. position without immediately ending the influence of 'new thinking' and terminating the constructive U.S.-Soviet relationship. This reduces to counterfactual history the question of how far the Bush administration would have gone to see Germany in NATO. It is quite clear, however, that the U.S. was heavily committed to this outcome. Moreover, to the extent that there was a consensus in the executive branch on this and to the extent that Congressional opinion was either part of that consensus or politically insignificant, it is not certain that one can identify a normative dilemma for the United States as it approached the prospect of German reunification. Whether that consensus would have persisted in the face of more determined opposition from the Soviet Union is again a matter of counterfactual history. The extent to which that commitment was maintained reveals the massive influence of liberal internationalism. It cannot be overlooked as is done by the Realist commentaries that pay scant attention to the normative content of American foreign policy. It is also testament to the skill of the Bush administration's handling of what was clearly a delicate situation that America's dilemma was reduced to almost imperceptible levels.

Ending the Cold War - Collapse of the Soviet Union

The same cannot be said of America's approach to the collapse of the Soviet Union itself. Without casting judgement on the administration's policy it is clear from the politically significant opposition to Bush's policy, that America faced a security dilemma on how best to respond to the declarations of independence by the Soviet republics, notably those in the Baltics.

America's Baltic dilemma was at its most intense in March 1990 and January 1991. Under the freedom provided by *Glasnost*, Baltic independence movements or 'National Fronts' had grown in popularity. Under *democratization* this trend made regional Communists realise that their position was threatened if they were seen to be mere puppets of the CPSU. In December 1989, therefore, the Communist Party of Lithuania declared its independence from the CPSU despite Gorbachev's insistence that Moscow maintain control. The initial crisis transpired when after the March 1990 elections the Lithuanian Supreme Council was dominated by those campaigning on an independence platform. It wasted no time in declaring national independence on March 11 and electing the noncommunist nationalist leader Vyataus Landsbergis as President. The

Soviets reacted by imposing an embargo on Lithuania in an attempt to coerce the withdrawal of the declaration. A way out was proposed when the law of secession was passed in April. This stipulated that a referendum requiring a two-thirds majority would start a process of negotiations. Before those negotiations could begin, however, the declaration of independence had to be withdrawn, something the Lithuanians were not prepared to do.

The American response to the subsequent standoff was bitterly contested. While the United States had never formerly recognised the Baltics as part of the Soviet Union, the Bush administration was all too aware of 'the reality of the situation' (Bush and Scowcroft, 1998, p.207). Scowcroft (Bush and Scowcroft, 1998, p.207) clearly identifies the administration's dilemma and implicitly indicates where its sympathies lay:

> We strongly supported self-determination as a matter of principle, as we were doing regarding German reunification. As a practical point, however, we were aware of Gorbachev's vulnerability to the political threat posed by nationalism. The people within the Party who most strongly opposed him on this issue were not those we would wish to see replacing him.

Bush (1998, p.207) makes clear once again his fear at the time that 'rhetoric might produce the military backlash and set back the cause of freedom throughout the Soviet Union rather than move it forward'. Furthermore, 'if there was violence, realistically, there was nothing the United States could do about it, and we would have blood on our own hands for encouraging the Lithuanian to bite off more than they could chew' (Bush and Scowcroft, 1998, p.215). Thus, in contrast to its position on German unification, the administration was not prepared to support Lithuanian self-determination in a manner that would hasten Gorbachev's downfall. '*[T]oo much was at stake*' Bush writes, 'in our relationship, and for other countries, to allow the situation in Lithuania to torpedo the painful progress we had made in U.S.-Soviet relations' (1998, p.276, emphasis added).

At every opportunity therefore the administration would counsel caution when in communication with independence leaders. Prior to the March 1990 declaration of independence, for instance, Ambassador Matlock met with a Lithuanian delegation who asked him how the U.S. would react to the forthcoming declaration. When he told them the Lithuanians would have U.S. sympathy but argued against early recognition on the grounds that it might encourage Soviet hardliners to use force, a sense of betrayal was evident. Matlock (1995, p.231) recalls that:

> One of the guests (I have forgotten who) looked me in the eye and observed, "So we're on our own. You're for democracy and self-determination, but we're on our own". The words stung. "Spiritually and politically, you're not entirely on your own", I said to put things in perspective. "We do not recognize that you are legally part of the Soviet Union, and we never will unless that is what the people of Lithuania freely choose. If there should be attempts to use force against you or apply an economic boycott, our reaction will be strong though nonviolent".

The personal dilemma is clearly evident here. Yet while Matlock thought the U.S. had to react to Moscow's punitive measures, he, like Bush and Scowcroft, saw a possible worsening of the situation if the U.S. overreacted (Matlock, 1995, p.355). *America's* normative dilemma was reflected in the political opposition the administration courted with this stance. On the 21 March, for example, the Senate voted on a resolution introduced by Senator Helms calling for the immediate recognition of Lithuania. While the administration managed to defeat that resolution by a vote of 59 to 36, Bush clearly identifies Congress as a continuing source of pressure and restraint (Bush and Scowcroft, 1998, p.216; p.226).

The Washington summit of June 1990, it will be recalled, was a crucial turning point in the diplomacy of German reunification. In anticipation of its importance, the administration sought ways that would allow Gorbachev to represent the summit as a success even though he would be conceding to the American position on German reunification. A trade agreement quickly became the focus of Gorbachev's and therefore the administration's attention. But Bush could not, as he put it, 'ignore Lithuania' (1998, p.280). He new that whatever he agreed with Gorbachev, Congress would not ratify it without progress on Lithuania. As Scowcroft put it at the time: "It would be hard to explain to Congress why we were negotiating economic agreements with Moscow that would help their economy at a time when they are using economic leverage to squeeze the Lithuanians" (1998, p.224). Congressional pressure, furthermore began to expose small cracks in the administration's response. While Baker, clearly favoured protecting the overall relationship with the Soviet Union, Scowcroft feared the policy was overlooking the interests America had in Lithuania itself. Sensitive to the consensus in the administration, however, Scowcroft decided a political challenge 'would be fruitless and a time wasting exercise' (1998, p.225).

Consensus in the administration, however, doesn't remove the fact that the U.S. faced a dilemma. The Senate, for instance voted on May 1 to withold trade benefits from Moscow until the embargo against Lithuania was lifted. Despite getting his way on Germany, the Washington Summit of June 1990 presented Bush with a dilemma: appease Congressional and Lithuanian pressure by punishing Gorbachev's behviour in the Baltics at the risk of losing Gorbachev's support on German reunification; or reward Gorbachev's concession on Germany with a trade agreement at the risk of provoking a backlash in the U.S. Congress for the betrayal of Lithuania.

Once again the administration seemed to find an appropriate compromise between the position of the Congressional leadership and that of his own inclination to support Gorbachev. While the administration would sign a grain and trade agreement, it would not send the package to Congress until the Soviets completed the conditions it had publicly laid out for granting them MFN status: they had to pass legislation on emigration. A secret side of the agreement would be the link between the agreement and the embargo on Lithuania (1994, p.424). As Bush writes: 'We would hand Gorbachev a tangible success in the form of a signed agreement with public stipulations that he had a chance of meeting, but we made sure the agreement would not be implemented until there was substantive progress on Lithuania. There would be no public embarrassment for Gorbachev at home, and we would get the conditions we wanted' (1998, p.285).

The situation in the Baltics began to ease in the second half of 1990, particularly when the moratorium on the declaration of independence, proposed by the more moderate Lithuanian leader Kazimiera Prunskiene was approved by the Lithuanian parliament on 30 June. Tensions were renewed, however, with the draft of a new Union treaty that appeared in the press on 24 November. The draft treaty politically divided the Lithuanian government which resulted in the resignation of Prunskiene. Moscow took advantage of the political turmoil to issue a decree on 10 January instructing the Lithuanian Supreme Council immediately to rescind all 'unconstitutional' acts including the declaration of independence. When on the following day Soviet troops began to use force to occupy government buildings in Vilnius, Lithuanian officials issued a plea to Western governments to take 'determined action' to prevent the Soviet takeover (Matlock, 1995, p.450).

Much had been riding on a constructive U.S.-Soviet relationship in June 1990. The stakes were high as the diplomacy surrounding German unification approached its crucial stage. Yet with Germany reunified and a member of NATO, the administration still did not feel able to politically abandon Gorbachev. It still considered Gorbachev's position as central to the consolidation of the CFE Treaty and the conclusion of a START Treaty. What is more, with Iraq's invasion of Kuwait, Soviet support became crucial in assembling the political and military coalition that would prosecute Desert Shield and Desert Storm. In fact the timing of the Soviet crackdown was particularly sensitive given the fact that the administration had effectively decided to go to war against Iraq once the January 15 U.N. deadline had passed (Bush and Scowcroft, 1998, pp.496-497). The Soviet ability to upset the administration's plans had been illustrated by Soviet Foreign Minister, Yevgeny Primakov's 11th hour diplomacy which prompted one commentator to suggest U.S.-Soviet cooperation had given way to a second Cold War[17].

It is not necessary here to explain the diplomacy surrounding Desert Storm, suffice to say that the U.S. had no intention of risking Soviet support by supplying the "determined action" that the Lithuanians were calling for. Bush privately wrote to Gorbachev on the 23rd January threatening to suspend cooperation and in public the administration appealed to the Soviet Union to observe the human rights commitments under various CSCE documents. Yet the administration refused to recognise Lithuanian independence. In fact, given the U.S. public position that the Lithuanian government had to be in control of its own territory and given the strengthened Soviet military presence following the crackdown, it seemed the U.S. was even further from a position that bestowed diplomatic recognition[18].

In terms of the American reaction to wider political developments in the Soviet Union, the Bush administration's perceived loyalty to Gorbachev was contested by Congress particularly in light of Yeltsin's election as Russian President and his support for Baltic self-determination. For example, Senator Hatch expressed his anger at the administration's stance. 'If ten years ago' he stated in Congress:

> someone had told me that a major, democratic movement would rise in the Soviet Union but the United States would not lift a finger to help the movement prevail, I would have dismissed him totally out of touch with reality. Yet that seems to be what is happening today[19].

In addition to formalising relations with the Baltic states, various Senators proposed the extension of Support for East European Democracy (SEED) legislation to cover the Soviet republics. Yet in the same hearings, an opposite view was heard. Professor Cohen of Princeton University, for example, argued that U.S. did not 'have the wisdom, the power, and therefore, the right to intervene directly in the great and fateful struggles now underway inside the Soviet Union'. Reflecting the uncertainty that constituted America's normative dilemma, he attacked Senator Hatch's view, stating:

> I simply do not recognize this country where they see democrats everywhere, and only Gorbachev holding back the forces of democracy. I don't recognize that country[20].

Thus, despite accusations of betrayal and despite intelligence suggesting Gorbachev's political credibility had 'sunk to near zero'[21], the administration still considered the Soviet leader as the best means of securing American interests (Baker, 1995, p.272). It compromised on technical issues to conclude the START Treaty at the Moscow Summit in July 1991, delivered on the promise of credit guarantees and extended MFN status to the USSR while making special provision for the Baltic states. Moreover, the administration was equally cautious in its response to independence movements elsewhere in the Union. Following the Moscow Summit, for example, the President's speech in Ukraine was labelled by the press "Chicken Kiev" for its reluctance to recognise Ukranian aspirations for independence. In defence of the administration's stance, Scowcroft writes that the President's warning against local despotism was not a veiled attempt to encourage support for Gorbachev's Union Treaty. Rather it was the consequence of a genuine concern that the process of dissolution may be violent as in Yugoslavia and Moldova (Bush and Scowcroft, 1998, p.516). Nevertheless, it was not until the August Coup had removed both Gorbachev and the traditionalist opposition as credible political forces, that the administration felt able to recognise the Baltic and other states of the former Soviet Union.

Conclusion: normative dilemmas and the limits of statecraft

The history of the U.S. response to the collapse of the Soviet outer and inner empire illustrates the political characteristics of a state's normative dilemma. Firstly, in seeking to promote democracy through the diplomatic recognition and political support of its agents, and secondly, in seeking to consolidate the gains of democratic revolutions by extending the institutions of the western security community, the U.S. faced a trade-off. Such policies not only threatened the reform process itself by provoking a conservative backlash against democratic progress, but also endangered the construction of a 'new world order' where the rule of international law replaced the Realist rule of the jungle. The dilemma was, to repeat President Bush, 'figuring out exactly where the line was and what was likely to be seen by the Soviets as provocative' (Bush and Scowcroft, 1998, p.40).

America's dilemma was reflected by arguments that the administration's policy lacked ambition, was overly cautious and too committed to Gorbachev's political fate. There were those in politically significant positions within the administration, but mostly within Congress, who believed U.S. policy underestimated the scope for promoting democracy by overestimating the stakes involved. As Scowcroft retrospectively notes, he feared that the U.S. concern for Gorbachev's political standing overlooked the interests the U.S. had in Lithuanian independence. Yet there were also those who prioritised the stability that Gorbachev's policy could offer either because they valued less the idea of democracy and self determination or because they believed such an emphasis would provoke a undemocratic backlash and undermine an unsatisfactory but tolerable relationship with the Soviet Union. This latter view clearly had strong support in the administration with the President perhaps its strongest advocate.

What is clear, however, is that America's response to the Soviet collapse was a consequence of the Liberal and Realist strands prevalent in its foreign policy discourse. Its dilemma was reflected in the political battle to inform the particular mix of that coalition. On the issue of SNF modernisation, the liberal argument of NATO unity overcame Realist resistance to disarmament. On German reunification, the administration was clearly informed by the Wilsonian impulse and was willing to risk relations with the Soviet Union in order not to repeat the mistakes of 1919. Again NATO unity as an expression of the Wilsonian security community was the administration's priority. On Baltic independence, America's dilemma was more intense. The administration perceived the dangers of a conservative backlash in the Soviet Union to be greater on the Baltic question than on the issue of German reunification. Where the administration worked hard to influence the internal Soviet debate on Germany, it perceived little opportunity to repeat that success with regards to the Baltics. Furthermore, the administration prioritised those goals that were separate to the Baltic issue and required Soviet cooperation: German reunification, prosecution of the Gulf War and completion of arms control negotiations. Certainly, the administration was Realist in its approach but this was no less of a normative stance. There were, in its eyes, limits to America's influence and its ability to consolidate democracy's gains. It sometimes paid for that assessment, but as is clear from retrospective accounts of their role, key actors in the administration believe their prudent approach was justified.

Central to the American response, then, was its assessment of Soviet domestic politics. As in the case of German unification it sometimes made crucial transnational coalitions that assisted the political position of New Thinkers. Yet ultimately the direction of Soviet policy and the fate of the Soviet empire was decided by the political battle between traditionalists and civil society. Both Bush and Scowcroft (1998, p.565) recognise the limits of their role. Bush describes their main accomplishment as guiding and shaping, though not initiating, the critical events that ended the Cold War. Scowcroft is more explicit. He writes modestly:

> It would be gratifying to say that our Eastern European policy - altered from support of those states most rebellious toward the Soviet Union to backing moves for greater freedom - had been among the catalysts of the changes. It was not. But our policy did provide solid encouragement and allowed us to react properly to events (1998, p.180).

Similarly, Bush (1998, p.180) writes that the policy of his administration put the U.S. in a position to take 'full advantage of the wave of liberalism as it moved through the region'. Thus while the achievements of the Bush administration should not be underestimated it is important to recognise that they are limited. U.S. policy existed in the context of interstate relations that, being littered by military power, demanded prudence. While prudence was in this context a virtue it restricted the encouragement statesmen could give to the process of liberalisation and democratisation. The 'wave of liberalism' that swept through Eastern Europe was decisive in ending the Cold War and its decisive agents were found not in Washington but across European civil society. While the Bush administration, unlike the Reagan administration, did nothing to contradict their cause it was their political fight for democracy that ultimately decided the identity of their states and in due course ended the Cold War.

It is important to qualify this view that American foreign policy and European civil society complemented each other perfectly. While the anti-statist ideology of liberalism was certainly a motivating factor for transnational civil society, its view should not be confused with the neoliberalism that has, with American help, embedded itself in many states since 1989. Mary Kaldor, for example, notes that 'instead of forging a new *more responsive* relationship between state and society as civil society theorists of the 1980s had anticipated, the state simply withdrew from large parts of society. What was revealed underneath the layers of state control was not civil society, but uncivility' (Kaldor, 1999, p.203, emphasis added). As the following chapter notes, America's promotion of laissez-faire neoliberalism is undermining the ability of states to respond to the need of its citizens and as such is not only betraying the promise of democracy that was so clear in the events of 1989 but also undermining the foundations of possible security communities. If such a community is to be consolidated and if the western model is to claim victory in the long term then, as Kaldor notes elsewhere (1991, p.39), it too has to change its more recent neoliberal complexion. As the following chapter argues, a clearer understanding of American hegemony and its own democratic identity is central to that process.

Notes

[1] Another starting point for this kind of analysis has been the question of why Germany and Japan have not acted like traditional great powers and pursued policies that balanced American power (Deudney and Ikenberry, 1999, p.188).
[2] This rationale was originally articulated by Secretary of State, John Foster Dulles (Hampton, 1996, p.21). Post-Cold War continuity is clearly illustrated by Hutching's use of the same phrase to describe American thinking during the Bush administration (Hutchings, 1997, p.350).
[3] This institutionalisation of the human rights discourse was also assisted by the creation in Congress of the Commission on Security and Cooperation in Europe. This was the result of Representative Fenwick's secret meeting with human rights activists in Moscow. It would monitor compliance with the Helsinki Final Act, particularly in the human rights. The emerging transnational network of peace and human rights activists in the East and West gained a bureaucratic ally within the U.S. government (Thomas, 1999, p.212).
[4] CIA, Office of Soviet Analysis, 'Gorbachev's Domestic Gambles and Instability in the USSR. An Intelligence Assessment', September 1989. *The Soviet Estimate: U.S. Analysis of the Soviet Union, 1947-1991*, (Washington, D.C.: The National Security Archive & Chadwyck-Healy Inc., 1995), no.00602. See also Beschloss and Talbott, 1993, pp.142-143.
[5] CIA, Office of Soviet Analysis, 'Gorbachev's Domestic Gambles and Instability in the USSR. An Intelligence Assessment', September 1989. *The Soviet Estimate: U.S. Analysis of the Soviet Union, 1947-1991*, (Washington, D.C.: The National Security Archive & Chadwyck-Healy Inc., 1995), no.00602.
[6] *New York Times* 2 March, 1989.
[7] Report adopted by the Heads of State and Government of the North Atlantic Council, Brussels, 30 May 1989. *CD 1989.* pp.283-292.
[8] Bush actually overrode the objections of Admiral Crowe (Bush and Scowcroft, 1998, pp.73-4).
[9] The most infamous prediction can be found in Mearsheimer, 1990.
[10] The connection between the administration's position and earlier Wilsonianism is made even more explicit by Bush insider Robert Hutchings, who uses Dulles's phrase, 'NATO

was for as well as against something', to describe the administration's thinking (Hutchings, 1997, p.390).

[11] Scowcroft claims the administration had made this formulation by mid-November 1989. Bush and Scowcroft, 1998, p.190.

[12] The importance of the Versailles remedial to the Bush administration is clear when in the introduction to their book Bush and Scowcroft specifically claim that avoiding 'the shadow of Versailles' was one of their main foreign policy achievements. Bush and Scowcroft, 1998, p.xiv, p.230, p.242, p.263. On Kohl's sensitivity to the analogy see p.252.

[13] Scowcroft's main concern was that giving the Soviets a chance to bloc unification may force Kohl to trade Germany's membership of NATO for Soviet consent to reunification (Bush and Scowcroft, 1998, p.234).

[14] *O direktivakh dlya peregovrov ministra inostrannykh del SSSRs Prezidentom SShA Bushm I Gosudarstvennym sekretarem Beikerom (Vashington, 4-6 aprelya 1990).* Philip Zelikow Collection (Zelikow-Rice Papers), Box No.3, Hoover Institution Archives, Stanford University.

[15] Baker attributes this concession to the legalistic and logical manner in which Gorbachev approached the issue, but mainly to the emphasis the Soviets had long placed on the CSCE as its preferred security institution (Baker, 1995, pp.253-254).

[16] Shevardnadze could not avoid such a fate a fact that contributed to his resignation in December 1990.

[17] William Safire, *New York Times* 14 February 1991 (Garthoff, 1994, p.446).

[18] For example, Robert Zoellick told Congress in March 1991 that the US did not 'recognize the Baltic governments because they don't meet the tests that have been established, in terms of controlling their own territory, being able to implement legal agreements'. *Soviet Disunion: The American Response.* Hearings Before the Senate Committee on European Affairs of the Committee on Foreign Relations, 6 March 1991 (Washington D.C.: USGPO, 1991).

[19] *Soviet Disunion,* pp.4-5. This frustration with the administration's policy was also expressed by the American Ambassador in the Soviet Union who felt the administration should have been more forthcoming in its attitude to Yeltsin and other opponents of Gorbachev who were consistent with America's values and interests (Matlock, 1995, pp.250-251).

[20] *Soviet Disunion,* p.5.

[21] CIA, Office of Soviet Analysis, 'The Soviet Cauldron', April 1991, *The Soviet Estimate: U.S. Analysis of the Soviet Union, 1947-1991,* (Washington, D.C.: The National Security Archive & Chadwyck-Healy Inc., 1995), no.00603.

References

Baker, III, J.A. (with Thomas M. DeFrank) (1995), *The Politics of Diplomacy. Revolution, War and Peace, 1989-1992,* G.P.Putnam's, New York.

Beschloss, M.R. Talbott, S. (1993), *At the Highest Levels. The Inside Story of the End of the Cold War,* Little, Brown and Company, Boston, Toronto and London.

Bush, G. and Scowcroft, B. (1998), *A World Transformed,* Alfred A.Knopf, New York.

Chomsky, N. (1992), *Deterring Democracy,* Vintage, London.

Deudney, D. and Ikenberry, G.J. (1999), 'The nature and sources of liberal international order', *Review of International Studies,* Vol.25, pp.179-196.

Gaddis, J.L. (1998), *We Now Know. Rethinking Cold War History*, Oxford University Press, Oxford.

Gills, B., Rocamora, J. and Wilson, R. (1993), 'Low-Intensity Democracy', in Barry Gills, Joel Rocamora and Richard Wilson, *Low-Intensity Democracy. Political Power in the New World Order*, Pluto Press, London, pp.3-34.

Hampton, M.N. (1995), 'NATO at the creation: U.S. Foreign Policy, West Germany and the Wilsonian Impulse', *Security Studies*, Vol.4, pp.610-656.

Hampton, M.N. (1996), *The Wilsonian Impulse. U.S. Foreign Policy, the Alliance, and German Unification*, Praeger, Westport.

Hutchings, R.L. (1997), *American Diplomacy and the End of the Cold War. An Insider's Account of US Policy in Europe, 1989-1992*, Johns Hopkins University Press, Baltimore.

Ikenberry, G.J. (1989), 'Rethinking the Origins of American Hegemony', *Political Science Quarterly*, Vol.104, pp.375-400.

Ikenberry, G.J. (1999), 'Liberal Hegemony and the future of American postwar order', in T.V.Paul and J. Hall (eds.), *International Order and the Future of World Politics*, Cambridge University Press, Cambridge, pp.123-145.

Ikenberry, G.J and Kupchan, C.A. (1990), 'Socialization and hegemonic power', *International Organization*, Vol.44, pp.283-315.

Kaldor, M. (1991), 'After the Cold War', in Mary Kaldor (ed.), *Europe From Below. An East-West Dialogue*, Verso, London and New York, pp.27-48.

Kaldor, M. (1999), 'Transnational civil society', in Tim Dunne and Nicholas J. Wheeler, *Human Rights in Global Politics*, Cambridge University Press, Cambridge, pp.195-213.

Kirkpatrick, J.J. (1982), *Dictatorships and Double Standards: Rationalism and Reason in Politics*, Simon and Schuster, New York.

Litwak, R.S. (1984), *Détente and the Nixon Doctrine : American foreign policy and the pursuit of stability,1969-1976*, Cambridge University Press, Cambridge.

Lundestad, G. (1990), *The American 'Empire' and Other Studies of U.S. Foreign Policy in Comparative Perspective*, Oxford University Press and Norwegian University Press, Oxford.

Matlock, J. (1995), *Autopsy of an Empire. The Ambassador's Account of the Collapse of the Soviet Union*, Random House, New York.

Mearsheimer, J. (1990), 'Back to the Future: Instability in Europe After the Cold War', *International Security*, Vol.15, pp.5-56.

Melanson, R.A. (1996), *American foreign policy since the Vietnam War : the search for consensus from Nixon to Clinton*, M.E. Sharpe, Armonk, N.Y.

Rice, C. and Zelikow, P. (1995), *Germany Unified and Europe Transformed. A Study in Statecraft*, Harvard University Press, London, Cambridge, MA.

Risse-Kappen, T. (1995), *Cooperation Among Democracies: The European Influence on U.S. Foreign Policy*, Princeton University Press, Princeton, pp.357-399.

Risse-Kappen, T. (1996), 'Collective Identity in a Democratic Community: The Case of NATO', in P.J.Katzenstein (ed.), *The Culture of National Security. Norms and Identity in World Politics*, Columbia University Press, New York.

Robinson, W.I. (1998), *Promoting Polyarchy. Globalization, U.S. Intervention, and Hegemony*, Cambridge University Press, Cambridge.

Ruggie, J.G. (1993), 'Multilateralism: The Anatomy of an Institution', in John Gerard Ruggie (ed.), *Multilateralism Matters. The Theory and Praxis of an Institutional Form*, Columbia University Press, New York, pp.3-47.

Shevardnadze, E. (translated by Catherine A. Fitzpatrick) (1991), *The Future Belong to Freedom*, Sinclair-Stevenson Ltd., London.

Sicherman, H. (1999), 'Review Essay: George Bush, Reluctant Revolutionary', *Orbis*, Vol.43, pp.299-315.

Smith, T. (1994), *America's Mission. The United States and the Worldwide Struggle for Democracy in the Twentieth Century*, Princeton University Press, Princeton.

Steinmetz, S. (1994), *Democratic Transition and Human Rights: Perspectives on U.S. Foreign Policy*, State University of New York Press, New York.

Thomas, D.C. (1999), 'The Helsinki Accords and Political Change in Eastern Europe', in Thomas Risse, Stephen C. Ropp and Kathryn Sikkink (eds.), *The Power of Human Rights. International Norms and Domestic Change*, Cambridge University Press, Cambridge, pp.205-233.

Weber, S. (1993), 'Shaping the Postwar Balance of Power: Multilateralism in NATO', in John Gerard Ruggie (ed.), *Multilateralism Matters. The Theory and Praxis of an Institutional Form*, Columbia University Press, New York, pp.233-292.

Wohlforth, W. (ed.) (1996), *Witnesses to the End of the Cold War*, Johns Hopkins, Baltimore.

6 'American' Hegemony: the economic dimension

Introduction

Chapter four argued that order was only enduring so long as it was worthwhile in terms of individual needs and aspirations. Essentially order would be securitised if it failed to firstly provide for the basic human needs of individuals; secondly to guarantee individuals a significant voice in the dialogue that constructed order; and finally to respond to the aspirations of individuals in a manner that didn't impinge on the provision of the first two conditions. Transforming political community so that others become seen as extensions of the self, and common security becomes embedded in the culture of all political units, can only be legitimised along these lines. The ideal of a dialogic community justifies intervention in other political units so long as the consequence of that intervention is the inclusion of more individuals in such a dialogue. It is on this basis that chapters five and six assess the role played by American foreign policy and more generally its hegemonic position in the international system.

The foreign policy of the Bush administration at the end of the Cold War was appropriately prudent but was less than decisive in determining the democratic direction of the European revolutions. The most significant actors in steering events in that direction were those found across transnational civil society, notably the peace and human rights coalitions that emerged out of the period of détente. In the late 1980s these networks occupied the political space prudently vacated by the superpowers and made sure that it was held by democrats. In so far as these groups were encouraged and to a certain extent protected by the prospect of U.S.-Soviet cooperation, particularly during the Carter years, then American foreign policy had a role to play in their rise to power. The American role, however, was less than decisive. In fact by acting cautiously so as not to provoke a Soviet backlash, Bush's foreign policy can be considered a success more for what it didn't do than for what it did.

Hegemony is often identified by the political superstructure and the military 'armour of coercion' that sustains and protects a coherent social order (Robinson, 1998, p.22; Cox, 1999, p.12). Yet it is the nature of that social order that indicates the underlying strength of hegemony and the prospects of enduring stability. If American hegemony is to encourage enduring stability then it has to work towards meeting the conditions of an ideal dialogic community. The previous chapter suggested that its decentralised political structure did help foster dialogue by providing many points of access. It also argued that this helped foster consensus across Europe that the practice of multilateralism further consolidated. When seeking to extend the dialogic community, American policy was sometimes justified in compromising on these principles because the distribution of material capabilities among opponents of such policies would have made it imprudent to do otherwise. An intervention on behalf of democracy would not help democrats if it created international tension that either legitimised repression in the name of 'national security' or started a war, even nuclear war.

In this sense American foreign policy can be normatively justified in reneging on its promise to promote democracy if it is uncertain as to the consequences of that policy or is certain that it will exclude more individuals from the processes that construct community. This chapter takes a more critical view of American hegemony. It is less state centric and focuses on the economic order that the Bretton Woods institutions have overseen. For it is the contention here that the social order created by the liberal capitalist system is not meeting the ideal of a dialogic community. As liberals like Deudney and Ikenberry (1999) note, the capitalist system is fostering a common identity across states and for that reason can be considered progressive. Yet it fails to meet the ideal of a security community if that common identity exists only among those who have the financial and social mobility to benefit from capitalism. To those who do not, or to those who culturally reject the consumerist identity imposed by the marketplace, transnational capitalism is a threat not an opportunity. Danger arises when nothing is done to respond to these concerns and exclusivist identities become politically significant, in the form of a nationalist backlash or transnational networks that are undemocratic.

Here American hegemony is inconsistent with the ideal of a security community. Yet this time its excuse is not normatively justified by prudence. The obstacles to a more responsive American policy are those special interests that perceive it to be in their particular interests to promote a market system even though that system exacerbates social injustice. In the previous chapter it was argued that the decentralised nature of the American political system was a benefit in creating a dialogue the outcome of which was responsive to the needs of others beyond the U.S. This may be so, but when the politically significant positions of that system are penetrated by intellectual communities that ignore or conveniently explain away social injustice, then that system becomes unresponsive. It becomes an obstacle to the creation of a security community and potentially an object of securitisation.

Chapter three argued that the militarist culture that elevates exclusivist and exceptionalist ideas under which military-technical constituencies pursue their own particular interests, blocked a process of disarmament that was in the interest of a wider community. It is the contention of this chapter that America's political culture and a particular reading of its own socio-economic 'success', increases the significance of those ideas under which a transnational capitalist elite pursues its particular interest without responding to the demands of those alienated by the free market. The penetration of the American system by this intellectual community has marginalised many Americans who have simply given up on Washington. By extension, the capitalist penetration of Washington has assisted in the penetration of the international institutions of American hegemony, provoking transnational resistance among those disillusioned with free market capitalism. By listening more intently to the voice of a transnational elite, the liberal economic order has failed to create consensus across those areas it wishes to identify as a security community. So long as it fails to listen to those with values and identities that are not accommodated by free market capitalism then it cannot be considered a community. And so long as capitalism continues to produce social injustice, then the privileged have no right to declare that potential community as being secure.

This chapter traces the development of this unsatisfactory economic system. It argues that the consolidation of the transatlantic security community was assisted by a system that was responsive to the socio-economic and cultural difference of post-war Europe and Japan. As such it laid the foundations for a socially responsible capitalist system on which the Western security community was built. With the collapse of the Bretton Woods system, however, and with the globalisation of capital, power has shifted away from the kind of state that was accountable to its citizens. The mobility of capital now makes it virtually impossible to discipline power in a manner that is responsive to the needs of the community. It pursues its own particular agenda and conversely the needs and aspirations of the wider community are themselves disciplined by transnational capital in manner that facilitates its pursuit of more wealth and even greater power.

As chapter four demonstrated, nuclear weapons robbed the power of democratically elected politicians to respond to the security needs of their citizens. This created a cosmopolitan duty on the part of the nuclear 'haves' to consider the messages from other political units when making their own decisions. The distinction between particular and common security was blurred and New Thinkers recognised that the interests of all were dependent on the fulfillment of this duty. The logic of transnational capitalism should provoke the same response. As democratic states are now powerless to control transnational capital, then transnational capital has a duty to listen and respond to the needs of the powerless. Yet just as special interests like the military-technical complex blocked movement towards common security in the military-dimension, so particular interests among the transnational capitalist elite show little sign of enlightened self-interest by voluntarily adopting this cosmopolitan duty. It is essential, therefore, that their actions be held accountable to the people whose lives they affect by democratising those international institutions that have the scope to regulate transnational capital.

A discussion of cosmopolitan democracy is beyond the scope of this book (see Held, 1995). The question here is whether American hegemony and its influence on the international economic institutions it created can be made more responsive to the people of a potential international security community. This chapter argues that the contemporary neoliberal approach of American foreign policy cannot, but further argues that a more responsive approach is immanent in a particular reading of America's own socioeconomic development. Specifically, American foreign policy would do well to relearn the lessons of its own experience in the 1930s when free market capitalism failed to meet the needs of many and intervention was required to discipline power in a way that made it socially responsible.

Embedded Liberalism

America's policy in the immediate postwar era was not dominated by the issue of the U.S.-Soviet security dilemma (Ikenberry, 1999). As was suggested in chapter five, managing the relations of the victors and vanquished was as much a part of the rationale for NATO as was the defence of those states against the Soviet Union. Moreover, the main question of postwar order lay in the socioeconomic rather than military field. In fact it has been argued that the Soviet threat and the anti-communist rhetoric was a useful tool towards convincing isolationists/unilateralists to support the multilateral institutions of the liberal international order. John Gerard Ruggie, (1993, pp.30-31) for example, argues that the containment order was not only chronologically later than the Liberal order, but was created as an instrumental tool to sustain that order. The main question was how defeated and exhausted national governments could respond to the needs of their citizens while at the same time be integrated into a liberal international economy that would, in order to assure international cooperation, restrict a government's room for maneouver?

Failure to balance these competing requirements had led to the collapse of the liberal trading system in the interwar period. International regimes that relied on multilateral practices simply gave way to the pressure for unilateralist national responses that resulted from the renegotiation of the state-society contract during the 1930s. The rise of working-class constituencies combined with economic depression made demands for social protection nearly universal. As such, states were less willing to meet the requirements of international economic cooperation through the socially disruptive adjustment of their domestic economies. Economic nationalism prevailed which contributed to unilateralist conceptions of security interests which contributed to the causes of World War II. For most American policymakers, therefore, the task of postwar reconstruction was to maneuver between two unsatisfactory solutions. On the one hand liberals, particularly in the State Department, argued that economic nationalism in the name of social protection had to be avoided given its consequences for international relations. If goods could not cross borders, they feared, soldiers would (Ikenberry, 1989, p.382). On the other hand, the European allies and certain domestic constituencies, notably agriculture, feared that free trade in the name of economic efficiency and international cooperation would enforce too much discipline on domestic responses and thus risk the legitimacy of democratically elected national governments and social stability.

That the postwar order reflected American preferences more than any other state is not in doubt. Yet it has been persuasively argued that the postwar liberal order was less a result of American coercive power than it was a consequence of a compromise to European social concerns (Ruggie, 1982; Ikenberry, 1989; Ikenberry and Kupchan, 1990). The Bretton Woods regimes that emerged from negotiations between these competing views managed to find an appropriate balance. They were designed to facilitate free trade through fixed exchange rates while simultaneously assisting states to meet balance of payments difficulties. Through an international overdraft facility states could avoid the potentially devastating consequences of the structural adjustment that would otherwise have been necessary. As a result, the liberal philosophy of the State Department, while straying from the ideal of Smith and Ricardo, became embedded in the ideologies of the West European allies. And while European's on the left regretted some of the discipline imposed by the international markets, Keynes for instance argued for a larger IMF overdraft facility than was finally agreed (Ikenberry, 1989, pp.395-398), American New Dealers had recognised the need for international regimes to accommodate national responses to the social problems caused by structural adjustment (Burley, 1993). 'In terms of the ideals and plans it originally articulated', therefore, America 'got less than it wanted, in terms of direct involvement in the post war system it got more than it wanted. It used its power to make the system, but the system was not really of its own making' (Ikenberry, 1989, p.376).

This compromise, what Ruggie (1982) calls "embedded liberalism" and Ikenberry (1989) "welfare state liberalism", not only institutionalised an ideological consensus based on the lessons of the 1930s, but also strengthened that consensus by integrating potential challengers into the liberal order. The flexibility built in to the international regimes combined with Marshall Aid were all 'part of a strategy to make sure the European left developed in a democratic direction' (Ikenberry, 1989, p.396). By taking into account the concerns of European social democrats (or, more accurately, having been forced to listen to such concerns by the weakness of European economies) the postwar order was, Ikenberry concludes, 'as much a triumph of the welfare state as of the halting and partial emergence of liberal multilateralism' (Ikenberry, 1989, p.398).

Of course, U.S. policy was not beyond using undemocratic actions to reinforce this strategy. Covert political intervention, notably the CIA funding of non-communist parties in the 1948 elections, was motivated by the same ends. However, the successful socioeconomic integration not only of the transatlantic security community, but of the western liberal order that also included Japan, was based mainly on the compromise struck at Bretton Woods. A balance was found between universal and particular, international and national interests. By institutionalising free trade, the Bretton Woods regime assisted the process that would ultimately forge common interests and identities without disempowering those who looked to national government to meet there particular needs. Combined with what the previous chapter referred to as the reluctant, open and penetrated character of America, this compromise ultimately meant West Europeans across the politically significant part of the spectrum consented to American hegemony. If America had an empire it was an empire by invitation (Lundestadt, 1990).

America's Structural Dominance and the Liberal Order

In 1971 President Nixon abandoned the system of fixed exchange rates that had underpinned the Bretton Woods regime. Nixon effectively devalued the dollar in what was a response to the massive deficits accrued during a decade of war in Vietnam and social reform at home. To Realists this unilateral move signaled the beginning of the end of the multilateral trade regime and a collapse of the liberal order. Taking a neo-Gramscian perspective, however, Stephen Gill (1990) has argued that the liberal order survived this shift in the balance of material power because a transnational network of 'organic intellectuals' made sure the liberal 'mode of thought' continued to inform the western policies. That network was embodied in the Trilateral Commission that informed much of Carter's approach to the liberal community and the Third World. From the neo-Gramscian perspective then, the persistence of the liberal order was not determined by the material influence of transnational capitalism, though this was still important in creating the 'terrain more favourable to the dissemination of certain modes of thought'(Gill, 1990, p.42). Rather the liberal order was sustained by the ideological hegemony of a transnational liberal elite that found expression in the Trilateral Commission.

Yet the ideological hegemony of the late-1970s and 1980s, was very different to that which had informed the architects of the Bretton Woods system. With the collapse of the New Deal coalition in the U.S. 'welfare state liberalism' had given way to neoliberalism with its emphasis on small government, tax cuts and flexible capital and labour markets. Reaganomics took this to an extreme arguing that a 'supply-side revolution' and cuts in public spending would allow the U.S. to sustain a balanced budget even though tax cuts were combined with the largest increase in peacetime defence expenditure. A consequence of what its detractors labeled 'voodoo economics' was a budget deficit that would take decades to redress. As the U.S. and other states increasingly looked to private capital and not the IMF to fund its deficits the power of those private markets increased relative to those controlled by democratically elected government. The markets that were meant to be government slaves evolved into their masters (Strange, 1996, p.4; Ruggie, 1982, p.43). The rising international mobility and power of transnational capital made control over economic policy more difficult for individual capitalist states.

On the one hand this meant governments had a strong interest in cooperation and coordination of macroeconomic policy. Recognition of that interest was facilitated by the activities of networks like the Trilateral Commission. On the other hand it suggested states could gain a competitive advantage by making their domestic economies attractive to transnational capital. Such policies however, would mean low tax, low public spending economies that would threaten the provision of the public services that were part of the embedded liberal compromise.

Here the role played by U.S. policy remained central. Yet its influence was not so much exercised through its capacity to coerce states into cooperation, or its ability to provide the finance to underwrite intergovernmental institutions. Rather its influence came from the structural position its own economy occupied in the evolving global economy. The sheer size of the American market gave it an immediate advantage over other markets in the competition to attract inward investment. Given the 'structural dominance' of the American economy and its ability to attract capital, other states have been forced to compete by imitating its socioeconomic model. One response has been the integration of markets in a manner that makes investment prospects more attractive[1]. At the state level we see the rise of the neoliberal state of low taxation, flexible labour markets and minimal social spending. This of course places great strain on the embedded liberalism compromise that underpinned the liberal order since 1945. The more immediate point, however, is that the liberalisation of the global economy has increased the power of the United States and extended its period of hegemony. Yet the means through which hegemony is now exercised is less a matter of interstate coercion or persuasion, than it is a function of the socialising power of its own economy.

The idea that power resides in the economy rather than the state, however, problematises the notion that hegemony is American (Robinson, 1998, pp.26-27). The increasing internationalisation of national economies and the increasingly transnational character of capital, suggests that policies designed to compete for inward investment favour transnational rather than national interests. The two are not always mutually exclusive of course, but on certain issues they may be diametrically opposed. For example, Americans with capital to invest may benefit from the low tax and low inflation policies of neoliberal states. But for other Americans who rely on or prefer services traditionally supported by the state, they find themselves increasingly insecure or disillusioned. The same process is common across the liberal order.

In these terms, the influence wielded by the American economy may force other economies to liberalise but this is not necessarily in the interests of all Americans. The point is that the neoliberal ideas that informed American policy at the end of the Cold War are less a reflection of American interests than the interests of a transnational capitalist elite. It is that class which is hegemonic rather than 'America'. Moreover, because that class is transnational and because it has penetrated Washington in a manner that secures a policy that facilitates its particular interests, the idea of a 'foreign policy' is also contestable. As William Robinson (1998, p.41) notes, the objective of 'American foreign policy' is to promote at home *and* abroad the socio-political infrastructure that provides the consensual glue to legitimate the capitalist hegemony. He continues:

> The new U.S. political intervention can be conceived, in the broadest sense, as a transnational political practice by dominant sectors in the U.S., acting as the political leadership of an increasingly cohesive transnational elite, for the purpose of installing and stabilizing polyarchic political systems in the South.

Actions taken under the banner of 'American foreign policy' and particularly 'new political intervention' designed to 'promote democracy' should be truly understood in this context. Even during the Cold War, containing the Soviet Union was a related but secondary incentive for U.S intervention. 'The driving force was defence of a budding post-colonial international capitalism under U.S. domination' (Robinson, 1998, p.15). In the post- Cold War environment, the language of democracy promotion should not disguise the fact that American foreign policy seeks the election of an elite that is willing to undermine those national programmes that pose obstacles to the transnational capitalist agenda.

Democracy is not simply a matter of electing political elites. The act of voting is the end point of a complex social process that determines the nature of the choice electorates face. Recognising this process U.S. foreign policy has, according to Robinson, sought to penetrate the society of a transitional state in a manner that fosters organic support for the transnational neoliberal hegemony[2]. The political process of voting is largely insignificant when it comes to affecting social change, but it plays the crucial role in legitimising the socioeconomic structure that is penetrated by, and determined to suit the interests of, transnational capital. The voting process actually marginalises any counter-hegemonic blocs that are based on national responses to popular demands for market intervention. In this sense, the U.S. promotes *polyarchy* – a political system of accountability that leaves the socioeconomic substructure untouched. By promoting 'democracy' *and* free markets, U.S. policy in effect separates economic management from the wishes of the electorate. Voters have a 'free' choice but on socioeconomic issues it is a choice between capitalism or more capitalism (Robinson, 1998, pp.49-56).

The liberal order, then, has been transformed in two ways. Firstly the ideas that inform hegemony have changed. It is no longer guided by the ideas of New Dealers who struck the Bretton Woods compromise with European Social Democrats. Rather, hegemonic power is now guided by a Neoliberal philosophy of free markets and harsh structural and cultural adjustment programmes. Secondly the hegemon itself has changed. The growth of private capital markets has limited the power of national governments to deliver policies that are inconsistent with the neoliberal programme. To this extent power has shifted to a transnational capitalist elite. This process has been encouraged by the U.S. government's unwillingness to regulate its own economy and its political intervention abroad.

As a transnational coalition that contributes to the breakdown of national identities and the marginalisation of unilateralist responses, this neoliberal bloc is an important part of creating peace between states. Globalisation can contribute to the internationalisation of a state's identity in a way that is necessary for states to transcend the security dilemma. Yet contemporary internationalisation is controlled by a neoliberal hegemonic bloc that excludes many from influencing the way that process is managed. As power shifts away from states, and democratically elected governments become increasingly distant from decisions with social consequences, a counter-hegemonic bloc is likely to emerge among those groups who do not benefit from free-market capitalism. This is by no means a security issue. There is nothing inevitable about a counter-hegemonic bloc being violent. But it is an issue of democracy and the potential for securitisation is there. The present process of internationalisation is denying many of what they used to have or at least expected to have, that is an ability to influence the way society evolves. Globalisation is not necessarily democratisation and as such its contribution to consolidating and extending a security community is questionable.

Disembedded Liberalism

Among liberal commentators on American hegemony, there is an optimism that the spread of capitalism contributes to international stability. Deudney and Ikenberry (1999, pp.193-194), for example, argue that at the interstate level capitalism has overcome the relative gains problem that Neorealists believe will always make cooperation between states expedient and temporary. At the societal level they identify a common civic identity – what Strange (1988) called the 'business civilization'[3] - that is 'intimately associated with capitalism and its business and commodity cultures'. In a passage that clearly resonates with Deutsch's definition of a security community and clearly implies that the West has unquestionably achieved that status, Deudney and Ikenberry write:

> The cumulative weight of these international homogenizing and interacting forces has been to create an increasingly common identity and culture - a powerful sense that "we" constitutes more than the traditional community of the nation-state. As civic and capitalist identities have strengthened, ethnic and national identity has declined.

Toleration, they suggest, has replaced the chauvinism and parochialism of pre-modern societies. As a result, the American backed rules and institutions of the liberal order have become firmly embedded in the wider structures of society. What is more, it is becoming increasingly difficult they suggest for "alternative institutions" or "alternative leadership" to seriously emerge.

John Gerrard Ruggie (1994) is less optimistic that the changing nature of the liberal order can maintain the stability it produced in the immediate post-War era. To Ruggie the increasing liberalisation of the global economy means greater intrusion into domestic domains and the politicisation of issues that were considered the sole prerogative of national governments. As international barriers to trade are reduced to insignificant levels then domestic structures become the focus for accusations of discriminatory trade practices. If political systems diverge and if they have effects on trade flows, then it potentially becomes an international problem.

This reinforces the point running through this book that domestic structure is significant in the process of constructing a security community. A common democratic identity is essential for a security community to exist. The danger is here, however, that efforts to promote a common capitalist identity by the liberalisation of markets is undermining the respect for national differences and the ability of national politicians to respond to those local requirements. The complexities of the new financial world have undermined the 'taken for granted cause-effect relations between exchange rates and trade balances…or between interest rates and exchange rates', making it more difficult to manage the economy in pursuit of particular (i.e. not neoliberal) conceptions of social justice. Similarly national institutions that the domestic social compact deems necessary for social or national cohesion come under attack. The neoliberal hegemony poses a double threat to such institutions. Firstly it legitimises the claims made by outsiders that such institutions are 'unfair' and thus pose an obstacle to increased economic efficiency. Secondly, it supports the claim made by insiders that the state cannot afford such institutions and society must adapt to a life without them.

The key point is that the neoliberal hegemony is undermining the compromise that was central to post-war stability in the West. The liberal order would encourage free trade but not to the extent that it would undermine the institutions that democratically elected national governments deemed necessary to preserve social justice and stability. Only on this basis was liberalism sufficiently embedded in western states and the liberal order stabilised. Now Ruggie fears that 'the new world economy is increasingly disembedded from the domestic social compact between state and society'.

Deudney and Ikenberry's optimism is not that strong that they can ignore this issue. If states abandon their commitment to national institutions that are considered vital to the traditional social compact, Deudney and Ikenberry recognise that 'motivation for their support of a liberal economic system would decline' (1999, p.190). At the time of writing they believed the opponents of the neoliberal hegemony were 'a loud but small minority of the alienated and economically dislocated. Their voices are not, however, a cause for a crisis of self-confidence' (1999, p.195). Yet as Ruggie points out (1995, p.522), there are voices 'among the most irrepressible and articulate advocates ... of free markets and free trade', who recognise that the social compact between state and society is being undermined. The *Economist* and the *Financial Times* he notes applauded the 'new deal' that the Clinton administration offered the American public: 'you accept change (such as NAFTA) and we'll help to give you the [occupational, health care and personal] security'.

Unfortunately, such promises have not been fulfilled and Washington is becoming increasingly remote not only from transnational communities, but also from many Americans themselves. Robert Reich (1999) summarises the indifference and apathy that pervades American politics. He writes:

> So long as Right-wing Republicans and a centrist White House remain unwilling to do anything of importance about health care, education, Social Security, Medicare, or campaign finance,

Washington's irrelevance will solidify into a gelatinous mass of indigestible spin.

The difficulties of changing the ideological grip that neoliberalism has on the American politics is considered in greater detail below. The more immediate point is that there are voices of political significance that are concerned that the present process of globalisation is threatening the liberal democratic community. In this sense globalisation is creating a societal security dilemma across that community. On the one hand there are those who are materially and ideologically motivated to transfer loyalties to transnational agendas thus deepening the sense of community across nations. On the other hand there are those who fail to see the material and cultural benefits of globalisation and become more ideologically inclined to regard it as a threat.

Extending the Liberal Security Community

Within the established liberal community the voices of those disillusioned with the liberal order are far from inaudible. Indeed the volume is slowly increasing. The intensity of the dilemma, however, increases once one moves outside the established liberal community and examines those societies less certain about the neoliberal hegemony. As Benjamin Barber (1995) notes, the failure to deliver on the expectations that were created by capitalists at the end of the Cold War can quickly lead to disillusionment. Extending the liberal security community to embrace former Communist states for instance was driven in part by the promise of greater economic prosperity. Should the socio-economic costs of the market place prove too costly then societies used to a relatively secure but admittedly poor standard of living may seek alternative means to meet their needs and aspirations.

Yet Barber also notes that the West should not only be concerned about capitalism's economic failure. Proclaiming capitalism a success because it meets the standards set by capitalists is also dangerous. Creating a common identity and extending the idea of political community is considered an essential part of the critical project of a security community. The culture that provides 'the consensual glue' for contemporary capitalism, however, is not as tolerant of other identities as liberals like to think. As noted above, by undermining those local conceptions of truth that deny individuals their voice in a dialogue on their future, the information that is required to make capitalism function is a positive force

(Robinson, 1998, pp.37-38). As is further noted, however, capitalism may simply replace one restricted dialogue for another if the previous power holders are simply replaced by an unaccountable transnational elite. Their hegemony, moreover, is maintained not through democracy but through a culture of consumerism that fosters consent for the economic system. The point Barber makes, however, is even if capitalism succeeds in meeting the material needs and aspirations of individuals, not all individuals want to be consumers and may resent the capitalist culture that they associate with America.

Sensitivity to difference is a central requirement of the ideal dialogic community (Linklater 1998). Insensitivity can easily lead to what Barber calls a 'Jihad' against 'McWorld'. It may lead to the securitisation of the liberal order that undermines its status as a security community. Yet it is the increasing disparities in material wealth and the increasing insignificance of the 'have nots' in a system where 'money talks' that is perhaps the greatest concern for the future extension of a worthwhile order required of a security communities.

Where civil society is underdeveloped the void left by the retreat of the state is exploited by less than democratic political movements. The 'exclusionary populism' that Cox (1999, p.14) identifies in this context is anathema to the idea of a security community. The 'covert forces' of extreme right political movements, xenophobic racism and religious cults 'assume a functional relationship with neo-liberal deregulated economies. Covert power substitutes for legitimate authority in a totally unregulated market – contracts are enforced by goons and guns'.

Integration across transnational capitalist classes is accompanied by precariously linked supporting classes. Yet those unable to benefit from the internationalisation of capitalism have already securitised the neoliberal elite and set in train a process of disintegration. 'The most open challenge to the impact of globalisation on social and political structures', notes Cox (1999, p.23) has come from a new type of revolutionary movement, the *zapatista* rebellion of the Mayan Indians in the southern Mexican state of Chiapas that broke out on New Year's day 1994. This was the day on which the NAFTA came into effect, which symbolised the anti-globalisation message of the revolt'.

As chapter four notes, the internationalisation of the state is not necessarily consistent with the idea of a security community if the process excludes more individuals from the ideal of a dialogic community. Clearly the zapatista movement is one group that feels threatened rather than liberated by liberal internationalism. In the context of their insecurity, Security Studies cannot declare the integration of North and Central

America as a step towards a security community. Security Studies must take a critical perspective and expose the claims of those who do believe such processes create security.

As Robinson notes (1998, p.48) 'the assumptions of modernization theory continue to provide theoretical guidance for, and legitimization of, the economic dimensions of U.S. foreign policy, and particularly the neo-liberal model and its notion that the unfettered operation of transnational capital will bring about development'. Even if these assumptions can promise and deliver an economic system that responds to the material needs of an increasing number in the long run, it is far from democratic.

Contemporary capitalism already produces enough food to feed a global population but the political organisation of the world means the disenfranchised can still starve. The point is, meeting the needs of the human members of a security community is not simply a matter of increased material wealth, it is a matter of how that wealth is distributed relative to the requirements of a dialogic community. Presently global economic institutions listen harder to the requirements of transnational capital than they do those without access to its privileges. While these institutions profess and sometimes deliver on the cosmopolitan duty that the powerful should adopt in such situations, their responsiveness will always be challenged so long as their decisions are based on a dialogue, however enlightened, of capitalists whose first priority is profit. In other words the global institutions that provide the forum for such a dialogue have to listen as hard to the concerns of environmentalists, transnational labour and poor individuals (and not necessarily their governments) as much as they listen to the concerns of transnational capital.

The role played by the U.S. government is obviously central to that process of democratisation. So long as U.S. foreign policy is dominated by transnational capital and notionally legitimised by academic proponents of modernisation theory and neoliberalism, American agency will be undemocratic and potentially destabilising. Yet democrats need not necessarily give up on Washington as many Americans themselves seem to be doing. While the policies emanating from contemporary Washington are indeed unresponsive to the needs of a global dialogue the fact that they are also unresponsive to the needs of many Americans suggests that progressive reform is immanent in the American polity. Seeing U.S. foreign policy as 'the final phase of a complex policymaking process largely determined by forces in civil society' (Robinson, 1998, p.27), suggests transnational political activism across civil society, by tapping into the resentment that exists across large sections of American society, can alter American foreign policy. Neoliberalism may have penetrated contemporary Washington, but it has not always held a hegemonic position, nor need it. The making of American foreign economic policy is indeed complex. The final section sets out the obstacles that intellectual communities lobbying Washington for more responsive policies will have to face.

American Democracy: open in means restricted in ends[4]

Robinson's main complaint against U.S. foreign policy is that it promotes a system of governance - polyarchy - that is inappropriate to addressing the needs of a majority. By assisting a transnational capitalist elite to penetrate civil society, U.S. foreign policy restricts political choice to varieties of capitalism. In this sense democracy is not open in its ends. Policy may follow the wishes of the electorate, but the choice of the electorate is heavily restricted by social structures that privilege those who benefit from the capitalist system. Robinson contrasts polyarchy with popular democracy. Popular democracy:

> is seen as an emancipatory project of both form and content that links the distinct spheres of the social totality, in which the construction of a democratic political order enjoys a theoretically internal relation to the construction of a democratic socioeconomic order. Democratic participation, in order to be truly effective, requires that democracy be a tool of changing unjust social and economic structures, national as well as international. In sharp contrast to polyarchy, popular democracy is concerned with *both process and outcome.*

Thus while Robinson does not deny the importance of constitutional liberalism and its emphasis on political and civil rights, democracy is more than simply guaranteeing individual protection against the political process. Rather democracy is about empowering individuals so that their voice is heard in the construction of a just society. They may choose inequality, but that choice can only be legitimate if it is done from a position of equality.

Equal access to the processes that construct society is idealistic, but as Habermas notes, the power of that ideal comes from the action taken to approximate that ideal. Why then does America persist in its promotion of constitutional liberalism and free market capitalism in a manner that fails to address these concerns? For Robinson, the answer lies in the penetration of the extended American state by a transnational capitalist elite. It is argued here that this process is assisted by cultural and institutional structures that are at the core of America's political identity. It is further argued, however, that a policy that is potentially more responsive to the needs of the global population is immanent in the American experience, specifically the New Deal's response to capitalism's failure in the 1930s.

It is well known that the Founding Father's feared the tyranny of the majority as much as they feared the tyranny of monarchy, and the system of checks and balances they set up to prevent this is also well known. What is overlooked, or at least is in dispute, is the social consequence of such a system. For instance, it often assumed that American democracy is open in its ends. That is, if the electorate did not like the social consequences of a certain policy they would simply vote in the next election to change it. A capitalist policy of unrestrained free markets, therefore, is simply responding to the needs and aspirations of the American people. Yet it is clear that the system of checks and balances in the American system gives a minority opinion an exaggerated influence. As such it can effectively veto the wishes of the majority. This, of course, is exactly what the Founding Fathers intended. But what has effectively happened, at least since the collapse of the New Deal coalition in the 1960s, is that power in Washington has been controlled by minority interests who use their material wealth to gain access to Congress and the White House. In this way institutional structures have assisted the capitalist elite in their control of American foreign policy.

Here the decentralisation of political power can be considered an obstacle to appropriate responses to the needs of individuals threatened by forces beyond their control. By extension this lack of responsiveness can handicap the construction of a security community. In previous chapters, decentralisation is said to assist the process of overcoming the security dilemma. It creates transparency, greater possibility to influence the policy of another and the likelihood that defection from cooperation will be gradual and therefore avoidable. Yet these conclusions all see the security dilemma in terms of inter-state relations. The issue here is the state's relationship with society and its ability to respond to the needs of individuals within that society. Here it is suggested that decentralisation on the American model exaggerates the influence of minority groups that can then have an effective veto of any state policy that seeks to respond to the needs or demands of the majority. In America's case a capitalist elite has had an effective veto such that the state and those that compete for its power do not challenge their interests. As was noted in chapter four, however, the influence of domestic political structure is indeterminate.

Domestic political structure mediates the influence of ideas, but it is the ability of those ideas to mobilise political support that is of decisive influence. Social and cultural structures exist independent of state institutions.

A consequence of the decentralised system has been the fusion of capitalism and democracy in America's political culture. The system of checks and balances disaggregated democratic mandates so that they could not be abused by elected politicians. Thus, '[i]nstead of the government being constituted and informed by the single beam of a popular mandate in a unified election, it takes on the character of a kaleidoscope, full of colourful activity but possessing very little in the way of coherence and direction' (Foley, 1991, p.77). In this sense the evolution of American society had less to do with any socioeconomic ideology that was implemented from above. Rather it has been a consequence of a political system that fractures such attempts and allows exceptional socio-economic circumstances the freedom to shape civil-society.

The fluidity of early social conditions in the United States and the Protestant tradition all contributed to an economic individualism that meant capitalism could prosper (Foley, 1991, pp.64-64). For example, the frontier acted both as a safety valve for the propertyless workers and as a continuous drain on the working population of the Eastern cities, with the result that the labour supply remained limited and industrial wages were kept high. The relative affluence and mobility of the American workers compared with their European counterpart was thought to have made them far less receptive to radical politics and far more interested in moving up the ladder of social status. Even for those workers who were not so taken with the individualist promises of success and who favoured greater solidarity with one another, they found that any collective consciousness stopped at racial, ethnic and religious barriers, which were consistently reinforced by the flow of immigrants (Foley, 1991, pp.56-57). Moreover, the disaggregative effects of local laws in the federal system meant that 'there was, in effect, no national pattern of law, legitimisation or repression to confirm a socialist critique'[5]. Finally the American 'celebration of its exceptionalism as a counterweight to socialism and as a rebuttal of Marxism undoubtedly contributed towards the civic integration of the United States' (Foley, 1991, p.59).

Thus the systemic guarantees against mob rule were in effect redundant as a majority challenge to the socio-economic order was diluted by the particular circumstances of that order. America's initial 'success', in other words, had less to do with liberal political management of democratic majorities than exceptional socio-economic circumstances. Yet because capitalism thrived under those circumstances, and because America was democratic in the sense that it accommodated free (although not universal) elections, capitalism became equated with democracy in the American psyche. As Foley (1991, p.65) puts it, capitalism is seen as 'embodying such American ideals as liberty, individualism, emancipation, democracy and even equality'. No other people, he suggests, 'are more dependent upon the meaning and value of capitalism for the conception of themselves, their history and their purpose in the world' (Foley, 1991, p.64).

These institutional and cultural influences have combined to limit the choice of the American electorate. Moreover it is this culture and this political system that has led a majority of Americans to turn their back on Washington and handed control of U.S. foreign policy to the transnational capitalist elite. Once in control of policy, this group has argued that free market global capitalism is consistent with democratisation. When they are challenged on this point, they point to this particular reading of the American experience to support their argument. Yet there is a major flaw in that kind of defence. Even if it were considered an example of good governance (the derisory turnout figures for elections to national office suggest that it is not) the American experience is exceptional. In other states, trade unions and welfare states have responded to the needs and aspirations of communities in ways that the free market could not. When America promotes capitalism, either through its structural position in the global economy or directly through political intervention, it risks undermining institutions that are often a necessary part of the social contract within other states. But because such institutions have not figured strongly in the American experience, American foreign policy fails to see the inconsistency.

The Need for Social Democracy

The system resting on this cultural acceptance of capitalism was secure so long as the exceptional socio-economic circumstances that favoured the free-market were sustained. Yet as those circumstances changed with depression in the 1930s, a repressed majority looked to the state. The question facing the system was whether it could translate this democratic need into political action, or would the liberal safeguards against a dictatorship of the majority protect the privileged few who had the power to survive, even exploit those circumstances?

The implementation of Roosevelt's New Deal and the rise of a socio-economic liberalism that sought to construct and then defend a welfare state demonstrated that in this instance the system was responsive to the needs of the majority even when constitutional liberalism continued to protect the rights of the minority. While Roosevelt's legacy remains mixed, it is clear that when socio-economic circumstances changed from the exceptional, and exceptionally fortunate ones that founded the American state, questions confronted the liberal democratic political system that had allowed free market economics to continue uninterrupted. In this sense questions should be levelled at the present American foreign policy of promoting the kind of democracy it does when the global socio-economic circumstances are not amenable to global free market economics. More importantly, because the circumstances that underpinned America's success were exceptional, it is unlikely that other societies will ever be able to accommodate a U.S. type system. A U.S. foreign policy that insists on promoting the free market alongside liberal democracy is likely to find its task complicated by the resistance of local political culture.

In *America's Mission*, Tony Smith (1994) makes the distinction between American policies that have been sensitive to the particular socio-economic circumstances of a state and those that simply seek to impose a liberal democratic regime. As noted above, America's success in promoting democracy across the transatlantic community and Japan was a consequence of administrations that were willing to compromise on the goal of free trade in order to assist societies manage the social adjustments that capitalism constantly requires. Contemporary American foreign policy has forgotten that lesson because New Dealers have been politically marginalised by the neoliberal hegemony. While it would be naïve to argue for a reconstruction of the New Deal coalition, a broader point is, however, more appropriate. If liberal democracy is to be embedded in the political cultures of transitional states, and if the democratic security community is to be consolidated and extended, American policymakers must relearn the lessons of its past. Not, as Fareed Zakaria (1997) claimed, by recalling its tradition of constitutional liberalism, it has not forgotten that, but by recalling that the foundations of the transatlantic community were based on liberal *and* social democracy.

Whose 'satisfactory solution'? Politicizing the Washington Consensus

The roots of the present liberal order lay in America's vision of the world as an extension of the New Deal state. On this basis it is logical to argue, as Anne-Marie Burley (1993, p.146) does, that the character of world order is likely, 'to wax and wane roughly in line with swings of domestic attitudes towards governmental regulation'. While the waning of the New Deal coalition may have contributed to the present situation the waxing of a similar coalition is by no means certain. As Robert Cox notes, reactions to globalisation are not always benign. 'Covert society' has taken root in America and, as portrayed so graphically in the film *Fight Club*, has the potential to feed off discontentment with consumerist culture.

The question that needs asking is whether contemporary American society contains within itself a counter-hegemonic bloc? Can the apathy and disrespect that presently pervades attitudes towards Washington (Gill, 1996; Cox, 1999, pp.12-13) be discarded and a political coalition mobilised to penetrate Washington and make it, and by extension, American foreign policy more responsive to the needs of a community that extends beyond the capitalist elite?

Of course the character of that response is essential when considering the process of building a transnational security community. The contemporary debate is framed not in terms of competing conceptions of internationalism and multilateralism, but how best to achieve particular conceptions of America's interests. An aggressive approach to market liberalisation that attacks 'unfair' trading practices of allies may gain broad support at home, particularly among neoliberals, but, for reasons noted above, it may undermine the compromise between local and international demands that have so far integrated other states into the security community. On the other hand, American unilateralism, frustrated by the unwillingness of its trading partners to liberalise further, may force restrictions and contribute to the kind of the trade war that liberals fear most. Ruggie (1995, p.521) for instance fears that discontent may find expression in mercantilist state policies. 'If governments find their array of policy tools, including the relatively benign option of the 'new protectionism', no longer suffices to achieve their objectives, there is no telling what measure they may turn to in exasperation'. This is dangerous because whichever way this particular debate is resolved the contemporary order is jeopardised.

In these terms the security dilemma facing American policy lies in finding the correct balance between international and national interests. National responses to local demands, even when they are democratically articulated, should not be allowed to threaten the transnational identity that capitalism encourages. On the other hand, policies that cater solely for the interests of transnational capitalism should not be allowed to neglect those who cannot or do not want to benefit from the 'opportunities' offered by globalisation. The present danger is that contemporary American foreign policy does not recognise this dilemma. Through the ideology of 'market democracy' it can accommodate the interests of a transnational financial elite. By marginalising the voices of those who do not benefit from globalisation, this discourse has resolved America's particular dilemma.

Yet this particular 'satisfactory solution', is creating unsatisfactory solutions elsewhere. In effect the liberalisation of markets is creating security dilemmas for other states and societies. That dilemma is unlikely to be 'resolved' in the way America resolves its own dilemma. A backlash against the liberal order, or at the very least, a missed opportunity to extend the concept of community, is likely to result.

To avoid this scenario, American policy must pursue its interests in a multilateral framework. That means finding a middle ground between the 'aggressive unilateralism' (Bhagwati and Patrick, 1990) of the free market (i.e. attacks on the protectionist responses of others to their socioeconomic requirements i.e. 'barriers to trade') and the protective unilateralism of nationalist responses (ie erecting its own 'barriers to trade' of its own). The political support for this lies in resurrecting the ideas that informed the internationalism of the New Deal. Political support for such ideas would benefit from a process that politicises America's own local 'solution' to globalisation. America's present response is 'satisfactory' because those unsatisfied are marginal in the political 'debate'. Listening to the section of American society that is socioeconomically disempowered and the half that is so disillusioned it does not bother to vote, may weaken America's embrace of globalisation and thus signify its own societal dilemma. Yet it at least creates a dialogue the outcome of which may be a policy that is more suited not only to sustaining the liberal community that presently exists across the 'west', but has a greater chance of embedding liberalism and thus extending the security community in other countries.

Conclusion

Chapter five suggested that there were elements of its political structure and identity that meant American hegemony was a positive force in the consolidation and extension of transnational security communities. Yet this chapter has argued that the same political system and culture has allowed transnational capital to veto political intervention designed to democratise American and transnational society by addressing socioeconomic inequalities. Liberals are right to suggest that the reluctant and penetrated character of American hegemony assists the creation of peaceful relations between states, but attention must also be paid to its affects within and across states.

The question that is a constant theme throughout this study, continues to be relevant: 'peace for whom?'. The liberal analysis of American hegemony must also be challenged with the question 'penetrated by whom?'. For American policy has been penetrated by a transnational capitalist elite who certainly have strong interests in peace between states, and that is to be welcomed. Yet its other interests, mobility of capital, creates a disregard for democracy within states. It would be unrealistic and therefore hopeless, even if it was warranted, to argue that America's legislative system must change in order to sustain a positive role in promoting a democratic peace. Rather, the benefits of the American system should be recognised and used to address the present failings of the policies that pass through it. In other words, a movement that mobilises the sections of transnational civil society that globalisation has overlooked can and must be directed at penetrating the hegemonic bloc that operates through Washington. Here the work of Cox (1999, p.13) and others highlight the promise of transnational civil society. A political focus of that movement must be the penetration of Washington and by extension the global institutions which are heavily influenced by it.

Notes

[1] Europe the obvious example, but also South America, Mercosur, see Hurrell, 1998.

[2] Cox also identifies this process arguing that 'subsidies to NGOs, for instance, incline the latter's objectives towards conformity with the established order and thus enhance the legitimacy of the prevailing order' (Cox, 1999, p.11).

[3] Gill uses Strange's phrase 'market civilization' to denote the idea that capitalism is a civilising force. However, he quickly adds that 'market civilisation' is an oxymoron. 'To be civilised involves a respect for and tolerance of other ways of organising society. Although one clearly has to appreciate the gains to society that have stemmed from greater productive power, treasured aspects of earlier or contemporary civilisations are more fundamentally appropriated and commodified in capitalist societies (Gill, 1996, p.211).

[4] Parts of this section are taken from my chapter, 'High Stakes and Low Intensity Democracy. Understanding America's Policy of Promoting Democracy', in Michael Cox, G.John Ikenberry and Takashi Inoguchi, *American Democracy Promotion. Impulses, Strategies, and Impacts*, Oxford University Press, 2000.

[5] Theodore J. Lowi, 'Why Is There No Socialism In The United States? A Federal Analysis', *International Political Science Review*, Vol.5 No.4 1984 p.377. Cited in Foley, 1991, p.58.

References

Barber, B. (1995), *McWorld versus Jihad*, Ballantine Books, New York.

Bhagwati, J. and Patrick, H. (eds.) (1990), *Aggressive Unilateralism: America's 301 Trade Policy and the World Trading System*, University of Michigan Press, Ann Arbor.

Burley, A. (1993), 'Regulating the World: Multilateralism, International Law, and the Projection of the New Deal Regulatory State', in John Gerrard Ruggie (ed.), *Multilateralism Matters. The theory and practice of an Institutional Form*, Columbia University Press, New York, pp.125-156.

Cox, R. (1999), 'Civil society at the turn of the millennium: prospects for an alternative world order', *Review of International Studies*, Vol.25, pp.3-28.

Deudney, D. and Ikenberry, G.J. (1999), 'The nature and sources of liberal international order', *Review of International Studies*, Vol.25, pp.179-196.

Foley, M. (1991), *American Political Ideas. Traditions and Usages*, Manchester University Press, Manchester and New York.

Gill, S. (1990), *American Hegemony and the Trilateral Commission*, Cambridge University Press, Cambridge.

Gill, S. (1996), 'Globalization, Democratization and the Politics of Indifference', in James H. Mittelman, *Globalization. Critical Reflections*, Lynne Reinner, Boulder, Colorado, pp.205-228.

Gill, S. (1999), 'Globalisation, Market Civilisation and Disciplinary Neoliberalism', *Millennium. Journal of International Studies*, Vol.24, pp.399-425.

Held, D. (1995), *Democracy and Global Order. From the Modern State to Cosmopolitan Governance*, Polity Press, Oxford.

Hurrell, A. (1998), 'An emerging security community in South America?', in E. Adler and M.Barnett, *Security Communities*, Cambridge University Press, Cambridge, pp.228-264.

Ikenberry, G.J. (1989), 'Rethinking the Origins of American Hegemony', *Political Science Quarterly*, Vol.104, pp.375-400.

Ikenberry, G.J. (1999), 'Liberal Hegemony and the future of American postwar order', in T.V. Paul and John A. Hall (eds.), *International Order and the Future of World Politics*, Cambridge University Press, Cambridge, pp.123-145.

Ikenberry, G.J. and Kupchan, C.A. (1990), 'Socialization and hegemonic power', *International Organization*, Vol.44, pp.283-315.

Linklater, A. (1998), *The Transformation of Political Community*, Polity, Cambridge.

Lundestad, G. (1990), *The American 'Empire' and Other Studies of U.S. Foreign Policy in a Comparative Perspective*, Oxford University Press and Norwegian University Press, Oxford.

Reich, R.B. (1999), 'The New Power', *The American Prospect*, November 23.

Robinson, W. (1998), *Promoting Polyarchy. Globalization, U.S. Intervention and Hegemony*, Cambridge University Press, Cambridge.

Ruggie, J.G. (1982), 'International regimes, transaction, and change: embedded liberalism in the postwar economic order', *International Organization*, Vol.33, pp.379-415.

Ruggie, J.G. (1993), 'Multilateralism: The Anatomy of an Institution', in John Gerard Ruggie (ed.), *Multilateralism Matters. The theory and practice of an Institutional Form*, Columbia University Press, New York, pp.3-47.

Ruggie, J.G. (1994), 'At Home Abroad, Abroad at Home: International Liberalism and Domestic Stability in the New World Economy', *Millennium: Journal of International Studies*, Vol.24, pp.507-526.

Smith, T. (1994), *America's Mission. The United States and the Worldwide Struggle for Democracy in the Twentieth Century*, Princeton University Press, Princeton.

Strange, S. (1996), *The Retreat of the State. The Diffusion of Power in the World Economy*, Cambridge University Press, Cambridge.

Zakaria, F. (1997), 'The Rise of Illiberal Democracy', *Foreign Affairs*, Vol.76, pp.22-43.

7 Conclusions

The need to lend suffering a voice is the precondition of all truth.
Theodor W. Adorno.[1]

Critical Security Studies and the Security Dilemma

If reality is socially constructed then seeking truth is a matter of making sure all take part in that social process. Security Studies cannot objectively identify the conditions of peace if the social structures that would otherwise pass as reality exclude individuals from the process that constructed them. Some may be able to identify a particular situation as peaceful, but if that definition has been reached without consulting all those affected by the social practices that sustain that condition then there is little truth to it. Social processes that are free of coercion would most probably construct a different reality to that which results from any dialogue that is mediated by power. As such, truth can only result from an unmediated dialogue involving everyone. The need to lend the silenced victims of coercion a voice is indeed the precondition of truth. Until intellectuals dealing with Security Studies work towards that end then their knowledge of what constitutes peace and security will be incomplete.

This book has advanced more pragmatic reasoning for the need to place universal human security at the center of the Security Studies discipline. If security is defined as the absence of threats to the self then the self must recognise the capacity it has for threatening others. There is no guarantee, of course, that the self will feel secure even if it poses no threat to the other, but it is likely to provoke a threat against itself if the insecurity of the other is considered a precondition of its own security. When the self recognises the security needs of the other, the likelihood that it will not feel threatened by the other increases. The benign interaction of particularities is dependent on this kind of compromise. The security of the particular can

176

only be realised in the long term if the security of all in the community is also realised.

The traditional discipline of Security Studies dealt with state security. The security dilemma has been used to explain why moves to address one state's security concerns unavoidably threatens another state. As one state rearms for defensive ends, other states cannot be certain that its intention is not aggressive. They in turn feel threatened and rearm themselves. Through the misperception of the original intent these potentially benign particularities are caught in a spiral of mistrust characterised by illusory incompatibility. Because the uncertainty of the anarchic international system is unresolvable, the power competition that characterises the security dilemma is considered a permanent feature of international politics.

At the centre of this definition of the security dilemma are unwarranted ontological and epistemological assumptions. John Herz's definition of the security dilemma (1950, p.157), for example, is dependent on 'a world of competing units'. It assumes that the purpose of a state is simply to prevent a military attack on a particular territory and that it will maximise material power to achieve that end. Yet the purpose of the state is not merely the defence of what Herz called 'territoriality'. The state is a consequence of human agency that is motivated by political ideals. State security is only a normative goal to those who believe the state can still advance those ideals. As chapter one noted, social institutions like the state are only secure so long as they meet the interests of human agents. Moreover, what the state deems valuable and therefore worth defending will also depend on human agency. The point is that a state's identity is contingent on the social practices of individuals and as such, making the assumption that the state is a power-maximising rational and egoistic defender of territory is not always warranted.

To recognise that reality is socially contingent is to recognise the social responsibility that is attached to knowledge. Knowledge can legitimise or challenge those structures that have been created through coercion. It can be conservative or revolutionary. It is argued in this book that the security dilemma as it is defined by the traditional approach to Security Studies is intrinsically conservative. By placing the state at the center of its concerns and by arguing that states are condemned to a competition for material power that can only be mitigated by cooperation between statist elites, the security dilemma legitimises, firstly, the assumption that states could provide security if only it wasn't for other states, and, secondly, the view that a military technical solution is the only one possible. Knowledge is always for someone and for some purpose (Cox, 1986), and the security dilemma has been used to legitimise the privileged position of a statist and militarist elite. To define international relations in terms of unresolvable uncertainty and a vicious circle of power accumulation, is to be a political ally of those special interests.

Yet certain states can and do provide a political order that is worthwhile in terms of universal human security. What chapter four identified as the international-democratic state is an ideal to aspire to. By responding to the needs and aspirations of its citizens without threatening the ability of other states to respond to the needs of their citizens, and in the absence of such a response, to be able to meet those needs directly, such states can provide the building blocs of a security community. The object of security is the individual, but to the extent that international-democratic states provide for that without doing anything to threaten other individuals, it too can be considered worthy of protection. The security dilemma arises when powerful agents of different values threaten the ability of states to pursue their internationalist and democratic interests. On the one hand the state can only be secure in a world of other internationalist and democratic states that responds to the needs of a global community of individuals, yet on the other hand, remaining true to those principles, acting in accord with them and seeking wider observance of them, may make such a state vulnerable to the coercion of political units with different values and may even, should the costs prove too high, weaken its own commitment to those principles.

This is a dilemma of normative human agency, not one dictated by structural circumstances beyond human influence. It is still characterised by dilemmas of interpretation and response but the threat is not to a state per se, but to the internationalist and democratic values of civil society. What opportunities are there to promote these values without threatening interstate cooperation and thereby undermine the international order that allows these values to be practiced? What threat is posed to these values in an effort to maintain international order by cooperating with states that threaten and deny such values? Answers to these questions and other similar questions will differ according to preconceptions, vested interests and attempts at objective assessments of threats and opportunities. A genuine dilemma is usually reflected by the political battle between Realists who see less opportunity to promote internationalist-democratic values and are more inclined to compromise these principles in the name of power politics, and liberals who are likely to see greater opportunity to advance this ideological agenda and less need to compromise a commitment to that agenda because of the power relationship with states of opposing ideologies.

This is a genuine normative dilemma because both sides are other-, as well as self- regarding. There is no point in promoting internationalist-democratic values if it provokes ideological opponents to launch a nuclear war. Equally there is little point in pursuing international order if it means compromising internationalist-democratic values to the extent that they become rhetorical and politically insignificant. Of course, the prescriptions based on the readings of other-regarding Realists and Liberals can be hijacked by selfish interests that use the internationalist-democratic agenda as a cover for the pursuit of particular interests that are wholly inconsistent with that agenda. It is the first task of Critical Security Studies to expose their practices and assist in the process of their political marginalisation. It is the second and obviously related task to demonstrate how the genuine security dilemma identified above can be transcended.

Transcending the Security Dilemma

In the absence of organic support for internationalist and democratic values certain efforts to promote such values may prove counterproductive. Intervening in the domestic politics of another state can only be justified if the chances of embedding internationalist and democratic values are high and the risks of violent disorder are low. The dilemma lies in weighing the risks and opportunities of this process. Sometimes the support an internationalist-democratic state can give to ideological allies is necessarily restricted by the limited capacity it has for advancing those ideals. Where direct intervention cannot do good the state can only make sure it does nothing to make things worse.

Compromising support for internationalist and democratic values in this manner is a threat to the state's own identity and to the prospect of a wider security community. Yet it is justified in terms of prudence and the recognition that the state is not the only agent of these values. Indeed prudence of this kind, so long as it is other-regarding and not corrupted by the selfish ends of special interests, is central to normative statecraft. The fact that most if not all states are not ideal international-democractic states and that they do pander to particular interests, however, means such prudence is not always normatively justified. It is, to use Booth's terms

(1994), 'rhetorical' rather than 'technical', or as Jackson (1995) notes, 'instrumental' rather than 'normative'. Either way there are limits on the role states can play in the process of constructing a security community. The context of the interstate system, littered as it is by military power that immediately raises the stakes of any disorder, and/or the existence of particularist interests less inclined to support internationalist and democratic values, will place limits on the state's normative commitment to a wider community.

This is not to conclude that a state's security dilemma, defined as how best to protect and promote the values that underpin a security community, remains a constant feature of international politics. The dilemma arises only when the political significance of an opposing ideology mobilises sufficient material power to threaten the internationalist-democratic agenda. The key to transcending the dilemma is to recognise that its structure is not immutable. The political significance of intellectual communities opposing an internationalist-democratic agenda can vary. Moreover, the significance of political ideologies is a consequence of a debate between societal groups made up of individuals with an interest in seeing how that contest is resolved. As chapter four noted, in an increasingly interdependent world states taking a unilateralist perspective have increasingly failed to meet the needs and expectations of their citizens. Political ideologies that advocate unilateralist security policies have been politically marginalised. Their approach has been dismissed as out of touch by individuals concerned about nuclear, socioeconomic and environmental threats that cannot be addressed unilaterally. More positively, with increased opportunity to travel individuals have realised the opportunities for self-fulfillment increase through internationalist ideologies and have become frustrated by the parochial outlook of nationalist and exclusivist approaches. The internationalist identity of many states has not been enforced nor even encouraged by other states. Rather it has grown from individual aspirations to change their more immediate society in a manner that replicates the confidence and opportunity experienced by those living in the internationalist-democratic states that make up security communities.

The decisive work in transcending the security dilemma, then, takes place at the societal level and is dependent on the political significance of transnational civil society. This is not to argue that the international-democratic state plays no role in either consolidating or extending the values of a security community. As an extension of society it is, of course, dependent on internationalist-democratic values being embedded in that society. But in moments of transition when the possibility exits that such values will become disembedded, state intervention can be decisive. If it is responsive to the needs and aspirations of its citizens without compromising its internationalist identity by doing anything that negates the needs of other individuals, then the state can be a positive force in the creation of a security community.

The key here is the state's internationalist identity. This does not necessarily mean cooperating with other states. Rather it means applying the same democratic principles to the citizens of other states that it applies to its own citizens. Deutsch's argument that a security community rests on giving adequate weight to the messages of other political units is an excellent guide. The only appropriate 'political unit', of course is the individual, and 'giving adequate weight' means making sure that their needs are not neglected and their aspirations encouraged when they do not clash with those of one's own citizens. The dilemma arises in the uncertainty that accompanies any intervention on behalf of internationalist-democratic forces in a transitional state. Intervention may make things worse or it may increase the political significance of internationalist-democratic forces. The key is, however, that the stronger those forces are at the societal level, the less intense the dilemma is for the internationalist-democratic state when considering intervention. Moreover, should internationalist-democratic values become embedded in the identity of what was once considered a transitional state, then the security dilemma can be transcended.

Lessons from the Cold War

In practice these conclusions are reinforced by the lessons of the Cold War. This section draws on the empirical analysis offered in chapters three and five to make two points that should inform the foreign policy of internationalist and democratic states. They will be introduced under the sub-headings: Multilateralism, and Détente and Disarmament.

Multilateralism

Multilateralism does indeed matter (Ruggie, 1993). Both empirical chapters focused on the role NATO played during the Cold War. Clearly

NATO was a collective defence organisation that was very much part of the Realist policy of containing the Soviet Union. Yet in the absence of the Soviet threat it may still have been necessary to invent it. Such a conclusion is reinforced by the fact that NATO continues to exist long after the Soviet Union stopped being a military threat. As chapter five made clear NATO was for as well as against something and as recent histories have noted (Risse-Kappen, 1996; Hampton, 1996) NATO has existed as an expression of a liberal democratic security community.

For NATO membership, being a liberal democracy was, of course, less important than being anti-Soviet. The case of Turkey, an illiberal, undemocratic but geostrategically very important state, is often cited by sceptics of the liberal argument. Their point is an important one. By highlighting what Hampton called the 'hybrid' identity of NATO one should qualify the less critical claims that NATO is the defender of democracy. It is equally important, however, not to dismiss the implications of the liberal analysis at the first sign of an inconsistency. Not all states may have been democratic, but they were all subject to the practice of multilateralism that bound NATO together in a manner that was much more effective than the coercive practices of the Soviet controlled Warsaw Pact. Multilateral practices between statist elites do not make a security community. Chapter four made that clear. Yet by giving states a voice in the dialogue that constructed NATO policy and by compromising in the name of consensus, NATO's practices encouraged the internationalist identity that is an essential component of a security community.

In fact, if one can temporarily operate at the interstate level of analysis, one can draw an analogy between NATO and the dialogic community that chapter four used as the basis for a security community. The foundation of this community were certain principles, national self-determination and non-discrimination (Hampton, 1996). Beyond that NATO's policy was open to discussion. Obviously practice did not approximate the ideal and the discussion was mediated by the realities of power relations. Yet the outcome was in no way preordained by the distribution of material power. As Risse-Kappen (1995) shows, less powerful states often did influence the policy of the United States. Interests were not given by the distribution of material capabilities they were politically contingent. Not only that, other states as well as transnational non-governmental actors were all influential on decisions that defined American interests.

The multilateral management of relations between member states was considered by liberals to be the original and most important function of the alliance. To this end consensus between those states became an end in itself. Consensus certainly helped in deterring the Soviet Union, and the argument that the Soviet Union needed deterring helped achieve consensus. The main purpose of NATO, according to Liberals however, was the management of transatlantic relations in a way that avoided security issues arising between them. Fundamental to the success of American policy here was not only a commitment to the foundations on which this dialogue was based, but also a willingness to compromise if the consequences of that dialogue and the requirements of consensus necessitated that.

The power of what Hampton called the 'Versailles remedial' – that discrimination against Germany or any other state could threaten American security – was central to the Liberal task of persuading Realists that their conception of 'America' could not be secured in separation from other states. Being embedded in the State Department this idea had a constant influence on U.S. policy and had a transformative effect on American identity. To repeat Thomas Risse-Kappen (1995, pp.176-181):

> U.S. membership in an alliance of democratic states shaped the process by which American decision makers struggled over the definition of American interests and preferences.... [It] affected the identity of American actors in the sense that 'we' in whose name the President decided incorporated the European allies.

If NATO was not necessarily made up of democratic states the 'we' feeling identified here, suggests it approximates the security community identified by Deutsch. By assisting the processes that embedded internationalism in state's identities, NATO's practice of multilateralism helped secure the transatlantic community.

Defending these principles and practices was, therefore, central to America's interest and identity. The dilemma posed by the Soviet Union was not so much how to defend the territory of NATO without provoking a Soviet attack, it was how to manage relations with the Soviet state without compromising the internationalist and democratic values that kept peace across the transatlantic security community and held open the prospect of peace with Eastern Europe. Chapter five illustrates how this dilemma played out across the issue of German unification, nuclear arms control and nuclear proliferation. The U.S. could not compromise its principles without risking the transatlantic security community, but it could not hope to reduce tensions with the Soviet Union without compromising on those issues.

As the end of the Cold War illustrated this dilemma was by no means immutable. The pressure exerted by transnational civil society changed the interests and identity of the Soviet Union and East European states. They changed, moreover, in a way that, at first sight, reflected the international-democratic values of the transatlantic community. Encouraged by the political freedom given by Gorbachev's reforms and, as will be noted below, reassured by the process of conventional and nuclear disarmament, transnational supporters of civil society gained political significance in states across Eastern Europe. As their significance grew at the societal level, America's security dilemma was moderated. Sticking to its principles of self-determination and non-discrimination was less risky because the Soviets themselves were espousing them.

That is not to underestimate the difficulties facing American statecraft in 1989-1990. New Political Thinking had far from embedded itself in the Soviet Union and the uncompromising pursuit of German self-determination and its consequences (i.e. NATO membership) risked, undermining the improved relations with the USSR. When civil society toppled the Berlin Wall in 1989 the transatlantic security community was faced with dangers and opportunities. Conscious of the former but determined not to let the latter slip, the Bush administration displayed fine judgement and skillful diplomacy to consolidate and extend that community. While Germany in NATO gave Soviet traditionalists a temporary political boost, the forces of internationalism and democracy in the USSR were by no means defeated.

The assessment of the Bush administration on Lithuanian independence was rightly different. The political opposition in Moscow was strong enough to suggest that it would have been imprudent on the part of the U.S. to have recognised Lithuanian independence in 1990 and extend NATO membership to it there and then. Yet once again, that does not mean that dilemma was determined by absolute political realities. A year later the Bush administration had no difficulty in extending recognition to all the Baltic states, and while NATO membership may remain imprudent, further changes in Russia's identity may moderate the dilemma posed by that issue.

The main point to draw from this argument is not that NATO is central to the future of a transatlantic security community and that by extending it one is extending the zone of peace. Clearly NATO remains a hybrid institution. Its meaning for Lithuanians is clearly different to that interpreted by many Russians. Claims that Soviet New Thinkers were under the impression that NATO would evolve into a purely political alliance would partly explain why many Russians are so opposed to its use of military force in the Balkans. The more important point is that *the principles* embodied by NATO and not necessarily the organisation itself are central to the future of the transatlantic security community. Self-determination, non-discrimination and dialogue have helped produce a new identity among the states of North America, Western and Central Europe.

As important a point is the realisation that NATO is not the only organisation that embodies these principles. The OSCE plays a vital role in extending these practices beyond NATO's jurisdiction. Indeed the fact that the Helsinki Principles were central to the way the U.S. ended the Cold War is often overlooked. NATO may have been the institution that integrated Germany and other states into the transatlantic community but the fact that this took place without too much disruption was because Soviet New Thinkers did not see any inconsistency with the Helsinki Principles. Gorbachev's key concession at the 1990 Washington Summit was prompted by the American argument that Germany had a right to choose its own alliance under the Helsinki Principles (Baker, 1995, pp.253-254; Bush and Scowcroft, 1998, p.282)[2]. Like the Versailles remedial helps internationalists convince American exceptionalists that its interests lie in defending the principles of the security community, so the Helsinki Principles, further the arguments of internationalists in Russia, more so than NATO principles.

Détente and Disarmament

Of course the Helsinki Principles were formulated in a period of détente between the United States and the Soviet Union. Recognising this gives some indication of the way interstate relations impacted on the support for transnational civil society. Moreover, because the political fortunes of civil society have been identified as central to the end of the Cold War, pointing to the impact that U.S. policy towards the Soviet Union had on civil society will help identify what kind of policies helped end the Cold War.

Again chapters three and five shed important light on this question. Together they conclude that a cooperative policy towards an ideological opponent should be pursued as far as this is not inconsistent with the internationalist and democratic values that are central to the long term prospects of a security community. Cooperating to achieve the increased security and prosperity of a state that withholds those benefits from its own citizens is at first sight contrary to the ideals of a security community. Yet the lesson of the Cold War suggests that an aggressive approach towards totalitarian states may satisfy oversimplified moral arguments, but it does very little to advance the values on which enduring peace is based.

Chapter five, for example argued that the internationalist and democratic values became politically significant across East European society during the period of détente. Despite strong political opposition that saw détente as appeasement and a betrayal of democracy, the signing of the Helsinki Final Act proved revolutionary. The human rights accords contained in the Final Act inspired civil society to hold Communist states accountable to their own promises. By also giving them legitimacy in their own society and by linking their welfare to the state's interest in arms control and trade, the Helsinki process increased the political significance of internationalist and democratic values.

The key point for U.S. policy was that totalitarian states were willing to make 'tactical concessions' (Thomas 1999) to human rights activists so long as the prospect of trade and arms control was real. Chapter five presented evidence of a direct link between President Carter's willingness to cooperate with the states of the Soviet bloc, his emphasis on human rights and the increased political freedom that was given to human rights activists in the late 1970s. It also suggested, it can do no more than that, that Reagan's confrontational policies and his unwillingness to negotiate seriously with totalitarian states, contributed to the crackdown on political opposition in the early 1980s, most notably in Poland. This argument, of course, rests on hypothetical arguments, but it is clear, as chapter five concluded, that the Reagan administration, for all its condemnation of Soviet practices, was powerless to stop the repression.

The very fact that the agents of democracy were also advocates of superpower cooperation tends to reinforce this argument. The transnational agents of internationalism and democratisation across Europe were fully aware that nuclear war was the ultimate violation of human rights. Peace, moreover, rested on democracy, but democracy could only flourish when international tension was low and states could not use the threat of war with an external enemy as an excuse for internal repression.

Further support for this argument is provided by a close examination of America's policy in 1989 when the democratic revolutions actually took place. The U.S. was pursuing a policy of détente rather than confrontation and had been doing so with increasing commitment since 1984. Cooperating with the Soviet elite to reassure them that the United States did not intend to exploit the turmoil that accompanied Gorbachev's reforms reinforced the political standing of New Thinkers in the Soviet Union. Indeed once the revolutionary potential of those reforms became clear, the Bush administration realised that the principles of deterrence and strategic stability were in fact an obstacle to democratisation. It recognised that more could be achieved through disarmament, than arms control.

Chapters three and five clearly demonstrate that the rationale for conventional and nuclear disarmament was political. Primarily, NATO unity demanded such a compromise. But there was also an understanding that political reform in Eastern Europe and the Soviet Union would lead to some kind of disorder. To make sure internationalism and democracy prevailed it was necessary to make sure the ensuing battle was a conflict of ideas, free from the threat of military coercion. If military power had been decisive then it is likely that the 1989 revolutions would have been condemned to emulate the 1956 and 1968 uprisings. The United States, moreover, would have had to continue to 'temper duty with prudence' for longer than even George Bush would have wished.

Inherent in political disorder is the possibility of violence. In that situation lies the possibility that violence can escalate to levels that necessarily limit the commitment one can give to ideological principles. Obviously the danger of war, particularly nuclear war, demands compromise with ideological opponents. Disarmament reduces the possibility that conflict will escalate to those levels where prudence means backing off one's principles. Disarmament across Europe in between 1989 and 1991 made it easier for Bush to set aside prudence and stick to the democratic agenda. This is not to conclude that disorder and low-intensity conflict in the name of democracy is a good thing. Rather it is to recognise that disarmament is a positive step towards achieving the ideal situation where ideologies are assessed solely on their ability respond to the needs and aspirations of individuals, and are not mediated by coercive power that is controlled and manipulated by special interests.

Security Communities and American Hegemony

Responsiveness is the foundation of any security community. Giving the messages of other political units adequate consideration was how Deutsch identified a security community. Chapter four made clear that the only political units worthy of security were those that responded to the needs of individuals and made sure their voice was heard in the process that constructed international society. It is on this basis that this book made an assessment of the role American foreign policy and, more generally, its international hegemony plays in the potential process of constructing a security community.

As was implied by the above summary of President Bush's achievements, the way America ended the Cold War was largely consistent with the normative role of a responsible great power (Bull, 1995). In helping to consolidate and extend the transatlantic security community, U.S. foreign policy struck the correct balance between duty and prudence. Yet there are structural features of that community that are increasingly a cause for concern. Moreover, those features are a large obstacle to the idea of extending the transatlantic security community or creating new communities based on similar principles.

Central to this argument is an understanding of the influence American exceptionalism has on the social processes that help constitute international relations. This final section looks at the role this plays in the military, political and socioeconomic dimensions of international relations. It concludes by pointing out that the Cold War could only end with a significant change to the identity of the Soviet Union. The consolidation of existing communities and the creation of a global one will involve significant changes in American identity.

The Military Dimension

A politically significant constituency in America's identity discourse sees itself as separate from the rest of the world with a duty to provide an example of peace and freedom. In military terms this sense of exceptionalism translates into a world view that denies any kind of responsibility for the security dilemmas of other states. America's nuclear weapons, according to this view, were to deter, whereas those weapons deployed by others with different values, were to attack. And because non-American values inspired aggressive ambition, America was justified in adopting offensive force postures if that was deemed necessary to deter. The threat to American values came not from this response, but from states with non-American values. America's nuclear weapons, according to this view, did not provoke, they were merely a response to the autonomous threat posed by others.

This aspect of American culture elevated the view that nuclear weapons were not necessarily a challenge to the impermeability of a state's territoriality (Herz, 1959). America could remain removed from the troubles of the old world, even in the nuclear age. Nuclear weapons were either capable of disarming an adversary in a preemptive, damage limitation strike, or technical solutions could be found to reconstruct the state's 'hard shell' (Herz, 1959). President Reagan's dream of the latter, of course, was the inspiration behind his conception of SDI. As Fitzgerald (2000, pp.22-25) notes, it was a vision that was perpetuated in American popular culture, a media that may even have kept the idea alive in Reagan's mind. Reagan's March 1983 speech announcing SDI used language very similar to the script of his earlier film *Murder in the Air*, and Paul Newman's *Torn Curtain*.

Liberal internationalists, of course, rejected this view. They embraced the idea of a nuclear revolution, recognised the interdependence of states under the nuclear threat and worked towards strengthening the norms of strategic stability. The ambiguity that surrounded (and continues to surround) the offer to share missile defence technology, demonstrates the difficulty of squaring the policies that stem from exceptionalism with the internationalism in American identity. Often the two sides were irreconcilable. At the Reykjavik summit, for instance, Reagan's dream of restoring national invulnerability through SDI clashed with the liberal view that strategic defences were merely a means of bargaining with the Soviets and strengthening the norm of strategic stability based on mutual vulnerability.

Ironically, the internationalist and exceptionalist strands of America's strategic policy threatened the preferred position of the American military. The Joint Chiefs opposed Reagan's vision of SDI because it threatened America's offensive capacity both conceptually, and, more to the point, financially. And for similar reasons they opposed the idea of a negotiated transition to a defense dominated world. The first step of the transition, as chapter three noted, was the elimination of ballistic missiles, something the Chiefs and their spokesman Admiral Crowe, opposed vehemently. Their opposition to the Reykjavik proposal as a starting point for such a transition was enough to sideline the idea of nuclear disarmament.

While nuclear disarmament has occurred since Reykjavik, it is clear that militarism and nuclearism are clearly embedded in America's internationalism. Moreover, the belief that military technology, either offensive or defensive, can deliver America from the threat of nuclear devastation stems from a politically significant sense of exceptionalism. The impression created by this mix of exceptionalism and internationalism is that America is unwilling to live with the vulnerability that the rest of the world accepts as part of the 'strategic stability' that America itself advocates. It is an impression of American hegemony that fails to encourage a sense of community with others.

The mutual vulnerability that liberals accept, has been a central part in fostering the internationalist identity between and across states. An "American" missile defence system sends the signal that all are not created equal and in fact Americans have greater right to security than others. This unilateralism is anathema to a security community where others are seen as an extension of the self. Nuclear weapons and the regime of strategic stability do less violence to the idea of community because it encourages a common identity. Yet that identity is one of common insecurity. Only by recognising that the interdependent nature of security goes beyond that highlighted by nuclear weapons and only then by abolishing nuclear weapons, can such a community be secure. America's exceptionalism and its faith in the idea that a military-technical solution can deliver America from insecurity, is an obstacle to that process.

Political Dimension

The unilateralism displayed in the military dimension of America's security discourse is also clearly evident in the political dimension of its security discourse. As noted above the practice of multilateralism is central to fostering a sense of common identity. By definition unilateralism demonstrates an unwillingness to compromise even if the messages of other political units have been given adequate consideration. American unilateralism in the field of missile defence and nuclear weapons risks the arms control and disarmament regime that could provide the basis for a wider security community. Its challenge to the ABM Treaty during the Reagan administration and subsequently was and is a threat not only to the security regime based on mutual vulnerability and thereby a threat to relations with Russia, but is also a direct threat to relations with the NATO allies. Multilateralism is fundamental to the NATO alliance and the ABM Treaty was and remains a fundamental part of the policy consensus that encourages NATO unity. As chapter five and the above comments made clear, NATO unity was and remains a security objective in itself. A unilateralist American approach on the ABM Treaty and the issue of missile defence has in the past threatened such unity. It will invariably do so in the future.

If its challenge to the ABM Treaty threatens to undermine the START regime and the NATO security community, so its inability to move beyond START threatens the Non-Proliferation Treaty (NPT) regime and the prospect of promoting the conditions on which to base a global security community. At the center of the NPT regime is the promise by the nuclear 'haves' to abolish their nuclear capability. This promise takes on political significance when aspirant states like India legitimise their weapons programme with reference to the poor disarmament record of the nuclear states. Again American foreign policy appears to recommend something it would not wish upon itself. Nuclear disarmament again appears central to the prospect of a wider security community.

Of course claims to an 'international community' often accompany the actions of the United Nations (U.N.). Yet U.S. policy towards the U.N. is illustrative of the distance the U.N. has to travel before embodying a true sense of community. The U.N. of course is based on the same multilateral principles as NATO. While NATO has been described as the only international institution loved across America's political spectrum, however, the U.N. has recently been the most reviled. The reason for the different American attitude is easily identified. The short term compromises that America has to make to see the long term benefits of the dialogue created by the U.N. is much larger than that which NATO has ever demanded. America's unwillingness to pay its financial dues to the U.N., to make a strong military commitment to its peacekeeping and humanitarian operations, and to cede its sovereignty to institutions such as the International Criminal Court, again demonstrate the tension between its exceptionalism and internationalism.

If a security community is to be extended further, and if phrases like the international community are to mean anything other than a rhetorical cover for what Booth (1994) calls a 'global protection racket', then democratic states cooperating through multilateral institutions like the U.N. is perhaps the best chance. If America is to contribute to that end then it must be willing to compromise to the dialogue that results from those institutions.

Economic Dimension

Similar conclusions stem from chapter six's analysis of the economic dimension of American hegemony. The extent to which capitalism can undermine repressive states, liberate the individual and use its creative energy to meet individual needs and aspirations more so than any other economic system, suggests that capitalism is consistent with the idea of a security community. Moreover, the globalisation of capitalism can, as liberals are quick to point out, break down the particularist identities of mercantilist nationalism that is anathema to a security community. This book would not argue with the claim that transnational capitalism can encourage the 'we' feeling that constitutes a community. There are, however, limits to the emancipatory capacity of free market capitalism.

An important conclusion to draw from chapter six is that global capitalism is merely reconfiguring the 'self' and 'the other'. Certain social groups that were previously seen in terms of a threatening other may now be seen as extensions of the self. National identity has little significance in the global market place and the 'we' feeling does transcend state boundaries. The community created by global capitalism may not discriminate in this way but it still differentiates an 'other' in terms of capitalist values and identifies its worth in terms of material wealth. Communities that are not considered attractive investment prospects may not be considered a threat, but they are certainly not truly considered part of the wider international community. Their own particular economic system or their own particular social values excludes them from such a community. They are not considered as extensions of the self because the capitalist self has nothing to gain from assisting them. These groups are excluded from the liberal community because of their inability or their unwillingness to contribute to the economic efficiency of that community.

Thus while the self-other relationship is being transcended amongst those with the social mobility to exploit the opportunities presented by the free market, new self-other relationships are being created. On the one hand there are those who can profit by this system and, on the other, those who cannot or do not want to. In other words, there are new conceptions of 'us' but there also new conceptions of 'them'. Free market capitalism does not extend the sense of community it reconfigures it. There may be integration of communities across states, but there is also a risk of the disintegration of communities that were previously located within states.

'America' may be considered to be at the heart of the new community based on liberal and capitalist values, but not all 'Americans' feel secure in that community. Where you stand on globalisation depends on how quickly you can move to exploit the opportunities capitalism presents. Without the mobility of capital, globalisation is rather threatening.

The two-thirds of American society that, according to Galbraith (1992), benefit from the contemporary economic system, combined with the cultural structures identified in chapter six, secures the capitalist system in America. Yet once again, the politically significant narratives fail to understand the significance of American exceptionalism. In other states the proportion of those benefiting from capitalism is far less than the two-thirds of Americans identified by Galbraith. Additionally the cultural structures that are required to make capitalism work do not always exist, nor do all cultures value the consequences of free market capitalism. For states to be integrated into a security community the internationalisation of their identity is essential. Capitalism can play a central role in that. But if the internationalising process of contemporary capitalism is equated with the rampant individualism of capitalist America then it will fail to produce the conditions of a security community.

If the agents of transnational capital fail see others as extensions of the self and treat their existence as inconsequential or even as a means to a particular end, then not only will the opportunity to extend the community be missed, but the liberal order will become an object of securitization. The liberal order is and will be an improvement on the realpolitik of the Westphalian system. But to transcend the old nation-state system is not to create a larger security community. To contribute to the extension rather than simply the reconfiguration of security communities, the opportunities that globalisation offers have to be distributed more widely. This is a plea for something approximating welfare-state liberalism at the international level, but that is not to be equated with Europeanisation. Its standard is taken from the ideal of a dialogic community that seeks to give all a voice in the way the new communities are constructed. Its argument is that the new communities of the liberal and capitalist order have the potential to repress as well as liberate and it is that danger that has to be guarded against.

The influence Washington has on globalisation is perhaps the most powerful of any one particular government. As the driving force behind the multilateral management of the global economy it has in many ways been successful in helping to create the internationalist identity of many states. The consolidation of the 'West' through welfare state liberalism (Ikenberry, 1989) was perhaps its greatest achievement. Yet chapter six argued further that Washington has become increasingly removed not only from the needs of nascent security communities, but also from many Americans themselves. Therein lies the possibility that Washington may be able to play a more responsible and responsive role. Washington and by extension the international institutions that are heavily influenced by it have been penetrated by a transnational capitalist elite, and while the cultural and institutional structures of American society facilitate this they by no means exclude the possibility that other groups cannot reorient U.S. policy. Transnational civil society has a potentially powerful ally in the large proportion of American society that has come increasingly disillusioned with Washington. If that potential can be mobilised, internationalists and democrats may find Washington more responsive to their concerns.

Notes

[1] Cited in Wyn Jones, 1995, p.312.
[2] It is also worth noting that during the coup that temporarily removed Gorbachev from power in 1991, Secretary of State James Baker resisted the initial advice to call an emergency NATO meeting. Fearing this would buttress the support of the coup plotters, Baker evoked the Helsinki Principles as a means of condemning them and appealing to civil society across the Soviet Union to oppose the coup (Baker, 1995, pp.517-518).

References

Baker, III, J.A. (with Thomas M. DeFrank) (1995), *The Politics of Diplomacy. Revolution, War and Peace, 1989-1992*, G.P.Putnam's, New York.

Booth, K. (1994), 'Military Intervention: Duty and Prudence', in L.Freedman (ed.), *Military Intervention in European Conflicts*, Blackwell, Oxford, pp.56-75.

Bush, G. and Scowcroft, B. (1998), *A World Transformed*, Alfred A.Knopf, New York.

Cox, R.W. (1986), 'Social Forces, States and World Orders: Beyond International Relations Theory', in Robert O. Keohane (ed.), *Neorealism and its Critics*, Columbia University Press, New York, pp.204-254.

Fitzgerald, F. (2000), *Way Out There in the Blue. Reagan, Star Wars and the End of the Cold War*, Simon and Schuster, New York.

Galbraith, J.K. (1992), *The Culture of Contentment*, Houghton Mifflin Co., Boston London.

Hampton, M.N. (1996), *The Wilsonian Impulse. U.S. Foreign Policy, the Alliance, and German Unification*, Praeger, Westport.

Herz, J. H. (1959), *International Politics in the Atomic Age*, Columbia University Press, New York.

Ikenberry, G.J. (1989), 'Rethinking the Origins of American Hegemony', *Political Science Quarterly*, Vol.104, pp.375-400.

Jackson, R. (1995), 'The Situational Ethics of Statecraft', in Cathal J.Nolan, *Ethics and Statecraft. The Moral Dimension of International Affairs*, Praeger, Westport. pp.21-36.

Risse-Kappen, T. (1995), *Cooperation Amongst Democracies: The European Influence on U.S. Foreign Policy*, Princeton University Press, Princeton.

Risse-Kappen, T. (1996), 'Collective Identity in a Democratic Community: The Case of NATO', in P.J.Katzenstein (ed.), *The Culture of National Security. Norms and Identity in World Politics*, Columbia University Press, New York, pp.357-399.

Ruggie, J.G. (ed.), (1993), *Multilateralism Matters. The Theory and Praxis of an Institutional Form*, Columbia University Press, New York.

Thomas, D.C. (1999), 'The Helsinki Accords and Political Change in Eastern Europe', in Thomas Risse, Stephen C. Ropp and Kathryn Sikkink (eds.), *The Power of Human Rights. International Norms and Domestic Change*, Cambridge University Press, Cambridge, pp.205-233.

Wyn Jones, R. (1995), '"Message in a Bottle"? Theory and Praxis in Critical Security Studies', *Contemporary Security Policy*, Vol.16, pp.299-319.

Bibliography

Acharya, A. (1998), 'Collective identity and conflict management in Southeast Asia', in E.Adler and M.Barnett, *Security Communities*, Cambridge University Press, Cambridge, pp.198-227.

Adler, E. (1992), 'The Emergence of Cooperation: national epistemic communities and the international evolution of the idea of arms control', *International Organization*, Vol.46, pp.101-146.

Adler, E. and Barnett, M. (1998a), 'Security Communities in theoretical perspective', in E.Adler, and M.Barnett, *Security Communities*, Cambridge University Press, Cambridge, pp.3-28.

Adler, E. and Barnett, M. (1998b), 'A Framework for the study of security communities', in E.Adler and M.Barnett, *Security Communities*, Cambridge University Press, Cambridge, pp.29-65.

Adler, E. and Barnett, M. (1998c), 'Studying Security Communities in theory, comparison and history', in E.Adler and M.Barnett, *Security Communities*, Cambridge University Press, Cambridge, pp.413-441.

Andrew, C. (1995), *For the President's Eyes Only. Secret Intelligence and the American Presidency From Washington to Bush*, Harper Collins, London.

Andrew, C. and Gordievsky, O. (1991), *KGB. The Inside Story of its Operations From Lenin to Gorbachev*, Sceptre, London.

Axelrod, R. (1984), *The Evolution of Cooperation*, Basic Books, New York.

Axelrod, R. and Keohane, R.O. (1993), 'Achieving Cooperation Under Anarchy: Strategies and Institutions', in David A. Baldwin (ed.) *Neorealism and Neoliberalism. The Contemporary Debate*, Columbia University Press, New York, pp.85-115.

Baker III, J.A. (1995) (with Thomas M. DeFrank), *The Politics of Diplomacy. Revolution, War and Peace, 1989-1992*, G.P.Putnam's Sons, New York.

Ball, D. (1982/3), 'U.S. Strategic Forces: How Would They Be Used?', *International Security*, Vol.7, pp.31-60.

Ball, D and Richelson, J. (eds.) (1986), *Strategic Nuclear Targeting*, Cornell University Press, Ithaca.

Barber, B. (1995), *McWorld versus Jihad*, Ballantine Books, New York.

Beschloss, M.R. and Talbott, S. (1993), *At the Highest Levels. The Inside Story of the End of the Cold War*, Little, Brown and Company, Boston, Toronto and London.

Beukel, E. (1989), *American Perceptions of the Soviet Union and a Nuclear Adversary From Kennedy to Bush*, Pinter in association with Spiers, London.

Bhagwati, J. and Patrick, H. (eds.) (1990), *Aggressive Unilateralism: America's 301 Trade Policy and the World Trading System*, University of Michigan Press, Ann Arbor.

Blair, B. (1993), *The Logic of Accidental Nuclear War*, Brookings, Washington, D.C.

Booth, K. (1994), 'Military Intervention: Duty and Prudence', in L.Freedman (ed.) *Military Intervention in European Conflicts*, Blackwell, Oxford, pp.56-75.

Booth, K. (1995), 'Human Wrongs in International Relations', *International Affairs*, Vol.71, pp.103-126.

Booth, K. (1998), 'Conclusion: security within global transformation?', in Ken Booth (ed.) *Statecraft and Security. The Cold War and Beyond*, Cambridge University Press, Cambridge.

Booth, K. (1999), 'Three Tyrannies', in Tim Dunne and Nicholas Wheeler (eds.), *Human Rights in Global Politics*, Cambridge University Press, Cambridge, pp.31-70.

Booth, K. and Wheeler, N. (1992) 'The Security Dilemma', in Baylis, J. and Rengger, N. (eds.) *Dilemmas in World Politics: International Issues in a Changing World*, Clarendon Press, Oxford, pp.29-60.

Boserup, A. and Nield, R. (eds.) (1990), *The Foundations of Defensive Defense*, St. Martins Press, New York.

Brodie, B. (1946) (ed.), 'Implications for Military Policy', in Bernard Brodie (ed.) *The Absolute Weapon: Atomic Power and World Order*, Harcourt and Company, New York, pp.70-107.

Brodie, B. (1959), *Strategy in the Missile Age*, Princeton University Press, Princeton.

Bull, H. (1980), 'The great irresponsibles? The United States, the Soviet Union and world order', *International Journal*, Vol.35, pp.437-447.

Bull, H. (1984), *Justice in International Relations*, The Hagey Lectures, University of Waterloo, Ontario.

Bull, H. (1995), *The Anarchical Society. A Study of Order in World Politics*, Macmillan, London.

Burley, A. (1993), 'Regulating the World: Multilateralism, International Law, and the Projection of the New Deal Regulatory State', in John Gerrard Ruggie (ed.) *Multilateralism Matters. The theory and practice of an Institutional Form*, Columbia University Press, New York, pp.126-156.

Bush, G. and Scowcroft, B. (1998), *A World Transformed*, Alfred A.Knopf, New York.

Butterfield, H. (1957), *History and Human Relations*, Collins, London.

Buzan, B. (1987), 'Common Security, Non-provocative Defence and the Future of Western Europe', *Review of International Studies*, Vol. 13, pp.265-279.

Buzan, B. (1993), 'Societal security, state security and internationalisation', in Ole Waever, Barry Buzan, Morten Kelstrup and Pierre Lemaitre, *Identity, Migration and the New Security Agenda in Europe*, Pinter Publishers Ltd, London, pp.41-88.

Buzan, B. and Waever, O. (1997), 'Slippery? Contradictory? Sociologically untenable? The Copenhagen school replies', *Review of International Studies*, Vol.23, pp.241-250.

Buzan, B., Waever, O. and de Wilde, J. (1998), *Security. A New Framework for Analysis*, Lynne Rienner, Boulder, Colorado.

Cahn, A.H. (1998), *Killing Détente. The Right Attacks the CIA*, Pennsylvania State University Press, Pennsylvania.

Checkel, J.T. (1997), *Ideas and International Political Change. Soviet/Russian Behaviour and the End of the Cold War*, Yale University Press, New Haven and London.

Chernoff, F. (1991), 'Ending the Cold War: The Soviet Retreat and the U.S. Military Build Up', *International Affairs*, Vol.67, pp.111-126.

Chiltern, P (1994), 'Mechanics of Change: Social Movements, Transnational Coalition and the Transformation Processes in Eastern Europe', *Democratization*, Vol.1, pp.151-181.

Chomsky, N. (1992), *Deterring Democracy*, Vintage, London.

Cohen, J. (1990), 'Discourse Ethics and Civil Society', in D.Rasmussen (ed.) *Universalism vs Communitarianism*, MIT Press, Cambridge, MA., pp.83-105.

Collins, A. (1995), *The Security Dilemma and the End of the Cold War*, New York, Keele University Press.

Corwin, E.S. (1940), *The President: Office and Powers*, New York University Press, New York.

Cote, O. (1991), 'The Trident and the Triad: collecting the D-5 dividend', *International Security*, Vol.16, pp.117-145.

Cox, R.W. (1986), 'Social Forces, States and World Orders: Beyond International Relations Theory', in Robert O. Keohane (ed.) *Neorealism and its Critics*, Columbia University Press, New York, pp.204-254.

Cox, R. (1999), 'Civil Society at the turn of the millennium: prospects for an alternative world order', *Review of International Studies*, Vol.25, pp.3-28.

Crowe, W.J. (1993) (with David Chanoff), *In the Line of Fire: from Washington to the Gulf, the Politics and battles of the New Military*, Simon and Schuster, New York.

Deudney, D. and Ikenberry, G.J. (1999), 'The nature and sources of liberal international order', *Review of International Studies*, Vol.25, pp.179-196.

Deutsch, K.W. (1957), et.al. *Political Community in the North Atlantic Area. International Organization in the Light of Historical Experience*, Princeton University Press, Princeton.

Etzioni, A. (1962), *The Hard Way to Peace: A New Strategy*, Collier Books, New York.

Evangelista, M. (1995), 'The Paradox of State Strength: Transnational Relations, Domestic Structures and Security Policy in Russia and the Soviet Union', *International Organization*, Vol.49, pp.1-38.

Evangelista, M. (1999), *Unarmed Forces. The Transnational Movement and the End of the Cold War*, Cornell University Press, Ithaca and London.

Feis, H. (1957), *Churchill, Roosevelt, Stalin : The War They Waged and the Peace They Sought*, Princeton University Press, Princeton.

Fitzgerald, F. (2000), *Way Out There in the Blue. Reagan, Star Wars and the End of the Cold War*, Simon and Schuster, New York.

Foley, M. (1991), *American Political Ideas. Traditions and Usages*, Manchester University Press, Manchester.

Frank, W.S. and Gillette, P.S. (1992), *Soviet Military Doctrine from Lenin to Gorbachev, 1915-1991*, Greenwood Press, London.

Freedman, L. (1981), *The Evolution of Nuclear Strategy*, Macmillan, London.

Friedberg, A.L. (1980), 'A History of U.S. Strategic "Doctrine" 1945 to 1980', *Journal of Strategic Studies*, Vol.3, pp.37-71.

Gaddis, J.L. (1989), 'Hanging Tough Paid Off', Bulletin of Atomic Scientists, Vol.45, pp.11-14.

Gaddis, J.L. (1998), *We Now Know. Rethinking Cold War History*, Oxford University Press, Oxford.

Galbraith, J.K. (1992), *The Culture of Contentment*, Houghton Mifflin Co., Boston London.

Garthoff, R.L. (1985), *Détente and Confrontation. American-Soviet Relation from Nixon to Reagan*, Brookings, Washington, D.C.

Garthoff, R.L. (1994), *The Great Transition. American-Soviet Relations and the End of the Cold War*, Brookings, Washington, D.C.

Gill, S. (1991), *American Hegemony and the Trilateral Commission*, Cambridge University Press, Cambridge.

Gill, S. (1996), 'Globalization, Democratization and the Politics of Indifference', in James H. Mittelman, *Globalization. Critical Reflections*, Lynne Reinner, Boulder, Colorado, pp.205-228.

Gill, S. (1999), 'Globalisation, Market Civilisation and Disciplinary Neoliberalism', *Millennium. Journal of International Studies*, Vol.24 , pp.399-425.

Gills, B., Rocamora, J. and Wilson, R. (1993), 'Low-Intensity Democracy', in Barry Gills, Joel Rocamora and Richard Wilson, *Low-Intensity Democracy. Political Power in the New World Order*, Pluto Press, London, pp.3-34.

Glaser, C.L. (1990), *Analyzing Strategic Nuclear Policy*, Princeton University Press, Princeton.

Glaser, C.L. (1992), 'Political Consequences of Military Strategy. Expanding and Refining the Spiral and Deterrence Models', *World Politics*, Vol.44, pp.497-538.

Glaser, C.L. and Kaufmann, C. (1998), 'What is the Offense-Defense Balance and Can We Measure It?', *International Security*, Vol.22, pp.44-82.

Goldmann, K. (1995), 'Bargaining, Power, Domestic Politics and Security Dilemmas: Soviet "New Thinking" as Evidence', in Pierre Allan and Kjell Goldmann, *The End of the Cold War. Evaluating Theories of International Relations*, Kluwer Law, Dordecht, pp.82-103.

Gonzalez, G. and Haggard, S. (1998), 'The United States and Mexico: a pluralistic security community?', in Emanuel Adler and Michael Barnett (eds.) *Security Communities*, Cambridge University Press, Cambridge, pp.295-332.

Gray, C. (1993), *Weapons Don't Make War: Policy, Strategy and Military Technology*, University Press of Kansas, Lawrence, Kansas.

Gray, C. and Payne, K. (1980), 'Victory is Possible', *Foreign Policy*, Vol.39, pp.14-27.

Greenberg, D.L. (2000), 'Review Essay: The Empire Strikes Out. Why Star Wars Did Not End the Cold War,' *Foreign Affairs*, Vol.79, pp.136-142.

Greenstein, F.I. and Wohlforth, W.C. (eds) (1994), *Retrospective on the End of the Cold War*, Center of International Studies, Monograph Series Number 6, Princeton University.

Grieco, J.M. (1993), 'Anarchy and the Limits of Cooperation: A Realist Critique of New Liberal Institutionalism', in Baldwin, *Neoliberalism and Neorealism. The Contemporary Debate*, Columbia University Press, New York, pp.60-84.

Gross Stein, J. (1994), 'Political Learning By Doing: Gorbachev as Uncommitted Thinker and Motivated Learner', *International Organization*, Vol.48, pp.155-183.

Grunberg, I. and Risse-Kappen, T. (1995), 'A Time of Reckoning? Theories of International Relations and the End of the Cold War', in Pierre Allan and Kjell Goldmann, *The End of the Cold War. Evaluating Theories of International Relations*, Kluwer Law, Dordrecht, pp.104-146.

Haas, E. (1980), 'Why Collaborate? Issue-Linkage and International Regimes', *World Politics*, Vol.32, pp.357-378.

Haig, Jr. A. (1984), *Caveat: Realism, Reagan and Foreign Policy*, Macmillan, London.

Hampton, M.N. (1995), 'NATO at the creation: U.S. Foreign Policy, West Germany and the Wilsonian Impulse', *Security Studies*, Vol.4, pp.610-656.

Hampton, M.N. (1996), *The Wilsonian Impulse. U.S. Foreign Policy, the Alliance, and German Unification*, Praeger, Westport.

Held, D. (1995), *Democracy and Global Order. From the Modern State to Cosmopolitan Governance*, Polity Press, Oxford.

Herman, R.G. (1996), 'Identity, Norms, and National Security: The Soviet Foreign Policy Revolution and the End of the Cold War', in Peter J. Katzenstein (ed.) *The Culture of National Security. Norms and Identity in World Politics*, Columbia University Press, New York, pp.272-316.

Herz, J. (1950), 'Idealist Internationalism and the Security Dilemma', *World Politics*, Vol.2, pp.157-180.

Herz, J.H. (1959), *International Politics in the Atomic Age*, Columbia University Press, New York.

Hurrell, A. (1998), 'An emerging security community in South America?', in E. Adler and M.Barnett, *Security Communities*, Cambridge University Press, Cambridge, pp.228-264.

Hutchings, R.L. (1997), *American Diplomacy and the End of the Cold War. An Insider's Account of US Policy in Europe, 1989-1992*, Johns Hopkins University Press, Baltimore.

Ikenberry, G.J. (1989), 'Rethinking the Origins of American Hegemony', *Political Science Quarterly*, Vol.104, pp.375-400.

Ikenberry, G.J. (1999), 'Liberal Hegemony and the future of American postwar order', in T.V.Paul and J. Hall (eds.), *International Order and the Future of World Politics*, Cambridge University Press, Cambridge, pp.123-145.

Ikenberry, G.J and Kupchan, C.A. (1990), 'Socialization and hegemonic power', *International Organization*, Vol.44, pp.283-315.

Jackson, R. (1990), 'Martin Wight, International Theory and the Good Life', *Millennium: Journal of International Studies*, Vol.19, pp.261-272.

Jackson, R. (1996), 'The Political Theory of International Society', in Ken Booth and Steve Smith (eds.) *International Relations Theory Today*, Polity Press, Oxford, pp.110-128.

Jackson, R. and Sorensen, G. (1999), *Introduction to International Relations*, Oxford University Press, Oxford.

Jervis, R. (1976), *Perception and Misperception in International Politics*, Princeton University Press, Princeton.

Jervis, R. (1978), 'Cooperation Under the Security Dilemma', *World Politics*, Vol.30, pp.167-214.

Jervis, R. (1982), 'Security Regimes', *International Organization*, Vol.36, pp.357-378.

Jervis, R. (1989), *The Meaning of the Nuclear Revolution. Statecraft and the Prospect of Armageddon*, Cornell University Press, Cornell.

Johnson, R.H. (1983), 'Periods of Peril. The Window of Vulnerability and Other Myths', *Foreign Affairs*, Vol.16, pp.950-970.

Kahn, H. (1960), *On Thermonuclear War*, Princeton University Press, Princeton.

Kahn, H. (1962), *Thinking About the Unthinkable*, Horizon Press, New York.

Kaldor, M. (1991), 'After the Cold War', in Mary Kaldor (ed.), *Europe From Below. An East-West Dialogue*, Verso, London and New York, pp.27-43.

Kaldor, M. (1999), 'Transnational civil society', Tim Dunne and Nicholas J. Wheeler (eds.) *Human Rights in Global Politics*, Cambridge University Press, Cambridge, pp.195-213.

Kier, E. (1996), 'Culture and French Military Doctrine Before World War II', in Peter J. Katzenstein (ed.) *The Culture of National Security. Norms and Identity in World Politics*, Columbia University Press, New York, pp.186-215.

Kirkpatrick, J.J. (1982), *Dictatorships and Double Standards: Rationalism and Reason in Politics*, Simon and Schuster, New York.

Klein, B.S. (1994), *Strategic Studies and World Order. The Global Politics of Deterrence*, Cambridge University Press, Cambridge.

Knopf, J.W. (1997), 'The Nuclear Freeze Movement's Effect on Policy', in Thomas R. Rochon and David S. Meyer (eds.) *Coalitions and Political Movements. The Lessons of the Nuclear Freeze*, Lynne Rienner, Boulder, Colorado, pp.127-161.

Kramer, M. (1991), 'Warheads and Chaos. The Soviet Threat in Perspective', *The National Interest*, No.25, pp.94-97.

Krasner, S. (ed.) (1983), *International Regimes*, Cornell University Press, Ithaca.

Krause, K. and Williams, M.C. (1996), 'Broadening the Agenda of Security Studies: Politics and Methods', *Mershon International Studies Review*, Vol.40, pp.229-254.

Krause, K. and Williams, M.C. (1997), 'From Strategy to Security: Foundations of Critical Security Studies', in Keith Krause and Michael C. Williams, *Critical Security Studies. Concepts and Cases*, University of Minnesota Press, 1997.

Lebow, R.N. (1985), 'The Soviet Offensive in Europe: The Schlieffen Plan Revisited?', *International Security*, Vol.9, pp.47-78.

Lebow, R.N. (1995), 'The Long Peace, the End of the Cold War and the Failure of Realism', in Richard Ned Lebow and Thomas Risse-Kappen, (eds.) *International Political Theory and the End of the Cold War*, Columbia University Press, New York, pp.23-55.

Lebow, R.N. and Stein, J.G. (1994), *We All Lost the Cold War*, Princeton University Press, Princeton.

Lebow, R.N. and Stein, J. (1998), 'Nuclear Lessons of the Cold War', in Ken Booth (ed.) *Statecraft and Security, The Cold War and Beyond*, Cambridge University Press, Cambridge, pp.71-86.

Linklater, A. (1996), 'The achievements of critical theory', in M.Zalewski, K.Booth and S.Smith (eds.) *After Positivism*, Cambridge University Press, Cambridge, pp.279-298.

Linklater, A. (1998), *The Transformation of Political Community. Ethical Foundations of the Post-Westphalian Era*, Polity Press, Oxford.

Lipson, C. (1993), 'International Cooperation in Economic and Security Affairs', in David A. Baldwin (ed.) *Neorealism and Neoliberalism. The Contemporary Debate*, Columbia University Press, New York, pp.60-84.

Litwak, R.S. (1984), *Détente and the Nixon Doctrine : American foreign policy and the pursuit of stability,1969-1976*, Cambridge University Press, Cambridge.

Lundestad, G. (1990), *The American 'Empire' and Other Studies of U.S. Foreign Policy in a Comparative Perspective*, Oxford University Press and Norwegian University Press, Oxford.

Lynn Jones, S.M. (1995), 'Offense-Defense Theory and its Critics', *Security Studies*, Vol.4, pp.660-691.

Matlock, Jack F. (1995), *Autopsy of an Empire. The American Ambassador's Account of the Collapse of the Soviet Union*, Random House, New York.

McFarlane, R.C. (1994) (with Zofia Smardz), *Special Trust*, Cadell and Davies, New York.

McSweeney, B. (1996), 'Identity and security: Buzan and the Copenhagen School', *Review of International Studies*, Vol.22, pp.81-94.

McSweeney, B. (1998), 'Durkheim and the Copenhagen School: a response to Buzan and Waever', *Review of International Studies*, Vol.24, pp.137-140.

Mearsheimer, J. (1990), 'Back to the Future: Instability in Europe After the Cold War', *International Security*, Vol.15, pp.5-56.

Melanson, R.A. (1996), *American Foreign Policy Since the Vietnam War: the search for consensus from Nixon to Clinton*, M.E. Sharpe, Armonk, N.Y.

Nitze, P. (1976/7), 'Deterring Our Deterrent', *Foreign Policy*, Vol.25, pp.195-210.

Nolan, J.E. (1989), *Guardians of the Arsenal. The Politics of Nuclear Strategy*, Basic Books, New York.

Nye, J.S. (1987), 'Nuclear Learning and U.S.-Soviet Security Regimes', *International Organization*, Vol.41, pp.371-402.

Oberdorfer, D. (1991), *The Turn, From the Cold War to a New Era: the United States and the Soviet Union, 1983-1990*, Simon and Schuster, New York.

Osgood, C.E. (1962), *An Alternative to War and Surrender*, University of Illinois Press, Chicago.

Oye, K.A. (1995), 'Explaining the End of the Cold War: Morphological and Behavioural Adaptions to the Nuclear peace?', in Richard Ned Lebow and Thomas Risse-Kappen (eds.) *International Political Theory and the End of the Cold War*, Columbia University Press, New York, pp.57-83.

Palme, O. (1982), *Common Security: a programme for disarmament*, Pan Books, London.

Patman, R.G. (1999), 'Reagan, Gorbachev and the emergence of 'New Political Thinking'', *Review of International Studies*, Vol.25, pp.577-601.

Pipes, R. (1977), 'Why the Soviet Union thinks it could fight and win a nuclear war', *Commentary*, Vol.64, pp.21-34.

Posen, B.R. (1982), 'Inadvertent Nuclear War? Escalation and NATO's Northern Flank', *International Security*, Vol.7, pp.28-45.

Posen, B.R. (1984), *The Sources of Military Doctrine: France, Britain and Germany Between the World Wars*, Cornell University Press, Ithaca.

Ralph, J. (1999), 'GRIT, Collins and the End of the Cold War', *Review of International Studies*, Vol.25, pp.721-725.

Ralph, J. (2000), 'High Stakes and Low-Intensity Democracy. Understanding America's Policy of Promoting Democracy', in M.Cox, G.J.Ikenberry and T.Inoguchi, *American Democracy Promotion. Impulses, Strategies and Impacts*, Oxford University Press, Oxford.

Ravenal, E.C. (1982), 'Counterforce and the Alliance: The Ultimate Connection', *International Security*, Vol.6, pp.26-43.

Reich, R.B. (1999), 'The New Power', *The American Prospect*, November 23.

Rice, C. and Zelikow, P. (1995), *Germany Unified and Europe Transformed. A Study in Statecraft*, Harvard University Press, London, Cambridge, MA.

Richelson, J. (1983), 'PD-59, NSDD-13 and the Reagan Strategic Modernization Program', *Journal of Strategic Studies*, Vol.6, pp.125-146.

Risse-Kappen, T. (1994), 'Ideas do not float freely: transnational coalitions, domestic structures and the end of the Cold War', *International Organization*, Vol.48, pp.185-214.

Risse-Kappen, T. (1995), *Cooperation Amongst Democracies: The European Influence on U.S. Foreign Policy*, Princeton University Press, Princeton.

Risse-Kappen, T. (1996), 'Collective Identity in a Democratic Community: The Case of NATO', in P.J.Katzenstein (ed.) *The Culture of National Security. Norms and Identity in World Politics*, Columbia University Press, New York, pp.357-399.

Robinson, W.I. (1998), *Promoting Polyarchy. Globalization, U.S. Intervention, and Hegemony*, Cambridge University Press, Cambridge.

Ruggie, J.G. (1982), 'International regimes, transaction, and change: embedded liberalism in the postwar economic order', *International Organization*, Vol.33, pp.379-415.

Ruggie, J.G. (1993), 'Multilateralism: The Anatomy of an Institution', in John Gerard Ruggie (ed.) *Multilateralism Matters. The Theory and Praxis of an Institutional Form*, Columbia University Press, New York, pp.3-47.

Ruggie, J.G. (1994), 'At Home Abroad, Abroad at Home: International Liberalism and Domestic Stability in the New World Economy', *Millennium: Journal of International Studies*, Vol.24, pp.507-526.

Sagan, S.D. (1986), '1914 Revisited: Allies, Offense and Instability', *International Security*, Vol.11,pp.151-176.

Sagan, S.D. (1986/1987), 'Correspondence: The Origins of Offense and the Consequences of Counterforce', *International Security*, Vol.11, pp.193-198.

Sanders, J.W. (1983), *Peddlers of Crisis. The Committee on the Present Danger and the Politics of Containment*, South End Press, Boston, MA.

Shevardnadze, E. (translated by Catherine A. Fitzpatrick) (1991), *The Future Belong to Freedom*, Sinclair-Stevenson Ltd., London.

Shultz, G. (1993), *Turmoil and Triumph: My Years as Secretary of State*, Maxwell Macmillan International, New York.

Sicherman, H. (1999), 'Review Essay: George Bush, Reluctant Revolutionary', *Orbis*, Vol.43, pp.299-315.

Simpson, C. (1995), *National Security Directives of the Reagan and Bush Administrations. The Declassified History of U.S. Political and Military policy, 1981-1991*, Westview Press, Oxford.Stares, P. (1991), *Command*

SIPRI (1985), *Policies for Common Security*, Taylor and Francis, London and Philadelphia.

Smith, T. (1995), *America's Mission. The United States and the Worldwide Struggle for Democracy in the Twentieth Century*, Princeton University Press, Princeton.

Smoke, R. and Kortunov, A. (eds.) (1991), *Mutual Security: a new approach to Soviet-American Relations*, St.Martins Press, London.

Snyder, J. (1984), 'Civil-Military Relations and the Cult of the Offensive, 1914 and 1984', *International Security*, Vol.9, pp.93-146.

Snyder, J.L. (1985), 'Perception of the Security Dilemma in 1914', in R.Jervis, R.Ned Lebow, and J.Gross Stein (eds.), *Psychology and Deterrence*, Johns Hopkins University Press, Baltimore.

Stares, P. (1991), *Command Performance: the Neglected Dimension of European Security*, Brookings, Washington, D.C.

Steinmetz, S. (1994), *Democratic Transition and Human Rights: Perspectives on U.S. Foreign Policy*, State University of New York Press, New York.

Strange, S. (1996), *The Retreat of the State. The Diffusion of Power in the World Economy*, Cambridge University Press, Cambridge.

Talbott, S. (1988), *The Master of the Game : Paul Nitze and the Nuclear Peace*, Knopf, New York.

Tara, R. and Zeringue, M. (1992), 'Grand Strategy in a Post-Bipolar World. Interpreting the Final Soviet Response', *Review of International Studies*, Vol.18, pp.335-375.

Thomas, D.S. (1999), 'The Helsinki Accords and Political Change in Eastern Europe', in Thomas Risse, Stephen C. Ropp and Kathryn Sikkink (eds.) *The Power of Human Rights. International Norms and Domestic Change*, Cambridge University Press, Cambridge. pp.205-233.

Thompson, E.P. and Smith, D. (eds.) (1980), *Protest and Survive*, Penguin, Harmondsworth.

Van Evera, S. (1984), 'The Cult of the Offensive and the Origins of the First World War', *International Security*, Vol.9, pp.58-107.

Van Evera, S. (1998), 'Offense, Defense and the Causes of War', *International Security*, Vol.22, pp.5-43.

Vincent, R.J. and Wilson, P. (1993), 'Beyond Non-Intervention', in Ian Forbes and Mark Hoffman (eds.) *Political Theory, International Relations and the Ethics of Intervention*, St.Martins Press, New York, pp.122-132.

Waever, O. (1993), 'Societal Security: the concept', in Ole Waever, Barry Buzan, Morten Kelstrup and Pierre Lemaitre, *Identity, Migration and the New Security Agenda in Europe*, Pinter Publishers Ltd, London, pp.20-24.

Waever, O. (1995), 'Securitization and Desecuritization', in Lipschutz, R.D. (ed.), *On Security*, Columbia University Press, New York, pp.46-86.

Waever, O. (1998), 'Insecurity, security and asecurity in the West European non-war community', in E.Adler and M.Barnett, *Security Communities*, Cambridge University Press, Cambridge, pp.228-264.

Waltz, K. (1993), 'The Emerging Structure of International Politics', *International Security*, Vol.18, pp.44-79.

Warnke, P. (1975), 'Apes on a Treadmill', *Foreign Policy*, Vol.18, pp.12-29.

Weber, S. (1993), 'Shaping the Postwar Balance of Power: Multilateralism in NATO', in John Gerard Ruggie (ed.) *Multilateralism Matters. The Theory and Praxis of an Institutional Form*, Columbia University Press, New York, pp.233-292.

Wendt, A. (1992), 'Anarchy is what states make of it: the social construction of power politics', *International Organization*, Vol.46, pp.391-426.

Wendt, A. (1994), 'Collective Identity Formation and the International State', *American Political Science Review*, Vol.88, pp.384-396.

Wheeler, N.J. (1992), 'Pluralist or Solidarist Conceptions of International Society: Bull and Vincent on Humanitarian Intervention', *Millennium: Journal of International Studies*, Vol.21, pp.463-487.

Wheeler, N.J. (1996), 'Guardian Angel or Global Gangster: a Review of the Ethical Claims of International Society', *Political Studies*, Vol.44, pp.123-135.

Wight, M. (1966), 'Western Values in International Relations', in H.Butterfield and M.Wight (eds.) *Diplomatic Investigations*, Allen and Unwin, London, pp.89-131.

Windass, S. (ed.) (1985), *Avoiding Nuclear War: Common Security as a Strategy for the Defence of the West*, Brassey's London.

Winik, J. (1996), On the Brink: The Dramatic, Behind-the-Scenes Saga of the Reagan Era and the Men and Women Who Won the Cold War, Simon and Schuster, New York.

Wiseman, G. (1989), *Common Security and non-provocative defence: alternative approaches to the security dilemma*, Peace Research Centre, Australian National University, Canberra.

Wohlforth, W. (ed.) (1996), *Witnesses to the End of the Cold War*, Johns Hopkins, Baltimore.

Wyn Jones, R. (1995), "Messages in a Bottle'? Theory and Praxis in Critical Security Studies', *Contemporary Security Policy*, Vol.16, pp.299-319.

Zakaria, F. (1997), 'The Rise of Illiberal Democracy', *Foreign Affairs*, Vol.76, pp.22-43.

National Security Archives

RR IM 67-36 Intelligence Memorandum, 'Soviet Military Policy in 1967: The Challenges and Issues', June 1967, *The Soviet Estimate: U.S. Analysis of the Soviet Union, 1947-1991*, (Washington, D.C.: The National Security Archive & Chadwyck-Healy Inc., 1995), no.00421

SNIE 11-16-70, 'Soviet Attitudes Towards SALT', February 1970, *The Soviet Estimate: U.S. Analysis of the Soviet Union, 1947-1991*, (Washington, D.C.: The National Security Archive & Chadwyck-Healy Inc., 1995), no.00442

DIA Report, 'Détente and Soviet Strategy, September 1975', *The Soviet Estimate: U.S. Analysis of the Soviet Union, 1947-1991*, (Washington, D.C.: The National Security Archive & Chadwyck-Healy Inc., 1995), no.00486.

Intelligence Community Experiment in Competitive Analysis, 'Soviet Strategic Objectives, An Alternative View, Report of Team "B"', December 1976, *The Soviet Estimate: U.S. Analysis of the Soviet Union, 1947-1991*, (Washington, D.C.: The National Security Archive & Chadwyck-Healy Inc., 1995), no.00501.

NIE 11-3/8-76, 'Soviet Forces for Intercontinental Attack Through the mid-1980s', December 1976, *The Soviet Estimate: U.S. Analysis of the Soviet Union, 1947-1991*, (Washington, D.C.: The National Security Archive & Chadwyck-Healy Inc., 1995), no.00502

DIA 20-80 Warning Intelligence Appraisal, 'USSR: A Military Option', February 1980, *The Soviet Estimate: U.S. Analysis of the Soviet Union, 1947-1991*, (Washington, D.C.: The National Security Archive & Chadwyck-Healy Inc., 1995), no.00532.

NIE 11-3/8-82, 'Soviet Capabilities for Strategic Nuclear Conflict, 1982-1992. National Intelligence Estimate. Volume I – Key Judgements and Summary', February 1983, *The Soviet Estimate: U.S. Analysis of the Soviet Union, 1947-1991*, (Washington, D.C.: The National Security Archive & Chadwyck-Healy Inc., 1995), 00568.

CIA, Office of Soviet Analysis, 'Gorbachev: Steering the USSR into the 1990s. An Intelligence Estimate', July 1987, *The Soviet Estimate: U.S. Analysis of the Soviet Union, 1947-1991*, (Washington, D.C.: The National Security Archive & Chadwyck-Healy Inc., 1995), no.00594.

CIA, Office of Soviet Analysis, 'Soviet National Security Policy: Responses to the Changing Military and Economic Environment', June 1988, *The Soviet Estimate: U.S. Analysis of the Soviet Union, 1947-1991*, (Washington, D.C.: The National Security Archive & Chadwyck-Healy Inc., 1995), no.00598.

Defense Research comment 82-87, 'Gorbachev: Soviet Economic Modernization and the Military', November 1987, *The Soviet Estimate: U.S. Analysis of the Soviet Union, 1947-1991*, (Washington, D.C.: The National Security Archive & Chadwyck-Healy Inc., 1995), no.00595.

NIE11-3/8-83, 'Soviet capabilties for strategic nuclear conflict, 1983-1993. Volume I Key Judgements and Summary', 6 March 1984. *The Soviet Estimate: U.S. Analysis of the Soviet Union, 1947-1991*, (Washington, D.C.: The National Security Archive & Chadwyck-Healy Inc., 1995).

NIC M 83-10017, 'Possible Soviet Responses to the US Strategic Defense Initiative', 12 September 1983, *The Soviet Estimate: U.S. Analysis of the Soviet Union, 1947-1991*, (Washington, D.C.: The National Security Archive & Chadwyck-Healy Inc., 1995).

CIA 'Intelligence Forecasts of Soviet Intercontinental Attack Forces: An Evaluation of the Record. A Research Paper, April 1989', *The Soviet Estimate: U.S. Analysis of the Soviet Union, 1947-1991*, (Washington, D.C.: The National Security Archive & Chadwyck-Healy Inc., 1995), no.00601.

CIA, Office of Soviet Analysis, 'Gorbachev's Domestic Gambles and Instability in the USSR. An Intelligence Assessment', September 1989. *The Soviet Estimate: U.S. Analysis of the Soviet Union, 1947-1991*, (Washington, D.C.: The National Security Archive & Chadwyck-Healy Inc., 1995), no.00602.

CIA, Office of Soviet Analysis, 'The Soviet Cauldron', April 1991, *The Soviet Estimate: U.S. Analysis of the Soviet Union, 1947-1991*, (Washington, D.C.: The National Security Archive & Chadwyck-Healy Inc., 1995), no.00603.

(Not published)

SNIE 11-10-84 'Implications of Recent Soviet Military-Political Activities', Washington, D.C., The National Security Archive.

NSDD210 'Allied Consultations on the U.S. response to General Secretary Gorbachev's 14 January 1986 Arms Control Proposal', February, 1986. Washington, D.C., The National Security Archive.

Ronald Reagan Library

NSDD249, 'Additional Instructions for the Current NST [Nuclear and Space talks] Negotiating Round', October, 1986. The Ronald Reagan Library.

NSDD250 'Post –Reykjavik Follow-Up', November 1986, The Ronald Reagan Library.

Congressional Hearings and Reports

Statement by the Secretary of Defense (Weinberger), 'Foundations of Defense policy', U.S. 98th Congress, House Committee, Defense Appropriations, FY84, 8 February, 1983.

Theater Nuclear Warfare Issues, Senate Armed Services Committee, 98th Congress, 15 March 1983.

House Committee on Defense Appropriations FY85. 98th Congress, 1 March 1984.

The Reykjavik Process: preparation for the Conduct of the Icelandic Summit and its Implications for Arms Control Policy, Report of the Defense Council of the Committee on Armed Services. House of Representatives. 99th Cong. 2nd Sess. (Washington: USPGO, 1987).

Reykjavik and American Security, Report of the Defense Policy Panel of the Committee on Armed Services House of Representatives. 99th Cong. 2nd Sess. February 1987. Committee Print No.26.

Impact of Gorbachev's Reform Movement on the Soviet Military, Hearing Before the House Armed Services Committee, 100th Cong. 2nd Sess. March 1988.

The Future of U.S.-Soviet Relations, Hearing Before the Senate Committee on Foreign Relations. 101st Cong. 1st Sess. June 1989.

Soviet Disunion: The American Response, Hearing Before the Senate Committee on European Affairs of the Committee on Foreign Relations, 6 March 1991.

The SDI as it relates to the ABM Treaty, Hearing before the Senate Congressional Committee on Foreign Relations 102nd Cong. 1st Sess. 24 April 1991.

Command and Control of Soviet Nuclear Weapons: Dangers and Opportunities Arising from the August Revolution, Hearing Before the Senate Subcommittee on European Affairs of the Committee on Foreign Relations, 102nd Cong. 1st Sess. 24 September 1991

Miscellaneous

American Foreign Policy: Current Documents, 1983 to 1991 (Washington, D.C.: GPO).

O direktivakh dlya peregovrov ministra inostrannykh del SSSRs Prezidentom SShA Bushm I Gosudarstvennym sekretarem Beikerom (Vashington, 4-6 aprelya 1990g). Philip Zelikow Collection (Zelikow-Rice Papers), Box No.3, Hoover Institution Archives, Stanford University.

Index

References from Notes indicated by 'n' after page preference